Music and Autism

MUSIC AND AUTISM

Speaking for Ourselves

Michael B. Bakan

with

Mara Chasar, Graeme Gibson, Elizabeth J. Grace,
Zena Hamelson, Dotan Nitzberg,
Gordon Peterson, Maureen Pytlik, Donald Rindale,
Amy Sequenzia, and Addison Silar

OXFORD
UNIVERSITY PRESS

Oxford University Press is a department of the University of Oxford. It furthers
the University's objective of excellence in research, scholarship, and education
by publishing worldwide. Oxford is a registered trade mark of Oxford University
Press in the UK and certain other countries.

Published in the United States of America by Oxford University Press
198 Madison Avenue, New York, NY 10016, United States of America.

Library of Congress Cataloging-in-Publication Data
Names: Bakan, Michael B. author. | Chasar, Mara.
Title: Music and autism : speaking for ourselves /
Michael B. Bakan with Mara Chasar [and nine others].
Description: New York, NY : Oxford University Press, [2018] |
Includes bibliographical references and index.
Identifiers : LCCN 2017034412 | ISBN 9780190855833 (cloth) |
ISBN 9780197543122 (paperback) | ISBN 9780190855864 (oxford scholarly online) |
ISBN 9780190865573 (companion website)
Subjects: LCSH: Autistic musicians—Interviews. | Music—Psychological aspects.
Classification:LCCML3838.B182018| DDC 780.87/4—dc23
LC record available at https://lccn.loc.gov/2017034412

To Megan, my wife, who showed me how to love
To Isaac, my son, who showed me how to be calm
And to Leah, my daughter, who showed me how to sing.

To Paul, my father, who gave me the gift of curiosity
To Laura, my sister, who always keeps me humble
And to Joel, my brother, who taught me how to groove.

To Rita, my mother, who made me a writer
To Susu and Rosie, for making me laugh
And to Mark, my inspiration, who knows who he is.

CONTENTS

FIGURES

ABOUT THE COMPANION WEBSITE

Oxford University Press has created a password-protected website to accompany *Music and Autism: Speaking for Ourselves*. Video and audio recordings of musical and spoken-word performances discussed in the text, as well as supplementary photographs, videos, and links to further online resources, may be accessed via this site. Readers are encouraged to take advantage of these additional resources. Examples available online are indicated in the text with Oxford's symbol ⓟ. Note that this same website is also associated with the original hardback printing and earlier electronic and audio book editions of this book, which were titled *Speaking for Ourselves: Conversations on Life, Music, and Autism*.

COMPANION WEBSITE CONTENTS

2.1   (audio) "Oh That!" by Zena Hamelson, performed by the Artism Ensemble (2012)

3.1   (video) "Purple Eggs and Ham," by Mara Chasar, performed in rehearsal by the Artism Ensemble (2013)

4.1   (text) Links to music discussed in the chapter

5.1   (audio) "Codependence Song," composed and sung by Elizabeth J. "Ibby" Grace

5.2   (audio) "Johnny I Hardly Knew Ya," traditional Irish song sung by Elizbeth J. "Ibby" Grace

6.1   (video) "How to Teach Piano to People with Asperger" (lecture), by Dotan Nitzberg; presented at the 2012 World Piano Teachers Association international conference in Novi Sad, Serbia

6.2   (video) Franz Liszt, *Gnomenreigen* (Dance of the Gnomes), performed by Dotan Nitzberg

6.3   (video) Edvard Grieg, Piano Sonata in E Minor, Opus 7, performed by Dotan Nitzberg

6.4   (video) Franz Schubert, "Wanderer" Fantasy, performed by Dotan Nitzberg

7.1   (photo) Electric bass guitar built by Graeme Gibson and Daniel Ouellet

7.2   (photos) Graeme Gibson photo gallery: birds

7.3   (photos) Graeme Gibson photo gallery: world music instruments (from his collection)

7.4   (audio) Improvisation on Greek bouzouki by Graeme Gibson

7.5   (photo) Female red-winged blackbird (*Agelaius phoeniceus*), photographed by Graeme Gibson

ACKNOWLEDGMENTS

This book could never have come to be without the extraordinary commitment and contributions of my ten collaborators: Mara Chasar, Graeme Gibson, Ibby Grace, Zena Hamelson, Dotan Nitzberg, Gordon Peterson, Maureen Pytlik, Donald Rindale, Amy Sequenzia, and Addison Silar. My heartfelt thanks goes out to all of you and to your wonderful families and networks of support, among whom I will mention Susan, Barry, Layenie, Adriana, Lia Chasar, Mike Chasar, Jill Huxtable, Ven Sequenzia, Nurit and Benny Nitzberg, Deborah and Bill Gibson, and Mike and Terri.

To Suzanne Ryan, editor extraordinaire, you are an author's dream. Thank you for your unwavering support of this project over the course of many years now, and for the gluten-free fried chicken in Austin too! I am deeply indebted to the three anonymous reviewers for the Press who weighed in on the manuscript at various stages. Your insights and generosity have been invaluable in my efforts to bring this work up to the level of its potential. I am also grateful to the excellent editorial and production team at Oxford University Press who worked with me on this project, and especially to Jamie Kim, Norm Hirschy, Damian Penfold, and Patterson Lamb for their various forms of assistance.

My colleagues and students in the College of Music at Florida State University have been supportive, helpful, and inspirational in ways beyond telling. Special shout-outs are due to all of my friends in the Musicology area—Denise Von Glahn, Douglass Seaton, Frank Gunderson, Charlie Brewer, Sarah Eyerly, Michael Broyles, and Meg Jackson—as well as to Patricia Flowers, Jane Clendinning, Alice-Ann Darrow, Wendy Smith, Lauren Smith, Laura Gayle Green, Bill Fredrickson, Jennie Carpenter, Christian Dauble, Tiawana Meeks, and Danielle Davis.

Megan Bakan, Alexandria Carrico, Carrie Danielson, Jeff Edelstein, Stephanie Espie, Mayna Tyrrell, and Nikki Schommer devoted countless hours to reading and re-reading the manuscript and provided important criticisms, corrections, and recommendations. Big thanks and big hugs go out to all of you, with some extra ones reserved for Nikki, who additionally prepared the index and reference lists, a huge undertaking.

The Artism Ensemble and the Music-Play Project figure less prominently in this book than they might, but that doesn't mean that my debt to the legions of people involved in those programs is any the less. Thanks to the Artism gang: E.S., NICKstr, Coffeebot, Mara Chasar, Zena Hamelson, Carlos Odria, Mia Gormandy, Vivianne Asturizaga, Ramin Yazdanpanah, Carlos Silva, Jade Stagg, Brian Hall, Channing Griggs, Haiqiong Deng, Elyse Marrero, Michelle Jones, Chris Wilkey, Matthew Martin, Lia and Mike Chasar, Mary and Larry Coffee, Sophie Wacongne-Speer and Kevin Speer, Rick and Stefanie Voss, Leo Welch, Ryan Scherber, Rachel Hurd, Bethany Atwell, Peggy Brady and the good people at COCA, Rabbi Jack Romberg and Temple Israel, John Fitzgerald and Remo, Inc., the National Endowment for the Arts, Jennifer Hoesing and the Florida Department of State's Division of Cultural Affairs, the Tallahassee Museum, the Society for Disability Studies, and Sue and Barry.

To list all those who participated in the Music-Play Project would take more time and page space than any of us can afford, so it will have to suffice for me to just send a big "Thank you!" to the thirty children and families and everyone else that took part, though I'd be remiss if I didn't give a special nod to my friend and former colleague Ben Koen, the co-founder of that program.

Some materials in this book have appeared in previous publications and I am grateful to the editors and publishers of those journals and books for granting me reprint permissions. Special thanks are due to Stephen Stuempfle and Ellen Koskoff at *Ethnomusicology*, Marcia Ostashewski and Heather Sparling at *MUSICultures*, David G. Woods, Victor Fung, and Robbie Gunstream at *College Music Symposium*, Simone Krüger Bridge and the *Journal of World Popular Music* at Equinox Publishing, and Susan Hadley and Rune Rolvsjord at *Voices: A World Forum for Music Therapy*, not to mention Oxford University Press for permitting reprints of materials from my chapters in the Oxford Handbooks of applied ethnomusicology and music and disability studies. Thanks to the editors of those volumes as well— Svanibor Pettan, Jeff Todd Titon, Blake Howe, Stephanie Jensen-Moulton, Neil Lerner, and Joseph Straus—for their guiding hands in those works and in turn the present one. And speaking of Joseph Straus, he has been a true inspiration and mentor to me in this work. Thanks, Joe!

A great many other people have contributed to this project in ways too numerous to specify. Beyond those I have surely forgotten to acknowledge here (to whom I apologize), they include Eleanor Feierstein, Tim

Rice, Rebecca Jenkins, Derryck Smith, Pauline Westhead, Danny Bakan, Jonnie Bakan, Kent Hutchinson, Carolyn Ramzy, Randy Raine-Reusch, Cal Melton, Keith Ivey, Sherry Simpson, Henry Hall, Mary Ann Dixon, Terry Wyatt, Peggy and John Benton, Iris and Mark Palazesi, William Cheng, Zach Richter, Jeff Packman, Anna Hoefnagels, Kathy Armstrong, Harris Berger, Louise Wrazen, Kenneth Aigen, Aaron Fox, Kayleen Justus, Karen Wacks, Eli Newberger, Brita Heimarck, Lindee Morgan, Amy Wetherby, Andrew Killick, Gerd Grupe, Kendra Stepputat, Michael Rohrbacher, Larry Witzleben, Elizabeth Fein, Clarice Rios, Dawn Prince, Richard Grinker, Tom Weisner, Elinor Ochs, Olga Solomon, Laura Sterponi, Timothy Cooley, Gregory Melchor-Barz, Theresa Allison, Neil Lerner, Andrew Dell'Antonio, Jennifer Iverson, Alex Lubet, Emily Morris, Sally Kahn, Annika Bowers, Allegra Stout, and Rachel Goff.

Finally, to Megan, Isaac, and Leah: Thank you for letting me write this book. I couldn't have done it without you. I love you more than life itself.

PROLOGUE

We are having dinner at Mark's house, but Mark is nowhere to be seen.

Mark is three years old.[1] He is a relative of mine (his father Scott and I are cousins) and has recently been diagnosed with an autism spectrum condition called Asperger's syndrome.[2] Having visitors to the house makes Mark anxious, especially when they're people he doesn't know, like my new colleague Benjamin Koen, who is here too with his wife Saba and their baby daughter Naseem.

Mark is much happier alone in his bedroom at the back of the house than dealing with all the hubbub of a dinner party, and his parents realize that it makes more sense to let him have his quiet time than force him to "be social." Sure, it would be nice if he came out and joined us, his mother Jenny tells us, but we all know that's not likely to happen.

Dinner is over, and while the others indulge in some wine-infused cleaning up, Ben and I sit down to drum together. We both teach ethnomusicology at Florida State University in Tallahassee—I've been on the faculty for about a decade, Ben for a little over two weeks—and we are both experienced percussionists. Scott is also a musician, and he and Jenny have a house full of drums: drums from Cuba, Brazil, Ghana, China, Indonesia—from all over the place really. Ben is playing a West African–style *djembe*; I'm on Balinese *kendang*. This is the first time that we've ever played together and the groove is strong right from the start—our own thing, but kind of like a Cuban *rumba guaguancó*.

My eyes are shut, as they usually are when I drum, and the music is taking me away. Then I feel a light tap on my leg. It brings me back into the room, and there, sitting on the floor beside me, is Mark. After more than an hour alone in his bedroom, he has come to join us, drawn out by the sound of the drums. Mark looks me right in the eye—something he rarely does—then casts his gaze downward at a pair of *bongó* drums resting on the floor between us. He looks back up at me, as though to ask, "Can I play too?"

I smile and nod encouragingly, drumming all the while. Mark jumps right in. He immediately shifts the groove, taking Ben and me in a new rhythmic direction. We follow him there with excitement. Mark's eyes light up. He changes the groove again; we go there too and he smiles radiantly.

Then Mark begins to sing. His voice is strong and clear, intoning words in a language of his own invention, a language he calls Skoofie.

We are reveling in the beauty and magic of the moment when a sudden cry cuts through the room, bringing our musical ascent to a screeching halt. It's the baby, Naseem. Eight o'clock has arrived and she's done for the night.

Minutes later, the Koens are off in their minivan, headed for home. Mark has disappeared, back to his bedroom, I suppose. I put away the drums and take a seat next to my wife Megan on the couch. Scott and Jenny join us after finishing up in the kitchen. Soon, Mark comes back into the living room—another surprise in an evening of many. He walks over to Megan and me and starts talking to us, but not like he ever has before. He usually carries a lot of tension in his body and moves stiffly, awkwardly; but now he looks loose and relaxed. He usually speaks to us in Skoofie, and on those rare occasions when he does use English he delivers his words in a monotone, with little apparent intention of actually communicating; now, though, he is speaking English, lucidly and expressively, and he's emphasizing his words with illuminating hand gestures and body language. His parents, especially Scott, look to be as surprised by the change as I am.

Yet strangely, I'm not really able to hear what Mark is saying—not the meaning of the words anyhow—for I am transfixed by their musicality, their poetry, the choreography of their presentation. And I am thinking to myself: what has happened to this child, what has changed, and what did that brief but profound musical encounter of just minutes ago have to do with it all?

But as I am focused on these thoughts, Mark shuts down. He stops talking, abruptly turns away, and walks back to his room. And when I next see him only a couple of days later, he's pretty much his old self again—a little bit stiff, a little bit anxious, not so keen to communicate.

After our drumming session, I have a restless night's sleep. I keep waking up, thinking about the events of the evening, wondering what to make of it, where to go from here. Then it comes to me, at about 3:00 in the morning, and I continue to stir it around in my head until the earliest time I can politely call Ben, at 8:00. I tell him I have an idea, an idea for a music-and-play project for children on the autism spectrum and their families, one that would essentially recreate the conditions of our drum jam with Mark the night before, and hopefully with similarly wondrous results.[3]

That vision eventually becomes a reality, first as a program called the Music-Play Project (2005–2009),[4] later as a neurodiverse music group named the Artism Ensemble (2011–2013).[5] It ultimately morphs into something very different as well, a new project spanning the years 2011–2016 that centers on my conversations during that period with ten fascinating individuals. All of these people have two things in common: a life in which music figures prominently and an autism spectrum diagnosis. In this book, they tell their stories, in their own words and through the conversations in which we shared.

NOTES

1. Mark is a pseudonym, as are the names used for his parents. Certain other details in this account have been adjusted as well to protect the anonymity of Mark and his family.

2. In earlier editions of the American Psychiatric Association's *Diagnostic and Statistical Manual of Mental Disorders* (see, for example, American Psychiatric Association 2000), Asperger's disorder, also known as Asperger's syndrome, was identified as a separate diagnosis within the larger diagnostic category of autism spectrum disorder (ASD). Three other forms of ASD—autistic disorder, childhood disintegrative disorder, and pervasive developmental disorder-not otherwise specified (PDD-NOS)—were likewise separately identified. The fifth edition of the *Manual*, *DSM-5* (American Psychiatric Association 2013), brought major changes, subsuming all four categories of autism diagnosis under the single diagnostic classification of ASD: autism spectrum disorder. Thus, in the words of John Donvan and Caren Zucker, "Asperger's as a diagnosis was killed off" by the APA in *DSM-5* (Donvan and Zucker 2016, 528). This change generated controversy and debate in many quarters (Silberman 2015, 381–468; Donvan and Zucker 2016, 527–33), and within the autistic self-advocacy, neurodiversity, and disability studies communities, a distinction between Asperger's and other kinds of autism is frequently maintained. The distinction remained an important one for the majority of my collaborators on this project during the research period, and for that reason we have retained the status of Asperger's syndrome as an identifiable autism spectrum condition throughout this book, its removal from the current edition of the *DSM* notwithstanding.

3. It is important to note that while the musical experience recounted here had a lasting impact on me, both personally and professionally, this was by Mark's own report not the case for him. In September 2013, some ten years after our first time drumming together (there have been many others since then), I had occasion to ask Mark what he remembered about that evening and whether it had been significant for him. He replied that he didn't remember much but knew

about what had happened because he had heard me talk about it. He then added, "It wasn't really that important to me because I'm not that into music anyhow" (personal correspondence, September 18, 2013).

4. There are several publications on the Music-Play Project (Bakan 2009; Bakan, Koen, Bakan, et al. 2008; Bakan, Koen, Kobylarz, et al. 2008; Koen et al. 2008). A substantial literature exists in the area of medical ethnomusicology (Allison 2010; Barz 2006; Barz and Cohen 2011; Edwards, Melchor-Barz, and Binson 2015; Koen 2008).

5. Studies of the Artism Ensemble have yielded a series of publications (Bakan 2014a, 2014b, 2014c, 2015a, 2015b, 2016a, 2016b). Representative publications from applied ethnomusicology are varied in both topical focus and approach (Dirksen 2012; Harrison 2012; Harrison, Pettan, and Mackinlay 2010; Pettan and Titon 2015; Titon 1992; Van Buren 2010).

Music and Autism

CHAPTER 1

Introduction

How do autistic people make, experience, and find meaning in music? And why does it matter to them that they do? These are the guiding questions from which this book has emerged.

The strong identification with music that many autistic people[1] have, sometimes in tandem with exceptional musical abilities, has been observed frequently since the advent of autism studies in the 1940s.[2] Meanwhile, music therapists have made autism a central focus of research and clinical practice in their discipline,[3] and music scholars outside of music therapy have begun to examine the lives and careers of storied musicians like Glenn Gould and "Blind Tom" Wiggins, theorizing that their legendary eccentricities—and aspects of their musical genius as well—may have been attributable to what we would today classify as autistic traits.[4] Some scholars, such as Joseph Straus, have argued for the existence of a unique mode of "autistic hearing" that issues from "a distinctively autistic cognitive style": an "autistic listener," suggests Straus, is someone who tends to focus on the part rather than the whole of a musical work and may bring to the listening experience remarkable skills of pitch recognition and rote memory.[5]

I too am interested in understanding how and why so many autistic people identify so strongly with music, but with my ethnomusicologist's ear, I want more to understand how *particular* individuals think about themselves and their place in the world than to know about autistic people generally.[6] I want to learn what these individuals care about and value, what strategies they employ to confront the formidable life challenges they face, and how and why they choose to be creative, express themselves, and interact with other people—or in some cases, don't. And I want to get to know them, and to learn where they're coming from, with music as our shared point of departure.

These types of knowing and understanding happen through direct, interpersonal interaction, at least initially. They come from playing music together, listening together, having conversations, exchanging text messages and emails, "chatting" online, arguing and debating, sharing a joke, or sharing a meal.

In the context of this book, knowing, learning, and understanding take place mainly through dialogue. The ten people with whom I share conversations have been my primary collaborators throughout the project: with them, I talk about music, autism, and life in general; and through our dialogues, their words come to be *re-presented* rather than merely represented. It is the contributions of these collaborators, more than anything else, that define both what this work is and what it has the capacity to achieve.

COLLABORATORS

My collaborators range in age from seven to forty-seven and hail from several different countries. They are boys and girls, men and women. Some are straight, others gay. They alternately self-identify as neurodiverse or neuroqueer; as Autistic with a capital "A" or autistic without; as autists, Aspergers, people living with Asperger's syndrome, or Aspies; as Christians, Jews, Buddhists, or atheists; as musicians or non-musicians, professors or students, and disabled or alternately abled individuals. Some are proud, pro-active autistic self-advocates while others would gladly rid themselves of their autistic conditions altogether. Some are highly accomplished professional musicians with advanced degrees while others neither sing nor play a musical instrument at all. Some insist on being identified as autistic while others bristle at the very mention of the word, despite acknowledging their ASC, or autism spectrum condition, diagnosis. (My collaborators and I uniformly prefer the designation autism spectrum *condition*, or ASC, to the more common designation autism spectrum *disorder*, or ASD.)

The first members of this eclectic cohort that we will meet are two girls diagnosed with Asperger's syndrome: ten-year-old Zena Hamelson (pseudonym) in Chapter 2 and twelve-year-old Mara Chasar in Chapter 3.[7] Both were participants in 2009 in the Music-Play Project (MPP), a program that centered on child-directed, improvisatory music-play sessions featuring groups of three to four children on the autism spectrum, their co-participating parents, and Ben Koen and myself as the designated music-play facilitators.[8]

About two years after the conclusion of MPP, in January 2011, Zena and Mara became original members of the Artism Ensemble. Artism built upon the music-play concept of MPP but on a larger scale, with more ambitious musical goals and an explicit public outreach mission. Over the course of its run, the group included five children on the spectrum, their parents, and a half dozen or more professional musicians/ethnomusicologists from around the world representing diverse musical and cultural traditions. Beyond meeting weekly for music-play sessions and rehearsals, the Artism Ensemble performed numerous concerts and other public events as part of a three-year National Endowment for the Arts–funded initiative to promote autism acceptance throughout the state of Florida and beyond.[9]

Following the 2011 Artism concert season, I sat down with Zena and her mother Suzanne (pseudonym) to discuss their MPP and Artism experiences. We had an extraordinary conversation. I enjoyed an equally enlightening exchange with Mara in 2013. These two dialogues, each in their way, compelled me to make this a book *of* conversations rather than a book merely based on conversations. They brought into focus a number of key topics and issues that became central to the project at large, such as musical stimming, alternative modes of musicking, autism acceptance, and the vagaries of normalcy.[10] (It should be noted that the conversation-based portion of Chapter 2 is both shorter and later in arriving than that of the subsequent chapters.)

Donald Rindale (pseudonym), my conversational partner in Chapter 4, is an ex-trombonist and former musicology graduate student, now an attorney. He was diagnosed with Asperger's in 2011 when he was in his early twenties. Our dialogues began about two-and-a-half years after that. They reflect Donald's trials and tribulations in both living undiagnosed for so long and coming to terms with his new ASC identity. Through texting-based online chat (chat for short), Donald was as comfortable discussing the operas of Richard Wagner and twentieth-century compositions for symphonic band as he was exploring distinctions between the phenomenological approaches of Heidegger and Merleau-Ponty, or the finer points of jurisprudence in disability rights legislation. From Chapter 4 on, the vast majority of conversations took place in chat sessions.

My conversations in Chapter 5 are with Dr. Elizabeth J. Grace, who usually goes by her nickname, Ibby. Ibby is a professor in the National College of Education at National-Louis University in Illinois. She is a widely published autistic self-advocate and social activist as well as an accomplished singer of Irish traditional music with an abiding passion for ethnomusicology. She asserts that her primary mode of cognition in life is to "think in music," an idea that she richly explores in the chapter. Thinking in music, Ibby claims, has not only increased her own ability to function well as an autistic person living in a largely unaccommodating society but has also enabled her to hear the hidden voices of other autistic people who, unlike herself, do not use speech. This special ability has helped her to be an effective advocate for many non-speaking autistics.

It was through Ibby that I was first introduced to the concept of autistic self-advocacy when I heard her speak at the Society for Disability Studies Conference in Orlando, Florida, in 2013. That same conference also brought to the fore a second concept that would become central to my research, neurodiversity, which the autistic scholar and self-advocate Nick Walker has defined as "the understanding of neurological variation [including ASC] as a natural form of human diversity, subject to the same societal dynamics as other forms of diversity," such as racial, cultural, sexual-orientation, and gender diversity.[11] The influence of works by Grace, Walker, and other autistic self-advocates and neurodiversity proponents are very much in evidence throughout this book.

Dotan Nitzberg (Chapter 6) is an Israeli concert pianist. At the time of our chat dialogues in 2014, he was a graduate student in piano performance at the University of North Texas. He would later transfer to Florida State University (FSU) in the fall of 2015 to pursue joint graduate degrees in piano performance and pedagogy (for which I served on his graduate supervisory committee). Dotan and I first became acquainted via email in February of 2014. Our mutual interests in music teaching methods for people on the autism spectrum was what brought us together. I have included in his chapter the text of a lecture on teaching piano to people with Asperger's, which Dotan wrote and presented at the 2012 World Piano Teachers Association conference in Novi Sad, Serbia.

My collaborator on Chapter 7, Graeme Gibson, lives in Vancouver, Canada. He collects musical instruments from around the world, builds his own high-quality instruments, and curates the website museumofworldmusic.com, which is subtitled "The Exploration of Traditional, Ethnic, 'World Music' and Experimental or Custom-made Musical Instruments" (Gibson 2015). Graeme sees parallels between world music and autism, as each "is a spectrum that includes numerous genres." He was diagnosed with classic autism as a young child and was the case study for his mother Deborah Gibson's Ph.D. dissertation on early childhood language development in autism.[12] Deborah participates in the conversations with Graeme and me; this gives them a character notably different from others in the book because of Graeme's preference for composing prepared written responses to questions emailed to him in advance over having to deal with the less predictable—and thus for him more stressful—dynamics of chat.

Maureen Pytlik (Chapter 8) also hails from Canada. She grew up in the nation's capital, Ottawa, where at the time of our dialogues she was pursuing degrees in both clarinet performance and mathematics at Carleton University. Maureen shares illuminating reflections on how having Asperger's impacted her approaches to clarinet playing, teaching clarinet, and teaching music theory, as well as navigating the complex dynamics of college social life. Perhaps most enlightening, however, is her vivid account of studying and performing West African dance and drumming while at Carleton. She explains how this experience was deeply transformative for her as a young woman, a classically trained musician, and a university student confronting the unique challenges of living with an autism spectrum condition.

In Chapter 9, I converse with the pseudonymous Gordon Peterson, a musicologist, early music specialist, composer, gigging musician, and former tenured music professor. I first encountered Gordon when he was a musicology graduate student at FSU in the mid-1990s. Some twenty years later, we reconnected when he sought me out after being diagnosed with Asperger's syndrome at the age of forty-five. Through Gordon's introspective journey into the musical and autistic workings of his labyrinthine mind—which he describes as being host to a "ribbon-like time line" that stretches back through music "from today all the way to the beginning of recorded history, and before"—we are invited into a breathtaking realm of imagination and autistic subjective experience.

Chapter 10 features Amy Sequenzia, who has achieved veritable celebrity status through her many published writings, widely read blogs, and committed activism on behalf of not only autistic people but many other historically disenfranchised groups as well. Amy is the one non-speaking member of this project's cohort of collaborators, but while she does not literally speak, she certainly does communicate, writing beautifully, in great volume, and with a voice that powerfully expresses her fighting passion for social justice. Our dialogues motivated Amy to explore an important dimension of her life that she had not paid much attention to before: the role and significance of music, which she experiences not as a performer or composer but strictly as a listener. The results of this focused attention are at times truly poetic as Amy seeks and finds words to capture the complex dance of emotions, sounds, colors, and synesthesia that animate her inner musical world.

Finally, in Chapter 11, Addison Silar (pseudonym) is my dialogue partner. He is another "non-musician" for whom music is nevertheless of immense importance. Diagnosed at the age of five with Asperger's syndrome,

Addison was a teenager with a passion for writing science fiction when we conducted our chats in June of 2014. Our conversations revealed an extraordinary process of musical engagement on Addison's part, one in which the music he listens to while writing not only inspires his creativity but is fully infused into the fictional worlds he invents. Music turns out to have multiple other functions in Addison's life as well, from ordering his thinking in ways that enable him to stay on task with homework assignments to filtering out all the "noise [and] different conversations going on at the same time, and other distracting mishaps" that "bombard" him as a matter of course in daily life.

AUTHORSHIP

Then there is the eleventh collaborator: me. Each chapter is grounded in a complete transcript of my conversations with the individual at its center. My voice is always present in the role of the main, and usually sole, conversational partner; and my editor self is consistently in the mix as well, judiciously inserting ellipses,[13] grammatical tweaks, and "missing" words and punctuation marks. Through all, I attempt to keep the original dialogues intact to the greatest extent possible, and I worked closely with each of my chapter collaborators to ensure that this was achieved.

Yet the ultimate shape and content of this work cannot help but be largely a product of my own invention. From the order of chapters to the presentation of materials in each, and from my decisions about what to leave in and what to leave out to the series of events that led to my conversations with these ten particular individuals in the first place, I am inescapably the primary author of this book.

Its principal voices, however, are those of my collaborators. Writing on behalf of her fellow autistic contributors to a landmark anthology, *Loud Hands: Autistic People, Speaking*, Julia Bascom asserts, "We are complete, complex, human beings leading rich and meaningful existences and deserving dignity, respect, human rights, and the primary voice in the conversation about us."[14] The same philosophy applies here: the voices that really count in this text, the ones that most urgently need to be heard— and *listened* to—are those of autistic people themselves. In common with Douglas Biklen in his book *Autism and the Myth of the Person Alone*, "most of all, I want to know how people who have been classified with autism interpret themselves and the world." But I would go one step further: I want people who read this book to be motivated to seek that kind of knowledge for themselves as well.[15]

With all that said, it takes two to tango, and in the end each conversation unfolds as a mutually transformative duet, encounters in which all parties come to the table (or computer or smartphone) with their own interests and agendas, and through which we eventually influence each other to think, perceive, and feel a bit differently than before. My collaborators were every bit as involved in questioning their own ideas, and mine, as the other way around. I can certainly say that my process of questioning and reflecting, of learning from and sometimes even arguing with my collaborators, has profoundly affected the way I think as a scholar, play as a musician, and am as a human being. Furthermore, I am not shy about allowing the results of that process to bubble up to the surface of the text, warts and all.

I would also venture to say that my collaborators and I were all deeply invested in changing our world for the better through the collaborative undertaking of this project, especially where the rights of autistic people are concerned and where unmet opportunities to foster better mutual understanding between autistic and non-autistic people exist. We have worked together essentially as applied ethnomusicologists, directing our individual voices and collective voice toward what Jeff Todd Titon defines as *applied ethnomusicology*: "the process of putting ethnomusicological research to practical use."[16] In that pursuit, we have gone beyond the project's stated goal of exploring how autistic people make and experience music, and why it matters to them that they do, to embrace a larger goal of radically transforming the misguided ways that non-autistic people and institutions have too often conceived of and responded to autism and the people who "have" it.

WHOSE AUTISM? WHOSE SPECTRUM?

As noted earlier, my ten collaborators, for all of their many differences, share at least two things in common: each has an autism spectrum diagnosis and music plays a central role in each of their lives. That seems a straightforward enough rationale for their participation in this project, but appearances can be deceptive, for the question of just what the autism spectrum is—and by extension, who is "on" it—is anything but self-evident.

Liz Bell is a prominent parent advocate and the mother of an autistic child. In 2009, she was invited to a public forum on autism with the then-governor of New Jersey, Jon Corzine.[17] Also in attendance was Ari Ne'eman, a young man with Asperger's syndrome who had founded the Autistic Self Advocacy Network (ASAN), a pioneering organization "run by and for Autistic adults seeking to increase the representation of Autistic people across society."[18] Ne'eman would eventually also serve on the US federal government's National Council on Disability, with his nomination for that post coming from President Barack Obama.

This was Bell's first encounter with the rising young star of autistic self-advocacy, neurodiversity, and national disability policy. Their exchange is chronicled in John Donvan and Caren Zucker's book *In a Different Key: The Story of Autism*, a sweeping historical study which, it should be noted, has received much criticism from within the autistic self-advocacy and neuro-diversity communities.[19]

According to Donvan and Zucker's account, "When Ne'eman was called on, he stood, faced the governor, and made his familiar two-prong argument—that people with autism did require supports, which should be provided, but that did not justify any attempts at a treatment, or cure, or any other response that would make an autistic person any less autistic."[20]

The first part of Ne'eman's argument made perfect sense to Bell, but she strongly disagreed with the second part: the notion that any effort to treat or cure autism was essentially unjustifiable. Donvan and Zucker write that, according to Bell, "the more activists like Ne'eman—talented, articulate, persuasive—proudly asserted their autistic identities, the more people seemed to forget about those with autism who had severe impairments," that is, about those "who would never speak, who had to be watched round-the-clock so that they didn't wander out at night and drown in a river or a swimming pool, who needed their diapers changed at least twice a day, even as adults."[21]

After the forum was over, Bell was introduced to Ne'eman and took him to task on several of the issues he had raised, most especially the cure issue: "If someday, Ari, my son and I can argue like you and I are arguing now, and he can make the case you're making against cures—then, yeah, I will be saying he was 'cured.'" Ne'eman, by Donvan and Zucker's report, listened respectfully to what Bell had to say, "but he stood his ground."[22]

Many neurodiversity proponents would contend that Bell's critique of Ne'eman (or at least of Donvan and Zucker's rendering of it) is misguided, that it fundamentally distorts the substance of Ne'eman's well-conceived positions regarding the rights and possibilities for advancement of *all* autistic people, not just those "like him."[23] These positions are clearly outlined in his influential essay "The Future (and the Past) of Autism Advocacy, or Why the ASA's Magazine, *The Advocate*, Wouldn't Publish This Piece," in which the author proclaims that "the traditional priorities of autism advo-cacy, which focus on eliminating the autism spectrum rather than pursuing quality of life, communication, and inclusion for all autistic people, need to be reset." In making his case, Ne'eman points out that autistic adults are chronically underserved "in crucial fields such as employment, community living supports, transportation, disability discrimination and rights protection"; that our public school systems are "rampant with violence and abuse against students with disabilities, with students on the spectrum subject to a particularly high risk of injury and even death"; and that "crucial barometers of inclusion with respect to community living and access show that to be on the autism spectrum is to be left out of many of the most important innovations of the disability rights movement of the last 20 years."

Meanwhile, Ne'eman continues, the main focus of attention with respect to autism has been on "discredited theories about vaccines, pseudoscientific treatments, and the rhetoric of pity and despair," while the lion's share of research dollars has been directed toward a misguided quest for treatments, interventions aimed at "normalization," and ideally a cure. "For many of us," he writes, "the prospect of cure and normalization denies essential aspects of our identity." While autism "does not represent the totality of who we are, it is indeed a significant part of us, and to pursue normalization instead of quality of life forces us into a struggle against ourselves."

But Ne'eman is not so naïve as to deny the very real and profound difficulties that arise from having autism. Of course we should "be engaged in trying to ameliorate the many challenges associated with being autistic," he states, but "we should target our efforts towards the real challenges we face, rather than towards a broader, nebulous concept of 'curing' autism that is offensive to many of the people that it aims to benefit. Second, we should in every instance consider the fact that it is often social barriers rather than disability itself that pose the problems we face."[24]

Ne'eman's arguments are compelling, but the "we" he claims to represent encompasses many people who do not share his views. Liz Bell is certainly one of those people, but so too is Donald Rindale, who informed me on multiple occasions during our dialogues that, given the opportunity to rid himself of his autistic condition, he would do so in a heartbeat. Unlike Ari, Donald *wants* to be cured.

And what about the legions of autistic people who neither speak nor type nor text, who do not—at least not yet—have any effective means of communication through which to share their wants and needs, their knowledge and their opinions? Can we necessarily assume that Ne'eman speaks for all of them, or even for any one of them in particular? Or that Bell does? Probably not. So much is still unknowable, and the whole matter is infinitely complex. Ne'eman's persuasive appeals notwithstanding, "the priorities of autism advocacy" are anything but obvious.

There is no getting around this dilemma. The best we can do is to, first, be as forthright as we can in recognizing and acknowledging the limitations of our understandings and points of view; second, accept that our intentions will not necessarily be matched by others' perceptions of them; and third, hope through it all that some good will come. These have been guiding priorities in the creation of this book, but knowing where to start required a viable working definition of *autism* to begin with. That definition came from the aforementioned autistic scholar Nick Walker.

NICK WALKER SPEAKS: "WHAT IS AUTISM?"

There can be no complete or universally agreed-upon answer to a question as complex as "What is autism?"[25] Nick Walker's response to that question, however, has been the most helpful to me.

On March 1, 2014, Walker posted a general introductory piece entitled "What Is Autism?" on his popular blog, "Neurocosmopolitanism: Nick Walker's Notes on Neurodiversity, Autism, and Cognitive Liberty."[26] His rationale for doing so, posted as a preface to the essay itself, is instructive, both in the perspective it offers on autism and in what it reveals about the position from which he writes.

"How many websites are there that have a page called something like 'What Is Autism?' or 'About Autism'?" the preface begins. "How often do organizations, professionals, scholars, and others need to include a few paragraphs of basic introductory 'What Is Autism?' text in a website, brochure, presentation, or academic paper?"

"I've seen so many versions of that obligatory 'What Is Autism' or 'About Autism' text," writes Walker. "And they're almost all terrible ... What is needed is some good basic introductory 'What Is Autism' text that is (1) consistent with current evidence; (2) not based in the pathology paradigm; (3) concise, simple, and accessible; [and] (4) formal enough for professional and academic use." And since he has been unable to find such a text anywhere, he says, "I wrote one. And here it is." He then grants permission to anyone "to reprint the text below, in whole or in part," free of charge, asking only for a credit or proper citation in return.

"Autism is a genetically-based human neurological variant," Walker establishes at the start of the piece proper. "The complex set of interrelated characteristics that distinguish autistic neurology from non-autistic neurology is not yet fully understood, but current evidence indicates that the central distinction is that autistic brains are characterized by particularly high levels of synaptic connectivity and responsiveness."

It is this unique feature of autistic neurology, Walker suggests, that makes the subjective experience of autistic individuals "more intense and chaotic than that of non-autistic individuals." He posits that autistic minds tend "to register more information" than non-autistic minds, with the result that "the impact of each bit of information tends to be both stronger and less predictable" in the autistic case. He goes on to explain that autism is a "developmental phenomenon, meaning that it begins *in utero* and has a pervasive influence on development, on multiple levels, throughout the lifespan." It produces a range of conditions marked by "distinctive, atypical ways of thinking, moving, interaction, and sensory and cognitive processing." Drawing a computer analogy, he explains that autistic people seem to have a different neurological operating system from those of their non-autistic counterparts.

Walker accurately indicates that according to current estimates, "somewhere between one percent and two percent of the world's population is autistic." He claims that while the number of individuals with an autism diagnosis has been growing continuously for several decades, "evidence suggests that this increase in diagnosis is the result of increased public and professional awareness, rather than an actual increase in the prevalence of autism." That claim, it should be noted, expresses just one position out of many in a highly contentious arena of debate; there is an array of competing theories concerning this dramatic rise in the rate of autism diagnosis.[27]

"Despite underlying neurological commonalities," Walker continues, "autistic individuals are vastly different from one another." Some, he says, "exhibit exceptional cognitive talents. However, in the context of a society designed around the sensory, cognitive, developmental, and social needs of non-autistic individuals, autistic individuals are almost always disabled to some degree—sometimes quite obviously, and sometimes more subtly."

Next, Walker turns his attention to the realm of social interaction, in which he suggests that "autistic individuals tend to consistently be disabled." He explains that because an autistic child's sensory experience of the world is generally more intense and chaotic than that of a child who is not autistic, "the ongoing task of navigating and integrating that experience" takes up "more of the autistic child's attention and energy. This means the autistic child has less attention and energy available to focus on the subtleties of social interaction," and this has consequences. "Difficulty meeting the social expectations of non-autistics often results in social rejection, which further compounds social difficulties and impedes social development. For this reason, autism has been frequently misconstrued as being essentially a set of 'social and communication deficits.'" Such a view is misleading according to Walker, since he believes that the social challenges faced by autistic individuals are, rather, "just by-products of the intense and chaotic nature of autistic sensory and cognitive experience."

Walker concludes the piece by debunking another pervasive stereotype. "Autism is still widely regarded as a 'disorder,'" he accurately reports, "but this view has been challenged in recent years by proponents of the neurodiversity model, which holds that autism and other neurocognitive variants are simply part of the natural spectrum of human biodiversity, like variations in ethnicity or sexual orientation (which have also been pathologized in the past). Ultimately," he states in closing, "to describe autism as a disorder represents a value judgment rather than a scientific fact."[28]

DOING THINGS WITH WORDS

Beyond the reality that all ten of my collaborators have an autism spectrum diagnosis and significant ties to music, they share a third important commonality as well. A reader of an earlier manuscript version of this book observed that everyone in it is someone who has not only made a life out of doing things with music, but also "out of doing things with words": they are, the reader states, "writers, graduate students, public speakers, rhetorical activists." They speak, write, type, and/or sign to communicate, and very eloquently (and all in English) at that. They are not only verbal, then, but exhibit high levels of verbal *ability*, and the one member of the cohort who does not literally speak, Amy Sequenzia, is as profoundly verbal as any of them. Amy uses words—typed using just one finger and with the aid of a full-time associate and advanced assistive technologies—with artful lucidity, this despite the "non-speaking, low-functioning autistic" label with which she has customarily been saddled, and which she has persuasively debunked in published writings.[29] Thus, there is an undeniable representational bias in this book, since the voices we hear from within it are of people who can and do use language to communicate.[30]

But as we have already seen, the autism spectrum is profusely heterogeneous, and one of the major ways in which people on it differ from one another is in the degree to which they use language to understand and engage with the world. Some never use language, some use it only minimally, some use it in idiosyncratic ways, some use it only when assisted by "facilitators" or "translators," and others use it with deft skill, even virtuosity.

It is to this latter category of skilled wordsmiths that each of my ten collaborators belongs, albeit in different ways and to varying degrees. This makes for compelling reading, but also a relatively limited scope of inquiry given the broad range of personhood that the autism spectrum encompasses and the profound impact language has on so many facets of human experience. Autistic people who neither speak nor write—and who neither type nor sign, let alone play music or talk about their experiences of it—are not heard from directly in these pages. Their conspicuous absence and the problems it raises, along with larger debates about representation and advocacy that their exclusion reveals, are addressed in the dialogues of several chapters—most notably those featuring Donald Rindale, Ibby Grace, and Amy Sequenzia—but this does not change the fact that this book ultimately covers a relatively small and exclusive slice of autistic life.

The severe problems that many autistic people face, such as self-injurious behaviors and a near-total inability to communicate with others, are topics that come up only rarely in these dialogues. There will be readers who resent, or at least criticize, the book's focus on a group of individuals whose autism-related challenges may seem relatively minor compared to their own, or compared to those of their autistic children, siblings, students, patients, or clients. Notwithstanding the fact that books in general are things of words populated by people who use words, I have no real answers to such charges, other than to state the obvious—that no single work can accomplish all things—and to profess my sincere hope that this book will pave the way for other works, and other kinds of works, that serve to bring a fuller spectrum of autistic neurodiversity to wide public attention.

PERFORMING ABILITY

Issues of ability and disability have loomed large throughout this project. In every case, my collaborators are people for whom ability *matters*, be that the ability to use language artfully, write musical sounds into poetry and prose, hear music as colors, "think in music," or capture the deepest emotional qualities of a Liszt piano etude in recital. Once again, they cannot be said to represent a truly broad cross-section of the autism spectrum; rather, they represent a relatively small subsection of it.[31] All might aptly be described as "talented" individuals, and both their particular talents and the ways these are appreciated—by themselves and by others (including me)—bring to mind Francesca Happé and Uta Frith's memorable phrase "the beautiful otherness of the autistic mind."[32]

Happé and Frith critique stereotypes that too readily pair autism with "exceptional talent" or "savant skills," and that on the flipside contrast that brand of autistic exceptionalism with its polar opposite: disability so profound that even the possibility of ability, let alone talent, is categorically denied.[33] The fetishization of extreme autistic talent and severe autistic impairment alike are fraught with liabilities. That said, it would be disingenuous for me to suggest that the talents of my conversational partners—their performances of ability—do not contribute significantly to what makes the conversations in this book thought-provoking and interesting.

MAKING UP (AUTISTIC) PEOPLE

The philosopher Ian Hacking has observed that "our sciences create kinds of people that in a certain sense did not exist before," and that once created, these kinds of people become all but impossible to ignore *as such*, for we are progressively entrapped by the modes of language and the frames of reference invented to account for them. Hacking identifies this human category-generating mechanism as the process of "making up people."[34] He invokes a passage from Nietzsche's *The Gay Science* to amplify his point. "There is something," wrote Nietzsche, "that causes me the greatest difficulty, and continues to do so without relief: unspeakably more depends on what things are called than on what they are."[35]

Hacking enlists the example of the autism spectrum to illustrate how all this works. He writes that in 1943, indeed even in 1973, "autism was a rare developmental disorder with a quite definite, narrowly characterised stereotype," but that this is no longer the case. "Today," Hacking observes, "we have the autistic spectrum. We have high-functioning people with autism. We have Asperger's, a name introduced into English in 1981 by the British psychiatric social worker Lorna Wing," who adapted it "from a diagnosis made in 1944 in Vienna by Hans Asperger, a distinguished paediatrician in the German-speaking world, whom Wing made prominent in English." Nowadays, he explains, the designation of Asperger's (or Asperger's syndrome) is typically applied "to people who had few difficulties acquiring language, but have all the other autistic symptoms," but whatever clarity that distinction might yield is compromised by the frequent identification of Asperger's as a condition "loosely synonymous with high-functioning autism." And then there are the many additional layers adding to all of this rich, albeit confounding, complexity. "High-functioning autists are beginning to crop up in fiction, much as multiple personalities did twenty years ago," Hacking notes, and some "high-functioning autistic people talk of forming an autism liberation front. Stop trying to make us like you. We do some things better than you, and you do some things better than us, so leave us be."[36]

Made up or otherwise, autism exists. It is a human invention that, once created, can never be truly undone, like race, or gender, or sexual orientation. But what the term "autism" is taken to mean, what the phrase "autism spectrum" is understood to connote, and how we choose to respond to the opportunities and challenges of our profuse neurodiversity at a historical moment demanding new and progressive approaches to old and deeply embedded problems—these are not fixed; these are not static. They are fluid, in constant motion, continually in flux. Choose well in our decisions and we can "make up" a better world than the one we have now: more inclusive, more humane, and more compassionate; a world in which our seemingly unassailable drive to classify and categorize one another directs us toward knowledge rather than fear, acceptance rather than exclusion, and conversation rather than objectification.

If the conversations that follow in some small way activate this process, turning Nietzsche's dialectic on its head by compelling us to relate to autistic people not as such, but rather as the resolutely distinct individuals that they are and conceive themselves to be, then this book will have served a useful purpose. After all, as Ibby Grace gently but firmly insists in the opening pages of *Typed Words, Loud Voices*, "An excellent way to understand us is to really listen to what we have to say." Or as Kassiane A. Sibley, another well-known autistic author and activist, puts it, albeit in rather more direct terms, "You don't get to tell me who and what I am. I do."[37]

NOTES

1. The issue of how best to refer to people with autism spectrum diagnoses—as autistic people, autistics, individuals with autism, etc.—has generated much debate. My approach aligns with that of the anthropologist of autism Elizabeth Fein, who writes: "In many disability contexts and communities, using 'person-first language' (i.e. *Steve is a person with autism*) is considered to be more respectful than using language that characterizes that person according to their condition (i.e. *Steve is autistic* or *Steve is an autistic*). However, in the autism world, this formulation of the relationship between person and condition is not so straightforward. Many in the autistic self-advocacy community have voiced a strong preference against person-first language, arguing that autism is not, in fact, separate from themselves in the way such language implies. . . . [I]n the absence of a single good answer to the thorny question of respectful language, I have chosen to use both of these formulations and alternate between them as seems appropriate for the context. Whenever possible, I follow the preferences of the person to or about whom I am speaking" (Fein 2012, ix).

2. In their article, "Music: A Unique Window into the World of Autism," Istvan Molnar-Szakacs and Pamela Heaton highlight Leo Kanner's prescient implication of "an unusual preoccupation with music" among the autistic children in the case studies for his seminal 1943 article "Autistic Disturbances of Affective Contact" (Kanner 1943; Molnar-Szakacs and Heaton 2012, 320). Since Kanner and up until the present, numerous other researchers have written on autistic musical proclivities. These include exceptional feats of memory and a disproportionate propensity for absolute pitch, which is often referred to alternately as "perfect pitch" (Brown et al. 2003; Dohn et al. 2012; Mottron et al. 1999).

   Contrary to popular misconceptions, the term *autistic* originated not with Kanner, but rather with the renowned Swiss psychiatrist Eugen Bleuler, who in a 1910 paper described "autistic withdrawal of the patient to his fantasies, against which any influence from outside becomes an intolerable disturbance" (Bernier and Gerdts 2010, 149). The use of "autistic" by Bleuler, however, was not in reference to a specific psychiatric condition; rather, it was presented in the context of a listing of symptoms of schizophrenia. The term *autistic* was also used by Hans Aspeger prior to its adaptation by Kanner (Bernier and Gerdts 2010, 149).
3. See Gold 2011, Reschke-Hernández 2011, Simpson and Keen 2011, and Edwards 2016 on music therapy in the treatment of autism.
4. S. Timothy Maloney has written on Gould (Maloney 2006), Stephanie Jensen-Moulton on Wiggins (Jensen-Moulton 2006). Other relevant writings may be found in the *Oxford Handbook of Music and Disability Studies* (Howe et al. 2016).
5. This topic is discussed in Straus's book *Extraordinary Measures* (Straus 2011, 163–65). Dave Headlam presents related arguments in his essay "Learning to Hear Autistically" (Headlam 2006).
6. For related approaches, see Dell'Antonio and Grace's co-authored piece "No Musicking about Us without Us!" (Dell'Antonio and Grace 2016), as well as Elyse Marrero's master's thesis, "Performing Neurodiversity" (Marrero 2012).
7. Decisions concerning whether to use pseudonyms (like Zena Hemelson) or actual names (like Mara Chasar) in reference to individuals included in this book were made by the individuals themselves (and/or by their parents in the case of minors). This protocol is in compliance with research requirements set by the Human Subjects Committee of the Institutional Review Board (IRB) at Florida State University, which annually reviewed the project and under whose guidance the research was conducted.
8. Four main publications came out of reports on the Music-Play Project (Bakan 2009; Bakan, Koen, Bakan, et al. 2008; Bakan, Koen, Kobylarz, et al. 2008; Koen et al. 2008). Notably, these works were focused not only on the ethnomusicology of autism but also on the ethnomusicology of children's musical lives and cultures. On ethnomusicological approaches to the study of children, Patricia Shehan Campbell and colleagues have done important work (Campbell 2010; Campbell and Wiggins 2013).
9. The Artism Ensemble was the subject of a series of articles and chapters published between 2014 and 2016 (Bakan 2014a, 2014b, 2014c, 2015a, 2015b, 2016a, 2016b).

10. The term *musicking* was first introduced by Christopher Small (Small 1998). Musicking activities involve not only performing or composing music but also listening to, dancing to, or otherwise relating to music.

11. This definition is drawn from Nick Walker's essay "Throw Away the Master's Tools" (Walker 2012). The term *neurodiversity* was first popularized by the sociologist Judy Singer in the late 1990s (Singer 1999; Fein 2012). Elizabeth Fein explains that it "connotes a pluralist acceptance and sometimes embrace of atypical neurological development," and notes that while in theory "the term encompasses all the many variations of human neurology[,] in practice, it is most often used by people on the autism spectrum who value their condition as an intrinsic and in some ways beneficial part of who they are" (Fein 2012, 16).

12. Gibson's dissertation is titled "The Early Lexical Acquisition of a Child with Autism Spectrum Disorder" (Gibson 2011).

13. Ellipsis marks indicating omission of passages of text are marked with periods separated by spaces (. . . or . . . .). Where three dots appear without spaces between them (...), these are from the original dialogue transcripts. In chat, email, and text messaging, people often use the marking "..." to imply something to the effect of, 'I'm still thinking about that' or 'There is more I could say about that.'

14. The quotation is from Bascom's *Loud Hands* foreword (Bascom 2012a, 10).

15. See Biklen's book *Autism and the Myth of the Person Alone* (Biklen 2005, 3). In these respects, the approach advanced here might also be productively compared to that of participatory action research (PAR) in the field of public health. As Baum, MacDougall, and Smith, writing in the *Journal of Epidemiology and Community Health*, explain, "PAR seeks to understand and improve the world by changing it. At its heart is collective, self reflective inquiry that researchers and participants undertake, so they can understand and improve upon the practices in which they participate and the situations in which they find themselves. The reflective process is directly linked to action, influenced by understanding of history, culture, and local context and embedded in social relationships. The process of PAR should be empowering and lead to people having increased control over their lives" (Baum, MacDougall, and Smith 2006). The Autistic Self Advocacy Network (ASAN) is a strong proponent of participatory action research in autism studies. Parallels between the approach of the present work and those employed by oral historians are also noteworthy (Frisch 2006; Perks and Thomson 2006; Ritchie 2015).

16. This definition is from Titon's Curry Lecture on applied ethnomusicology (Titon 2011). The issue of defining applied ethnomusicology is extensively addressed in *The Oxford Handbook of Applied Ethnomusicology* (Pettan and Titon 2015).

17. The account of the event provided here is derived from the book *In a Different Key* (Donvan and Zucker 2016, 525–26).

18. This quotation is from the narrative biography of Ari Ne'eman posted on the "Leadership" page of the Autistic Self Advocacy Network's website.

19. See, for example, Erin Human's review of *In a Different Key*, titled "Cognitive Difference in a Different Key" (Human 2016).

20. *In a Different Key* (Donvan and Zucker 2016, 525).

21. *In a Different Key* (Donvan and Zucker 2016, 525).

22. *In a Different Key* (Donvan and Zucker 2016, 526).

23. See Ne'eman's essay "The Future (and the Past) of Autism Advocacy" (Ne'eman 2012), as well as the related writings of others in the autistic self-advocacy and neurodiversity communities (Bascom 2012a, 2012b; Sequenzia and Grace 2015).

24. The quotations in this passage were excerpted from "The Future (and the Past) of Autism Advocacy" (Ne'eman 2012, 89–94).

25. The books *NeuroTribes* (Silberman 2015) and *In a Different Key* (Donvan and Zucker 2016) both offer substantive, albeit often starkly contrasting, historical perspectives on the ever-changing definitions of autism and the autism spectrum.

26. Nick Walker blogs at neurocosmopolitanism.com

27. An illuminating discussion may be found in *NeuroTribes* (Silberman 2015, 381–423).

28. See the relevant entry on Nick Walker's neurocosmopolitanism.com blog for the complete text (Walker 2014).

29. See Sequenzia's "Non-Speaking, 'Low-Functioning'" (Sequenzia 2012).

30. It should be noted, however, that in the research projects leading up to this one, and in the Music-Play Project especially, this was not the case. About a quarter of the more than thirty children who participated in the Music-Play Project between 2005 and 2009 used language in communication to only a limited degree, and in a few cases almost not at all. For an enlightening case study focused on one of these children, see "Following Frank" (Bakan, Koen, Kobylarz, et al. 2008).

31. Note that this statement applies specifically to the present research and not to earlier, related programs such as the Music-Play Project, which involved the participation of individuals representing a much broader cross-section of the autism spectrum and was discussed in an earlier series of publications (Bakan 2009; Bakan, Koen, Bakan, et al. 2008; Bakan, Koen, Kobylarz, et al. 2008).

32. The quotation is from Francesca Happé and Uta Frith's book *Autism and Talent* (Happé and Frith 2010, xi). Expanding on their idea of "the beautiful otherness of the autistic mind," Happé and Frith explain that in popular accounts of autism, "the existence of extraordinary talent in art, music, maths [mathematics], calendar calculation or memory, often referred to as savant skills, has become a stock in trade. As a result of this fascination, it is now very likely that any eccentric scientist or artist, living or dead, will come under scrutiny for having traits of autism or Asperger syndrome. But are geniuses, such as Newton or Einstein, personifications of the association of autism and talent? In our view, this notion misrepresents both autism and talent. Nevertheless, the association of autism with special talent, sometimes at the highest level, cannot be denied and provides one of the most tantalizing mysteries of this condition" (Happé and Frith 2010, xi).

33. On autistic musical savants, see also Joseph Straus's "Idiots Savants" (Straus 2014).

34. "Making Up People" (Hacking 2006).

35. Nietzsche, quoted in "Making Up People" (Hacking 2006); for original source see Nietzsche, *The Gay Science* (Nietzsche and Kaufmann 1974).

36. "Making Up People" (Hacking 2006).

37. The Grace quote is from *Typed Words, Loud Voices* (Sequenzia and Grace 2015, 14). The Sibley quote is from a piece titled "Kassiane A. Sibley's Open Letter to Identity Police (Part 1)" (Sibley 2013). Kasianne Sibley is part of an important

movement led by autistic women and transfolk of color who are helping to redefine the terrain of autistic and neurodiversity activism. She and other advocates such as Lydia Brown and Morenike Onaiwu, as well as organizations like the Autism Women's Network, have taken strong political stances in their efforts to reclaim and reshape the terms, conditions, and perceptions of autistic cultural identity relative to a much broader conception of ethnic/gendered intersectionality than has formerly been acknowledged.

CHAPTER 2
Zena Hamelson

I have characters in my head. I think about them a ton, *like probably more than I think about my own life. That's fine with me because they kind of relate to me. A lot of them have similar diagnosises [sic]. . . . And what's happening was, they were all musicians, the people in my head, and so I was imagining them playing the instruments.*

Zena Hamelson (2011)

Ten-year-old Zena sits in a chair staring blankly at the wall, flapping her hands, repeatedly straightening and bending her legs. Occasionally she looks down and twists and pulls on her fingers; sometimes she stands up and paces stiff-legged around the room.

Zena has a diagnosis of Asperger's syndrome, and the "odd, unusual, or repetitive behaviors, known as 'stimming,'" that she is performing conform to that diagnosis.[1] Stimming, short for self-stimulatory behaviors, "is common in many individuals with developmental disabilities; however, it appears to be more common in autism," explains Stephen Edelson of the Autism Research Institute, adding that stimming is associated "with some dysfunctional system in the brain or periphery" and tends to "interfere with attention and learning." There "are numerous ways to reduce or eliminate stereotypic behaviors," adds Edelson, "such as exercise as well as providing an individual with alternative, more socially-appropriate, forms of stimulation. . . ."[2] The implication is clear: reducing or eliminating stimming is a desirable goal.

As Zena stims, the people around her are making music—fun, uplifting music, improvised but with a compelling Afro-Peruvian *festejo* groove. There are about eighteen players taking part in all, a mix of professional musicians, adult "non-musicians," and five children ranging in age from seven to fourteen. Three of the children are girls: Zena, Mara, and E. S.; the two boys go by NICKstr and Coffeebot. All five kids have some kind of an autism spectrum diagnosis; none of the adults do. The "non-musician" adults are parents of the participating children, while the professional musicians are a combination of music students and faculty members from Florida State University and Florida A&M University who have variously found their way to Tallahassee from points of origin far and near: China, Peru, Bolivia, Canada, and various parts of the United States.

This is the first-ever meeting of the Artism Ensemble, our inaugural session. It is going remarkably well. Mara, NICKstr, and Coffeebot are moving about the room freely, trying out the various drums, shakers, thunder tubes, and other percussion instruments that have been laid out to create our E-WoMP, or Exploratory World Music Playground. I join them in their E-WoMP musical games; so to do their parents, though in more reserved fashion and usually on just a single instrument each. Meanwhile, Artism's staff musicians are seated in a semi-circle of chairs that half-surrounds me and the kids, parents, and percussion. They play on a variety of instruments: guitars, a stand-up bass, flutes, an Aboriginal Australian didgeridoo,

2.2 The Artism Ensemble rehearsing in the E-WoMP in 2013, Council on Culture and Arts (COCA) Building, Tallahassee, Florida. Left to right: Vivianne Asturizaga, Carlos Silva, Carlos Odria, Brian Hall, Michael Bakan, Coffeebot, NICKstr, Richard Voss, Michael Chasar, Elyse Marrero, Mara Chasar, E. S.

a Chinese *zheng* zither. All are professional-caliber players on their respective instruments, as well as highly skilled improvisers.

Thanks to a generous donation from the Remo instrument company, the kids, parents, and I have an array of enticing percussion instruments to choose from: djembes, congas, bongos, ocean drums, cuicas, a large gathering drum, tom-toms, egg shakers, and more. There is even a miniature drum set consisting of five flat, bodyless drums that are yoked together by a spider-like contraption of stands. That rig took me a long time to set up before the session, so I'm disappointed when none of the kids shows even the slightest interest in playing it. Most of the Remo instruments are modeled after traditional counterparts from West Africa, Latin America, Native America, East and Southeast Asia, and other world regions. There are a few additional drums that actually come from some of those places as well; these are from my personal collection.

The percussion instruments are distributed around the room in a way that creates an impression of randomness; at least that's the intention. We don't want the children to feel like they're in a formal music-making environment, let alone a clinical setting. Rather, we want this to be a place where they can have fun and basically do whatever they want to, free of any specific demands or expectations, musical or otherwise. The instruments themselves facilitate this. All are high yield for low input, meaning that they produce a satisfying sound immediately—no training or prior experience needed.

Beyond the instruments selected for the E-WoMP, the mallets and beaters used are important too. All are equipped with soft rubber or foam-padded ends to ensure that no one gets hurt by an inadvertent mallet strike to the head or drumstick poke to the eye. The soft-headed mallets also have the advantage of keeping the volume from getting too loud, though the two boys are putting that theory to the test as they whack on the biggest drums they can find as hard as possible. This doesn't appear to please E. S. much; she's rocking back and forth near a corner of the room and covering her ears, but when I come over to check on her and ask if she's doing okay, she smiles and nods enthusiastically. I tell the boys to lighten it up a bit anyhow and they do. Meanwhile, Mara has grabbed a couple of egg shakers and is dancing gleefully around the perimeter of the E-WoMP, singing with abandon as she goes. Somehow, this eclectic, intercultural, intergenerational, and neurodiverse band is putting it all together around the contagious festejo groove of the group's two Peruvian-born guitarists, Carlos Odria and Carlos Silva. Everyone appears to be having a good time and everyone is in sync.

Everyone, that is, except Zena. She seems entirely detached, and I am mystified by this. Back in 2009, Zena had been a shining star in the

Music-Play Project (MPP), Artism's predecessor program: musically active and creative, a natural leader of her music-play group, a fine ensemble player, a willing and talented improviser. Back in 2009, she had been consistently on task and rarely stimmed, and if she stimmed at all it was only for fleeting moments.

And now stimming is all she seems to do. Why? It is all the more vexing as her mother, Suzanne, has conveyed to me on a few occasions in recent weeks—in emails and on the phone—how excited Zena is about this new Artism project, how she can't wait to get started. It just doesn't add up for me, this seeming regression into an insular world of stimming and detachment by a girl who seemed entirely unlikely to go there.

The session ends. A week passes. Another Monday evening Artism session arrives, but this time Zena and Suzanne do not. I have heard nothing from them in the interim. I'm disappointed, but not surprised. I assume that they have dropped out of the program and just haven't gotten around to letting me know yet.

But the following week, they are back again.

This session unfolds much like the first one for Zena. She spends most of her time stimming and staring off blankly into space. She occasionally bangs out a rhythm or two on one of the E-WoMP instruments, but only when one of the other players or I hand her something to play and try to coax her into joining in; and when she does, it is only for fleeting, grudging moments of lackluster participation. She looks decidedly unhappy in those moments, which leads me to observe that by contrast she actually looks to be quite happy the rest of the time, that is, when she *is* stimming.

As we're putting away the instruments at session's end, Suzanne approaches me with Zena in tow. Can we step outside and talk for a moment, she asks me. Sure, I reply. She explains that Zena has a problem. She likes being in Artism and is really enjoying the sessions—especially listening to the two amazing guitarists, Carlos and Carlos, and the Chinese zheng virtuoso, Haiqiong—but she doesn't enjoy how other members of the group, myself included, keep trying to get her to join in with the playing. She wants to be able to listen and respond to the music "in her own way," Suzanne explains, even if that means just flapping her hands and twisting her fingers and pacing around the room. For now, at least, that is how she wishes to participate, and she wants to know, first, if that's okay with me, and second, assuming it is, whether I can pass along a request to the rest of the band to just let her do her own thing. Yes and yes, absolutely, I reply, embarrassed at the realization that this is how we should have been running the sessions all along.

With the change, things get better. Everyone respects Zena's desire to engage with the group on her own terms, and Zena seems liberated by the shift. Her stimming becomes more relaxed and expressive, her self-consciousness seems to melt away, and by the next rehearsal she is playing instruments and starting to interact with the other players, at least some of the time. She even introduces an original arrangement of the Beatles' "A Hard Day's Night" for the ensemble to play and directs it while leading from the steelpan (steel drum). Eventually she will create and lead other pieces as well, such as her West African–inspired, improvisation-driven percussion ensemble number "Oh That!," which may be heard at the companion website (CW 2.1 ▶).

Zena's more overt way of participating with the group grows stronger with each rehearsal, though it does not replace her stimming mode. Rather, she finds a new comfort zone moving fluidly between stimming in her way and playing on the E-WoMP instruments with the other ensemble members. I eventually figure out that for Zena, neither the stimming mode nor the playing mode is superior to the other. They are just two different ways of being engaged in the experience, each preferred at one time or another for reasons known only to her.

I come to accept and appreciate Zena's shifting modes of participation over time. Still, I can't help but wonder, even long after the fact, what happened back in the beginning. Why had Zena retreated into herself and her apparently closed-off world of stimming in Artism's early days? And what had eventually enabled her to return, at least provisionally, to the kind of engaged musical participation that she had exhibited back in 2009?

A CONVERSATION WITH ZENA

In May of 2011, about six weeks after the end of the Artism Ensemble's first concert season, an opportunity to ask these questions presents itself when I sit down with Zena and Suzanne at their Tallahassee home. We enjoy a brief drumming jam session together before settling into a lengthy conversation.

"So, let's talk about Artism for a minute," I propose.

"Okay," says Zena.

"'Cause you like that."

"Yes."

"During the first couple of weeks, you . . . were participating in your way . . . but you weren't playing, you weren't playing instruments very much at all—sometimes I think you didn't play them at all. Do you remember in [the] Music-Play Project [in 2009]? There you used to play quite a bit, I seem to recall."

"Well, there was a reason why I played a lot in that," Zena offers. "I was afraid that someone was going to tell me I had to play if I didn't. . . . There were people with video cameras. It was just a lot of pressure and I felt like I had to play the instruments, like [that] was why I was there. And I was kind of scared because this one boy's mom had, like, really gross, like, acne on her face, and it scared me to death . . . and, like, a bad sunburn. Her skin looked like leather, and it just really made me feel sick."

Suzanne looks surprised. She tells Zena that she had always thought the reason she had not played early on "was because with the addition of the other musicians and instruments, that it was *so* stimulating to you that you just couldn't—"

Zena cuts her mother off mid-sentence. "Oh, I have an explanation for that," she assures us. "[In] the Artism project"—her voice trails off; she squints pensively, then speaks again. "I have characters in my head," she explains, shifting course. "I think about them a *ton*, like probably more than I think about my own life. That's fine with me because they kind of relate to me. A lot of them have similar diagnosises [sic]."

"Umm-HMM!" Suzanne exclaims with evident curiosity. "Have they always? Because I know you've had these characters in your head for a very long time."

"Yes, yes," Zena affirms. " . . . Well, the thing is there's kind of like a lot."

"Oh *real*-ly!" Suzanne replies with a chuckle.

"Yeah, there's this one band of brothers and there are, let me count." Zena pauses. She stares upward and begins to silently mouth the numbers. "There are ten of them. And I have a few other bands of brothers who they, like, play with."

"You mean, like, bands, like music bands?" Suzanne inquires.

"No, no."

"Oh. Just bands of brothers."

"Yeah."

"Gotchya."

"And what's happening was, they were all musicians, the people in my head, and so I was imagining them playing the instruments, like I had one on the zheng and one on the djembe, and everything."

"Ah, very cool," I say.

By this point, Zena's little brother "Roger" has joined her and Suzanne on the living room couch. He has been to a few Artism concerts and decides to join the conversation. "And one of them on the sitar," he interjects, "and one on that weird Chinese instrument—"

"The zheng!" Zena and Suzanne shout out in unison. Roger launches into an "air zheng" performance, rolling his eyes upward and sweeping his body from side to side as he pretends to pluck the strings of a twenty-one-string Chinese zither. His impersonation of Artism's resident zheng master Haiqiong Deng (Figure 2.3) makes Suzanne and me laugh. Not Zena, though.

"That thing's cool!" Suzanne exclaims, a reference to the zheng. "I was spellbound by [Haiqiong's] performance . . . just watching her play and how much she loved it and all."

2.3 The Artism Ensemble in concert at the Tallahassee Museum, 2011. Front row, left to right: NICKstr, Mara Chasar, Lia Chasar, Elyse Marrero. Back row, left to right: Carlos Silva, Michael Bakan, Brian Hall, Haiqiong Deng (playing the zheng), Ramin Yazdanpanah. (Note: Zena and Suzanne are onstage performing but have been cropped from the photograph, at their request, to protect their anonymity.) [Photo credit: Kent Hutchinson]

"She's, like, amazing!" Zena chimes in, eyes wide with excitement. "She, like, goes into a trance and goes—"; now it's Zena's turn to impersonate Haiqiong playing. She, too, rolls her eyes upward and swoops down across the "strings."

"Yeah, it was really beautiful to watch *and* listen to—" Suzanne begins to say, but Zena jumps in before her mother can finish the sentence.

"So did she really grow up, did she grow up in China?" Zena asks me, bursting with curiosity.

"Yeah, she did."

"You know, the whole time I was [in Artism] I was fighting an urge to ask her a million questions about back when she was [in] China, how much she knew about Tiananmen Square."

"Oh!" I exclaim, surprised.

"I was desperate to ask her, 'Have you ever seen the famous picture of Tiananmen Square where there's a guy jumping on a tank? Have you?'"

Zena's excitement is palpable. She starts stimming vigorously, bouncing up and down in place while flapping her hands. Then she freezes. She looks down at the floor. She has suddenly become self-conscious, maybe even embarrassed.

"Well, I thought it might be rude [to ask]," she whispers, eyes still downcast.

I steer the conversation back to an earlier topic: ". . . [W]e were talking about how at the beginning [of Artism], how you didn't really play much, and now you've explained that because you've got these characters in your head and then they were playing the instruments [you didn't feel the need to play yourself]."

"Yes!" Zena replies. Her downcast stare is replaced by a warm smile. She seems glad to hear me picking up the thread of her earlier remarks. I continue: "But then, at a certain point, that changed, and then you became [involved] very actively [in] playing and composing and directing the band. So just sort of take me through the process of how the whole Artism project unfolded for you and what it's done for you, good, bad, or otherwise."

Zena clearly likes this prompt. She responds to it without a moment's pause. "At the beginning," she recalls, "I was a little nervous that I'd have to play like in the last one [that is, like in the 2009 Music-Play Project]. But after a while I realized it was cool if I could just express myself in any way. And in the end I felt comfortable enough and my characters kind of merged with it. That's when I started playing more."

This intrigues me. "Okay," I begin in reply. "So the main thing, then, it sounds like, there were two things: the characters sort of merging"—Zena cuts me off: "And it was also just me getting more comfortable with it," she asserts.

"So when you say the characters merged," I ask her, "did they become"—I pause—"you?"

Zena squints again as she stares out the living room window, seemingly deep in thought. She turns back to face Suzanne and me, but as she answers my question, it is into her mother's eyes that she stares intently: "Yes!" she exclaims finally. A glowing smile spreads across her face. And suddenly she looks different, or at least she does to me: a little bit older, more mature, more self-assured. Calm clarity replaces the furtive glances of moments before.

A pregnant pause hangs in the air. Suzanne finally breaks through it.

"Cool!" she whispers in quiet fascination, and in that same moment Zena, poised and composed up to now, starts stimming intensely. She shakes her foot, twirls her hair around her fingers, then chews on her T-shirt as she looks back and forth nervously between Suzanne and me, as though seeking reassurance that it's okay for her to have characters in her head, that it's okay for them to merge and become her, that it's okay for her to just be herself, just the way she is.

NOTES

1. The quotation is from the book *Teaching Music to Students with Autism* (Hammel and Hourigan 2013, 75).
2. This passage is from the online article "Self-Stimulatory Behavior" published on the website of the Autism Research Institute (Edelson, n.d.).

CHAPTER 3
Mara Chasar

You know, when I hear about people saying people with autism aren't "normal" and get sur-
prised when we do things like use big words or do things they can't, I just think: We are normal.
We learn things just like "normal" people do, we talk when we feel like it to who we feel like
talking to just like "normal" people do, we play and dream and laugh and love just like "normal"
people do, even if we're too shy to admit it sometimes.

Mara Chasar (2013)

Mara Chasar was diagnosed with Asperger's syndrome at the age of three. She was seven when we began playing music together in the Music-Play Project (MPP) in 2009. At that time, her mother Lia reported to me that Mara was on normal grade level for her age in school and was very capable verbally, but that social interaction and communication were difficult for her. She added that Mara could be "challenging behaviorally," that her feelings were "hurt easily," that she didn't "like competition or understand games," and that she was "very musically and rhythmically oriented."

In MPP, Mara participated in one of the program's six E-WoMP music-play groups. Her experiences varied greatly from session to session. Much of the time she seemed to enjoy herself, most especially when she was dancing, which she did often and beautifully, creating a vocabulary of movement and expression that was all her own. At other times, though, she would become despondent and frustrated, sometimes pouting and asking her parents to take her home. For all of the ups and downs, though, MPP was a positive experience for Mara, and when I formed the Artism Ensemble in 2011 and invited her and her parents Lia and Mike to join the group, they signed on immediately.

It takes Mara some time to acclimatize to the very un-MPP-like musical environment of Artism: here, rather than being part of a small music-play group, she is instead a member of a large band that is already scheduled to go out in public and play concerts, and it includes several professional musicians from diverse world cultures as well as her child peers and their parents. But Mara soon grows into Artism and indeed flourishes—as a percussionist, a dancer, and a composer.

One of Mara's compositions for the group, a dramatic adaptation of Dr. Seuss's *Green Eggs and Ham* that she titles "Purple Eggs and Ham," becomes an Artism crowd favorite. (A rehearsal performance of the piece may be seen at the companion website [CW 3.1 ▶].) Mara herself stars in the production as "Mara-I-Am," the alter ego to Seuss's beloved "Sam-I-Am" character. The piece receives a rousing standing ovation when Artism performs it as the closing number of our concert for the Opening General Session of the 2013 Society for Disability Studies Conference in Orlando, Florida. Mara wows the crowd, not just in the concert itself, but also in an open question-and-answer session with the audience immediately following the show. She takes on one question after another, addressing each with insight, wit, and wisdom well beyond her years. By evening's end, Mara has addressed a range of topics encompassing everything from the distinction between "autism acceptance" and "autism awareness" to the special challenges of living with Asperger's in a society short on accommodations and long on judgment. Her contributions make a strong impression on the audience, and on me as well.

WRITING WITH MARA

Six weeks have passed since the Artism Ensemble concert in Orlando. It is August in Tallahassee. We are slogging through the dog days of summer: relentless heat, unbearable humidity, daily thunderstorms. Life as usual in the steamy south.

I am trying to write a book, this book. The problem is that I can't figure out where or how to begin. My thoughts drift to memories, in particular to memories of Mara at the post-concert Q&A in Orlando. There should be a chapter in the book about Mara, I think to myself. Then it hits me: I don't want to write *about* Mara; I want to write *with* her. And immediately I know what I have to do.

I pick up the phone and dial the Chasars' number. Lia answers. We chat for a bit before getting to the main purpose of my call. I tell her about the book I'm starting to write, my plan for a chapter focusing on Mara, and my just-hatched idea to collaborate directly with Mara in writing it.

"I'm pretty sure she'd be into it," Lia tells me, "but let me check with her." She does, reporting back to me minutes later that Mara definitely wants to do this.

We all meet up at my office an hour or so later. Mara has never been here before. She looks around at the stacks of books and videos and CDs, the endless piles of papers and folders, the Balinese masks and puppets, the computer and sound equipment, the piano and the many drums and other percussion instruments. She seems nervous at first, but her apprehension melts away the moment she feasts her eyes on a nice black office chair next to my desk. She plops herself down on the chair and gives it a good kick-start.

"Whee!!" Mara exclaims with glee as she tucks up her knees and whirls about in the chair, over and over and over again. The downcast eyes light up and open wide. The frown becomes a radiant smile and her laughter fills the room.

"I *love* spinny chairs!" she shrieks. "Spinny chair! Everyone loves the spinny chair!!"

She spins and spins, round and round, and she continues spinning as she quickly modulates from her playful tone to a more serious one.

"So what do you want?" she asks me.

I'm a bit thrown off by the question.

"Want?" I say, pondering, searching for just the right way to put it. "Oh, what do I want—well, I just want to talk to you, about autism and Asperger's and stuff like that," I venture, not sure how that's going to go over. Mara continues to spin. "You know," I continue, "you had such wonderful things to say about all that stuff during the question-and-answer session after our Orlando concert with Artism, and since then I've been reading this book written by autistic people—it's called *Loud Hands: Autistic People, Speaking*—and what you were saying is really in line with what they're saying.[1] So now I'm trying to write about music, and autism, and Artism and all that, and I think it would be great if you could write with me, because you have such amazing insights and I think having you share those would make the things I'm working on way better than anything I could write by myself."

"So you want me to help you write a book?"

"Well, yeah, a book, some articles, a few different things actually. Is that OK?"

"I think that sounds cool."

"Great. So how about you talk and I'll type out what you say, or else you can just sit here at the computer and type yourself if you prefer. That's fine, too."

"You type," she says. "I like *spinny chairs!*"

"Remember how our concert in Orlando was at that conference, you know, the one for the Disability Studies society?"

"Yeah."

"Well, after the rest of you guys left, I stayed around for the rest of the conference. There was this one session that was run by people who do disability studies but who also have autism themselves, and they thought that our concert was sponsored by this big organization called Autism Speaks. It wasn't, but they thought it was because I had handed out this questionnaire to the audience and one of the questions had to do with 'promoting autism awareness.' Well, it turns out that 'autism awareness' is a phrase that these people, and a lot of other autistic people, too, really hate. They think it's offensive, because what they want is autism *acceptance*, not autism awareness, because a main mission of Autism Speaks is to find a *cure* for autism, to get rid of it, and these people with autism say they don't *want* to be cured, they just want to be who they are and to be accepted for being who they are.[2] So then—"

"Who says autism is a bad thing?" Mara interjects in a tone of righteous indignation. "It sounds like this [Autism Speaks] organization is treating autism like cholera. Autism isn't cholera; it isn't some disease you can just cure. It's just *there*. You don't *need* to be aware of it; you just have to accept that it's there. I mean, you can't accept cholera; it's a disease."

"You told me that a lot of people find this organization offensive," Mara continues, "and honestly, you know, [from what you've said about it,] I do too. Awareness and acceptance are a lot different from each other. Yeah. Awareness means you know it's there, but acceptance means you know it's there and it's not going to go away. Of course, you can't accept something if you don't know it's there, so I guess we have to be aware of it *and* accept it. So if that organization's thing is 'Autism Awareness,' maybe they should change it to 'Autism Awareness *and* Acceptance.' And honestly, curing autism doesn't come in some kind of a pill or medication. And there *is* no cure. There really isn't. It's just there, wound into your personality."

Mara has stopped spinning momentarily. Now she resumes. "Spinning chairs! Spinning chairs make *everyone* happy!" she sings. Then, in a mock serious tone, "I get distracted easily," and after that, throwing back her hair and laughing wildly, "*especially by things like this that are SPINNY CHAIRS!!*"

"You know," I say to Mara, laughing along with her as she continues to spin, "the scientists and the doctors and therapists and people like that who specialize in autism, and the people in those organizations like Autism Speaks, would say that what you're doing now—spinning and spinning and spinning while we have this conversation—is an example of *stimming*, that it's a 'symptom' of your Asperger's or your autism or whatever."

"Stim-*what*?" Mara asks, seemingly confused. "What *is* that?"

"Stimming," I repeat. "It's a word that they use to describe so-called 'self-stimulating behaviors' that autistic people do when they're, I don't know, feeling stressed or uncomfortable or whatever, or maybe the scientists don't know why they do those things but they know they do them and they say that's one of the things that makes them autistic."

Mara's laughter now escalates to a fever pitch.

"That's just *ridiculous*!" she states incredulously. "I mean, I bet that the president has a spinny chair and sometimes *he* spins around."

"Which president? The president of the United States [Obama] or the president of Autism Speaks?"

"Both of them," she fires back. "I'm sure they look around and see if their security guards are around, and if they see the coast is clear they just kind of silently spin around in their chair. They probably don't laugh like I do because the president doesn't laugh, or at least lots of people think that, but that's just another stereotype—but still. Spinny chairs. I *like* spinny chairs."

There is a brief pause in the conversation as Mara continues to spin.

"I like to talk a lot," she explains, "but the president likes to talk a lot too. And he gives all those speeches, so why don't they say that the president needs to be 'cured,' because the president talks a lot too. If he's like me in *any* way, he needs to be 'cured,' *doesn't* he?"

I chuckle. Mara stops spinning, leans forward, and points to the spot on my computer monitor where I have just transcribed her last remark.

"Just say that I said that sarcastically," she insists. "I don't want to offend the president."

"I have something else I wanted to say," Mara announces after another brief pause, resuming her spinning at the same time. "You know, I think there should be a type of therapy that involves spinny chairs. There should be a room where there are rows and rows of spinny chairs, and a bunch of people would file in and sit down, and they'd all talk to each other and say, 'I wonder what this new therapy is?' And then the therapist would walk in and tell everyone to be quiet, and then he or she would say, 'Now, spin around in your chairs really fast!' and everyone would at first be really skeptical, but then someone would try it, whirling around and around. They'd say, 'Hey, this is fun!' and everyone else would start to do it, and then the whole room would be spinning around and around, or at least to everyone in the spinny chairs. Or a therapy where everyone gets together and just types or writes stories together. When I'm bored or sad or stressed, I like to sit down, ignore everyone, and just *write* for hours on end."

"You know," Mara continues, "when I hear about people saying people with autism aren't 'normal' and get surprised when we do things like use big words or do things they can't, I just think: We *are* normal. We learn things just like 'normal' people do, we talk when we feel like it to who we feel like talking to just like 'normal' people do, we play and dream and laugh and love *just like 'normal' people do*, even if we're too shy to admit it sometimes."

"Some of us have a few problems, but why do 'normal' people have to be the ones to 'fix' them?" Mara asks rhetorically, after which she instructs me to be sure to put "scary quotes" around each appearance of "normal" and around the word "fix" in the preceding section.

"Why are all the therapists 'normal' and we're not?" she adds. "In fact, the therapists should be people who used to have severe autism or Asperger's, or *whatever*, and then found out how to deal with their problems. Having a Ph.D. in psychology doesn't always make you an expert."

"What about people like me," I ask, "you know, who aren't autistic but work with people who are?"

"Well, you people seem pretty nice," Mara answers matter-of-factly, "and you seem to know what you're talking about, so people like you would be pretty good for that role. But I still like the idea of doctors and stuff who have autism."

A few minutes later, Mara is back to spinning in her favorite chair. The conversation turns to the subject of the Artism Ensemble. As she spins, Mara provides me with an astute, comparative reading of the different musical approaches she and her fellow child composers in the group employed.

". . . [You] know, I like to make my songs funny. And NICKstr likes to make his songs really precise. E. S. liked [*sic*] to make her songs quiet. And Coffeebot likes to make his songs precise and sort of loud, and he really likes the steel drum. Me, I really like all their songs. They're always so great. I mean, I don't know how Coffeebot comes up with those awesome beats; and E. S. [is amazing]! NICKstr, I don't always understand his songs. They've never been very predictable, even though he likes them to be precise, and honestly it's really cool seeing all these kids come up with different styles of songs."[3]

"And of course the Autism Ensemble [*sic*] is not a cure," Mara continues. "I don't treat it like a cure, because it isn't, and if you call it a cure I will disagree with you. It's simply the kind of way you can calm down and, you know, help with the bad parts of autism without restricting the good parts." I ask her what she means by that. "Well, what I mean is, a lot of famous people were autistic or Asperger's or something," she explains. "[My] Mom tells us that people like Einstein and Marie Curie and a bunch of other famous people had it. Mom tells me that a lot of people who have autism and Asperger's can be more creative and insightful than other people, insightful in a way, you know, where they've experienced a lot of the emotions that they're either writing about in stories, or plays, or poems; because a lot of people who have autism can swing between different emotions really quickly. I'm like that. Someone will just say one word and I become like a stereotyped *emo*. (Once again, if you haven't heard it before, an *emo* is one of those really sad, dark people. I just go around telling people 'Life is pointless' when I'm like that.) Of course, the bad parts in my situation are that when I get angry, I get ANGRY!! I mean, like, yelling, slamming-door angry. Of course, I never get physical angry. I don't punch or hit or bite, though I have bitten someone, but that was in third grade. What I meant by helping with the bad parts but not restricting the good parts is that Artism kind of helps with my anger issues without restricting my creativity, and that's all I got to say."

"Well, okay," I respond. "I know we've been at this for a while, but can you just tell me a little bit more about how that works?"

"It's the fact that I'm allowed to bang on drums for a while—and any instrument I want (as long as I don't break it or it's not meant to be banged)—without anybody telling me I'm supposed to do it *this* way, or I'm supposed to do it *that* way, or I'm supposed to put *this* there or *that* THERE, or I'm doing it wrong."

"Is that the most important one," I ask, "the one about not being told you're doing it wrong?"

"Yeah."

"Why is that so important, not to be told you're doing it wrong?"

"Because I'm told that every day. I want a break from it!"

Mara laughs, changing up the mood momentarily. "*Spinny chairs!*" she proclaims in a triumphant reprise of her familiar refrain before finally returning to the topic of Artism. "It's just nice being there with other people without them telling me what to do, or just jabbering about all the things they can do that I can't," she says. ". . . We're all just kids in the end. I mean, that's the whole point. We're all just kids in the end. Who friggin' cares whether we're autistic or not? Why does it matter?"

1. *Loud Hands* (Bascom 2012b).
2. In late September of 2016, the Autism Speaks board of directors voted "to modify the organization's mission statement, marking the first such change since the nonprofit was established in 2005. The new iteration is shorter and strikes a markedly different tone," writes Michelle Diament on the developmental disability news source website disabilityscoop.com. "Gone are terms like 'struggle,' 'hardship' and 'crisis.' Also absent is any mention of seeking a cure for the developmental disorder" (Diament 2016).

   Here is the wording of the mission statement, as it appeared on the Autism Speaks website on October 15, 2016: "Autism Speaks is dedicated to promoting solutions, across the spectrum and throughout the lifespan, for the needs of individuals with autism and their families through advocacy and support; increasing understanding and acceptance of autism spectrum disorder; and advancing research into causes and better interventions for autism spectrum disorder and related conditions. Autism Speaks enhances lives today and is accelerating a spectrum of solutions for tomorrow" ("Mission" 2016).

   Initial reactions to the statement's modification from within the autistic self-advocacy community suggest that it has done little if anything to appease their very strong concerns. For example, the activist group Boycott Autism Speaks posted the following response on their blog on October 15, 2016. "Recently, Autism Speaks announced a change in its mission statement. They have removed the word 'cure' while keeping words like 'interventions,' 'solutions' and talk about research into the causes of autism, which still implies that they have not distanced themselves completely from eugenics and 'prevention' of autism. Autism Speaks claims to want to increase 'understanding and acceptance' after over a decade of working against those very things. This is not the language or intentions of autism acceptance. While this has been portrayed as a move forward, we at Boycott Autism Speaks are more than skeptical" ("#ActuallyAutistic People React to Autism Speaks 'Change' in Mission Statement" 2016).
3. Performances of works by some of these composers are available: "Joobai I," by E. S., may be accessed at http://www.youtube.com/watch?v=2ZVHiDQJLLo; "Steel Percussion," by NICKstr, at http://www.youtube.com/watch?v=SjkrjHf_cSI. These two performances were recorded during a concert by the Artism Ensemble at the Florida State University Museum of Fine Arts in the spring of 2013.

CHAPTER 4
Donald Rindale

For me, at least, musical performance was a method of applying my talents and knowledge towards an art form that I absolutely adored—and at which I did quite well—and provided opportunities to more or less "get away" from the often offensive and upsetting social situations in which I had to operate, social situations, that is, where people were talking to and about me (when their mouths were not occupied by mouthpieces and reeds of various shapes and sizes!). It was a great refuge indeed.

Donald Rindale (2014)

On February 11, 2013, I receive an email with the subject line "Introduction from a prospective FSU doctoral student." I open and read it:

Hello, Dr. Bakan. My name is Donald and I am a new graduate student and teaching assistant in the Department of Musicology at [Private] University. For nearly three years, I have been in contact with . . . members of the FSU Musicology faculty regarding their Masters and Doctoral programs in Musicology. I had the pleasure of meeting with [one of them] and several FSU students at the American Musicological Society conference in San Francisco back in 2011. Being on the autism spectrum myself, and having recently been made aware of your own extensive research on music and autism, and considering that this is an area in which I am becoming increasingly interested, I am now very much more interested in attending FSU for my Ph.D. studies.

I have attached my current CV to this email to introduce myself and my research activities. It appears that FSU would be an excellent "fit" for me given the historical musicological interests of the faculty members, your own work on music and autism, the excellent placement record of the program, and the presence of opportunities for supplementary certification in Arts Administration and Critical Theory.

I am wondering if we could set up a time to talk on the phone in the near future. Because it has been "a while" since my last communication with FSU, I would certainly appreciate the opportunity to learn about the fellowship/assistantship opportunities, application procedures, and other pertinent matters.

Please let me know if we could arrange something soon.

Thank you for your time and consideration.

Sincerely,
Donald Rindale[1]

Donald's CV is remarkable. His wide-ranging interests—from the operas of Richard Wagner to musical semiotics, and from human consciousness and perception to the musicological implications of LGBT and feminist philosophy—are matched point for point by a strong record of productivity: numerous conference presentations, published entries in the *New Grove Dictionary of American Music*, articles and reviews in online periodicals, and a host of newspaper articles as well. He has been lecturer-in-residence for a major New England opera company and has garnered a wealth of credits as a trombonist in concert bands, jazz ensembles, and opera orchestras. And as if all this were not enough, he is also an experienced conductor, having directed wind ensembles and musical theater orchestras at both the high school and college levels.

"A most impressive CV," I reply. "You're a busy guy!"

We arrange a time to meet by phone and have a nice conversation about FSU's musicology graduate program and related matters. After that, more than half a year passes before I hear from Donald.

"Hello again!" he emails me in late August. "I hope you have been doing well these past few months. I was pleased to see an announcement for a lecture that you gave at Columbia University about autism and ethnomusicology. If you wouldn't mind, would you please send me a copy of that presentation? I would love to read that!"

The timing is auspicious, since I am just then starting to expand the scope of my music-and-autism research to include adults as well as children. It occurs to me that Donald would be a great interview for this new phase of the project, so, after responding to his request about the Columbia paper, I ask him if he would be interested in taking part. Yes, most definitely, he replies. We discuss our options and decide to go with texting-based chat. A few weeks later, we convene online for our first chat session.

CONVERSATION 1: OCTOBER 11, 2013

Donald is already signed in by the time I arrive at my office and get logged on.

"Are you there now?" he has typed in the Google Hangouts text box.

"Yes, I am!" I reply.

"Cool. . . . I am available now to chat."

"Okay. Let's do it. Tell me a little bit about your background and training in music."

"Sure! As with everyone else, I took classes in general music throughout elementary school, beginning in kindergarten. However, I began serious instrumental study on the trombone when I was in the fourth grade, and maintained that throughout the rest of elementary school and high school. Halfway through college, I unfortunately had to stop playing due to the onset of Temporomandibular Joint Disorder [TMJ]. Also throughout high school, I conducted at rehearsals and concerts quite regularly. In college, I began as a music performance major, but due to my medical difficulties [with TMJ], I switched schools and also switched to an undergraduate major in musicology with a minor in philosophy. I have continued those studies until now."

"So you don't play music at all anymore?"

"Not really. I have not played trombone in several years and I only have a rudimentary proficiency on piano, so I don't really get involved with that either."

"So your musical life [now] is mainly as a listener, analyst, and critical thinker—i.e., musicological."

"Right now, yes," Donald agrees. "When I first had to make that change, it was pretty emotionally difficult. However, I found that I have enjoyed the new direction much more than I enjoyed performing, so I guess it was actually a positive change after all."

"That's good to hear! Prior to that, had you aspired to a professional career in music performance?"

"Oh, yes. It was the only love of my life," Donald proclaims. His follow-up remarks make it emphatically clear, however, that this is no longer the case. "Honestly, if my trombone got run over by a tank, I'd be delighted. I would have no intention of resuming it even if I physically could. It was a wonderful chapter of my life, but that page has long been turned."

Well, *that* was unexpected, I think to myself.

I'm not quite sure where to take the conversation from here. "Yes, life moves us where it does," I type finally, cringing at how cliché that sounds when the words pop up on the screen, "and, if we're lucky, to places we might not have been that are better than those that came before. Sounds like that's the case for you."

"Yep!" Donald affirms. "And now the same is happening with my transition to law. I suppose I have been lucky in that every move I have made has been a move 'up.'"

Transition to law? What transition to law? I have no context for this, so I ask Donald to explain.

"Well, after a long period of reflection," he begins, "I have decided that my talents and skills would be better applied in an area in which I could make a difference, specifically by being much more involved with real people and real problems than I could in musicology. Over the past year or so, law has become increasingly intriguing to me not only in itself, but also as it is a field where the same skills in research, writing, and public speaking which I have cultivated for a long time in musicology could be just as frequently and rigorously utilized."

I ask Donald if his new legal aspirations have anything to do with a desire to work on behalf of others on the autism spectrum.

"I think so," he replies. "Right now, my interests are quite varied, including constitutional, domestic and international human rights law, the laws of war—maybe those will actually be followed again some day—family law, labor law, etc. I try to do at least 1,000 pages per week of additional reading in law to really get my 'gears' going. But sure, I think disability law, generally construed, would be very appropriate in my case. I think there was actually a matter in Florida not too long ago where a court had found that the State simply had to provide medical coverage for various therapies that were necessary for autistic children, so it is nice to see some progress along those lines."

"So your shift from musicology to law sounds great," I tell Donald, "and it makes a lot of sense. I wonder, though, if you *were* going to continue into a career as a musicologist, say, as one who focuses on the music and musical experiences of autistic people in particular, like I do, what would be your primary goals and aspirations? I know that isn't your plan, but I'm interested in your response, especially with me being an 'ethnomusicologist of autism' who could perhaps be a proxy to driving the kinds of agendas that you envision for yourself and other autistic people through musicological inquiry and musical action."

"But wait a sec," I type after having posted my last entry. "Before you answer that, I should share a bit about what I envision my current role as an ethnomusicologist of autism to be, since I realize I haven't done that at all and the context is probably important. The basic idea is that as an ethnographer who focuses on music (i.e., as an ethnomusicologist) my goal is not to fix, cure, provide therapy for, diagnose, etc., people with autism. Nor is it specifically to lobby for or build new 'environments' that accommodate autistic 'disabilities.' Rather, [the ethnomusicological goal] is the same as it is if I go to Bali to study gamelan music or anywhere else in the world to study whatever music. I want to understand the people whose music is the subject of my investigations, and in turn to understand their music through the lens of their values, experiences, desires, [and] worldviews."

"Thus, if I'm studying 'music and autism,'" I continue, "I assume that the autistic people with whom I work are the 'experts' in their own cultural traditions, including communication and music, and proceed from that point; they are, in short, *experts at being who they are*. I do fieldwork: I observe, I ask questions, I participate in music making together with my autistic friends. Ultimately, my job is not to figure out what's 'wrong' and how it can be made 'better' and how music might contribute to that. It is, rather, to say, 'This is how these particular people, who are labeled autistic, make music and make culture and make community with one another and with their neurotypical counterparts.' I'm there to describe and advocate, always assuming that there is no 'better' to go for other than cultivating better mutual understanding, and mainly on the side of neurotypicals having a better understanding of autistics [rather than the other way around]."

"Sounds good," Donald responds. "As far as my interests in the implications of autism for musical listening/performance/conducting, etc., I have been primarily interested in how it is that, at least in my own case, my neurological configuration actually allows for the particular emotional experiences that I have during particular pieces, even down to minute elements like chord progressions, certain instrumentation-al timbres, etc. I have never really been interested in the social, interpersonal aspects of musical performance as it relates to autism. In my own case, I never found that I was unable to adequately act as a member of an ensemble because of my own [autistic] profile. In fact, I found ensemble performance to be a welcome refuge from the interpersonal engagements that I had to endure in the outside world. The music did not laugh, or judge, or make nasty comments, or quizzical facial expressions and gestures at the sight of some unexpected behavioral tendencies, among other things. For those reasons, I will always love it, whether I continue in musicology or not."

Donald now changes the subject, framing aspects of his own experiences with autism in relation to what he imagines other individuals who are differently affected might experience.

"I have some kind of capacity for 'simulation'—the 'technical' term for understanding body language, particularly facial expressions—as it would be incited in others in their dealings with me," he states. "I have to credit philosophy—you know, that 'useless major'—for allowing for that. Studying phenomenology in particular, and the sub-field of 'philosophy of mind,' has allowed me to understand with much greater clarity than before why I am how I am, and why others see me as different in the way that they do. However, just because I discern these things more clearly [than some others on the spectrum] does not mean that they are somehow not painful for me. For children who are more severely afflicted than myself, they might not be able to realize that others are making fun of them or are adopting a condescending or patronizing disposition towards them. Therefore, they are particularly vulnerable to such hostility, since those who perpetrate it are, presumably, neurotypical and therefore realize they have a 'sitting duck.'"

Donald stops typing for a minute or so, then resumes. "I, however, *am* able to tell such things, and when I realized that [others'] reactions were ones of confusion and derision, that hurt a lot, since I realized how different I am than other people and how I tend to 'lose out' on the jovial interactions and social engagements that they take so for granted."

"Sorry this is so long," Donald writes apologetically after a brief pause, "but now I will address your question in more detail. . . ."

I assure him that what he has written is not too long in the slightest. "It's great," I encourage him. "Please go on!"

He does: "I am actually going to be writing a seminar paper on the need for musicologists, and intellectual people generally understood, to assume a more public persona. Paul Hollander, Edward Said, and others have written extensively on such matters. In other words, the mental energy and acumen with which we, neurotypical and otherwise, are so fortunately endowed *must* also be applied to assisting 'those other people out there' in the 'real world.' (This is one of the inspirational factors for my switch to law.) I think the same kind of perspective should be practiced by musicologists. There really isn't any reason why it shouldn't be. We are all one people in one world, and if you (hypothetical 'you' here) get a five or six year full ride to a Ph.D. program to stroke your beard and think great thoughts, you simply must, as an ethically inclined creature, engage in a more public involvement with the real people and real problems to which I referred."

I stroke my beard and allow Donald's strong words to sink in.

"As this relates to autism advocacy," Donald adds, "I see this happening in two ways. First—and this might apply to you more specifically as [someone whose family has been affected by autism]—musicologists, and all intellectuals, should become advocates for increased financial and other resources to assist autistic people, particularly as they become ineligible for government resources in many jurisdictions after they reach a certain age. It is simply a matter of human decency and the need to be our brothers' keepers, in my view. Second, we can, and should, whether musicologists or not, change the way in which the diagnosis of autism in one's child is received and *perceived*. One of the most profoundly upsetting statements that I hear from parents of autistic children, particularly those rather severely disabled, is that 'it was like we were kicked in the gut' when we first heard. You know, the kind of *60 Minutes* or *20/20* interviews where this is discussed and then thoughts for the life he could have had emerge and the tears come and blah blah blah. I can certainly imagine that, when a parent receives such news, there is a period of mourning; mourning for the fact that the desires you may have wanted for him—good level of education and employment, independence, perhaps children of his own—are now substantially or even entirely impeded."

"Oh," Donald continues after a brief pause, "and I am also incensed by people who have killed their autistic children and then themselves in murder-suicides because the conditions became intolerable for the parents precisely *because* of inadequate assistance from the State in caring for its most vulnerable. People have to see children in such conditions *not* as hopeless people or receptacles of impossible dreams. Instead, they should see those children not merely as dignified beings deserving of their love and attention, but as people who can be 'used'—and I don't use that term pejoratively—to advance the cause of disability studies and to inform medical research, public policy and legislation, and other measures aimed at helping them live as full and prosperous lives as possible. It might actually be helpful and encouraging for parents of such children to see their children as 'means to an end,' insofar as they, and other people's similarly situated children, can be key players in the progress of neuroscience, psychology, etc., so that they and the *next* group of kids *after* them can get the tools that are necessary for them."

Another pause. I wait for Donald to continue.

"I think that's it!" he writes finally.

"That's wonderful, Donald."

What a fascinating experience this has been. I am already looking forward to our next session.

"Bye for now," I type. "Have a great weekend! Nice chatting with you!"

"Thanks, Michael! Please let me know when you'd like to chat again."

"Will do. Bye."

I sign off and take some time to scroll through the Hangouts transcript. As I read, I am awed by Donald's lucid prose, his probing intellect, his passion for the rights of autistic people. I am also unsettled by some of what he has written, especially his comments concerning how autistic children might be productively "used" as "means to an end" or as "tools" in the advancement of autism research. I make a note to return to that subject with him in our next conversation, though that will prove unnecessary when he beats me to it.

In any case, my first experiment in chat-based fieldwork has been an unqualified success, vastly exceeding my expectations and establishing the basis for a viable research method moving forward. The chat medium has facilitated a free-flowing exchange of ideas between Donald and me, and the precise transcript it has yielded—the very transcript that I am now reviewing—seems almost too good to be true: no tedious transcription process to deal with, no wondering whether I am hearing the words on the recording accurately, and so many possibilities for working collaboratively with Donald to craft the "raw data" of our text into a final, publishable document.

I am eager to resume the conversation. It takes more than six weeks for us to arrive at a mutually agreeable time, but it is well worth the wait.

CONVERSATION 2: NOVEMBER 26, 2013

By the time I get online for my second chat with Donald, it's 4:03 p.m. I'm three minutes late.

"Ready whenever you are," Donald has typed in the dialogue box.

"OK. Here I am," I type back. "How's it going?"

"Doing OK. How are you?

"Fine, thanks. Very rainy here. Thunderstorms and such."

"Oh gosh. Yes, it's sure cold around here!"

"So, any follow-up thoughts since our last conversation?" I ask.

"None other than to ask how you found the comments that I made. Have they been helpful at all, either for the book and/or for your own life? . . . I was hoping that my comments about how people could use their [autistic] kids as 'tools' for further research, such as in some kind of group setting for a big NIH [National Institutes of Health]-style research grant, experimental medication, etc., did not come off offensively." I am relieved that Donald is the one bringing this up, since I had wanted to but was afraid I might offend him in doing so. "Honestly," Donald continues, "I do not know what other term I could apply than 'tool' for the way I would want more parents of autistic children to view their kids; not as 'burdens' to the family, which will or can never be the same ever again, but as 'tools' for the process of uncovering the mysteries of the condition to help both themselves and others."

The word choice might be problematic, but Donald is clearly coming at the issue from a caring and compassionate place, from a desire to do good. I search my mind for a better word than "tool" to recommend to him. For some reason I come up blank; even the most obvious alternatives— participant, subject—escape me in the moment. I am tempted to pursue this autism research topic further with Donald, but there is so much else to explore. We move on to other subjects.

"You said some really wonderful stuff in that last conversation," I begin, "especially [toward the end] where you were talking about your phenomenological perspectives on being an autistic musician, and [about] what musicologists and others might do to both account and advocate for autistic people, children and adults. I was particularly struck by this passage: 'I have never really been interested in the social, interpersonal aspects of musical performance as it relates to autism. In my own case, I never found that I was unable to adequately act as a member of an ensemble because of my own [autistic] profile. In fact, I found ensemble performance to be a welcome refuge from the interpersonal engagements that I had to endure in the outside world. The music did not laugh, or judge, or make nasty comments, or quizzical facial expressions and gestures at the sight of some unexpected behavioral tendencies, among other things. For those reasons, I will always love it, whether I continue in musicology or not.'"

"Ah yes, I remember writing that," Donald affirms before adding a parenthetical aside: "(Gosh... I wrote that? ☺)"

"Well, maybe you could expand on [it]," I suggest. "It's interesting that you note that 'the music didn't laugh' at you; but what about the other musicians? Is there something different about the social environment of music making that moves musical experience out of the normal mode of social encounter, [which] can often be oppressive for autistic people?"

Donald's reply is enlightening. "I think that if there was some kind of special tendency for musical performance to afford that kind of departure from the normal experience, it might not be any greater or less than that afforded by other artistic experiences, like acting or drawing or anything else. For me, at least, musical performance was a method of applying my talents and knowledge towards an art form that I absolutely adored—and at which I did quite well—and provided opportunities to more or less 'get away' from the often offensive and upsetting social situations in which I had to operate, social situations, that is, where people were talking to and about me (when their mouths were not occupied by mouthpieces and reeds of various shapes and sizes!). It was a great refuge indeed. It allowed me to demonstrate to people that I was talented, smart, and capable like them, and could do anything they could do, even if I had some shortcomings as far as intimate interaction with them."

"That makes a lot of sense, Donald. I especially appreciate the line about the other musicians' mouths being otherwise occupied in ways that precluded their using them to be unkind and condescending. What about before or after rehearsals? Did the spirit of goodwill and communitas that the shared musical moment facilitated translate [to] outside the bounds of that moment itself? In other words, were musicians with whom you played in the ensembles, by virtue of sharing something meaningful and communicative with you in the making of music, elevated in their consciousness in ways that inspired them to treat you more humanely, more as an equal, than others in your peer group and/or in other situations? Did music form a bridge to other kinds of social connection with fellow musicians?"

"I think that they could have behaved in such a way if I had actually paid attention to it and tried to get them to do so," Donald speculates. "To be honest, I was so much in my proverbial 'own little world' before and after that I really did not communicate much at all with anyone else. Were I to [have done] so, I probably would have noticed at least an appreciable degree of collegiality around me."

Donald's last remark intrigues me, especially relative to some of his earlier ones. There is something paradoxical about the way he self-presents at times, though I can't quite put my finger on it. In one breath, he seems perfectly content to reside in his "own little world"; in the next, he expresses deep cravings for meaningful social connection. I decide to ask him about this.

"So, Donald, I'm curious about something. From these chat exchanges, you strike me as a rather social person. First, you're articulate and a compelling conversationalist; second, you seem very motivated to 'keep the conversation going,' as it were, which I really appreciate. What is the importance of a 'social life' to Donald? I get a sense that there are parallel realities, the one where you revel in the delights of, to quote you, your 'own little world,' the other where you seem quite intent to reach beyond it, connect, and make an impact, positively so, on the lives of others, whether through these chats, your aspirations in legal studies, etc. In short, what makes you 'tick'?"

"Well, I am not confined in my own 'little world' nearly as much as I was even two and a half years ago when I was first diagnosed. I think the main reason for this was taking philosophy courses in phenomenology and learning more and more about that whole perceptual framework. It allowed me to see just how different I was from other, neurotypical[,] people, and also, by implication, to infer what they must think of me and how they must see me. My capacity for [reading facial expressions and body language, that is, for] 'simulation,' to [again] use a phrase from philosophy of mind, seems to have correspondingly increased. And so, I actually am finding myself wanting a long-term partner and more relationships in general as a result of this 'temptation of normalcy.' Ascertaining what 'normalcy' is has not always been easy or fun, but at least I have been able to see how other people live, and understand how much different I am from others. Again, that has not always been pleasant; sometimes it has been very difficult."

It suddenly occurs to me that I lack some very basic information about Donald. "How old are you?" I ask him.

"Twenty-four."

"So you were diagnosed at about twenty-one?"

"Yep. Right before I turned twenty-two."

"So all those years that you were actually playing music, you did not 'know' you had Asperger's, right?"

"No, I didn't. I didn't know what was wrong."

"Would it have made a difference to know, in terms of how you might have pursued your musical life, do you think?"

"I don't think it would have made a difference in terms of how I would have pursued my musical life as much as it would just have clarified to me what was wrong and why I was the way that I was, whether in a musical context or not."

I bristle at Donald's repeated mentions of being somehow "wrong." I've been immersed of late in the writings of autistic self-advocates and neurodiversity proponents, in pronouncements like Julia Bascom's "*there is nothing wrong with us*,"[2] in proud assertions of autistic pride and unapologetic appeals for broad societal acceptance of autistic ways of being, as they are and on their own terms. I want Donald to buy into this positive, alternate vision of autism, and even though I know it is not my rightful place here to advocate on its behalf, I decide to do so anyhow, in effect challenging his right to be accepted as *he* is on *his* own terms.

"You've referred twice in the last couple of exchanges to being 'wrong': 'I didn't know what was wrong,' 'it would have just clarified to me what was wrong,'" I begin. "In the autistic self-advocacy [literature] there is a defiant thread of 'There is nothing wrong with me' that permeates the discourse. Do you really feel (as opposed to think) that something is 'wrong' with you, or is it more a question of living in a wrong-headed world that won't take you for what you are? I, for one, am finding you to be very much 'right' in the way you think, express yourself, etc. . . ."

"That reminds me of the website wrongplanet.net," Donald replies.[3] "I certainly do feel that it is the case of the world being 'wrong-headed' and not taking me for what I am, but when I do feel that way, I do wish that I wasn't this way. Certainly, having this condition has allowed me to apply a rather exceptional degree of focus to academic studies and has facilitated my success in certain professional respects. But if I was afforded the pro-verbial 'pill' or 'magic wand' to 'take this away,' I definitely would."

We turn our attention to one of Donald's favorite subjects: philosophy.

"Let's talk phenomenology for a bit, shall we?" I propose.

"Sure!"

"Which phenomenologists have been especially influential on you, and most especially on the drive to self-reflection that compelled you to seek out a diagnosis for your condition of social challenges?"

"I think Edmund Husserl and Martin Heidegger have been the most helpful in these regards, Husserl, of course, by virtue of being the first major exponent (after Brentano) of these principles, and Heidegger by virtue of his refinement of them (in the form of the *Dasein* [being in the world] ideas). Interestingly, Heidegger dedicated his magnum opus, *Being and Time*, to Husserl, who did not like it very much!"[4]

"Fussy philosophers—never know how to take a compliment!" I joke. "Okay, so how did phenomenological inquiry help you to reach your cur-rent self-concept and level of self-awareness relative to your ASC?"

I wait patiently as Donald composes an erudite response.

"Well, in my own case, my condition is not so severe as to prohibit the realization of the applicability and value of those kinds of concepts to try-ing to make sense of my own life. I suppose that different people will have different degrees of difficulty in making sense of things. I suppose that any notion of reading texts such as Husserl's and Heidegger's with a view to getting their own condition more thoroughly understood or evaluated would not be uniformly appropriate, given the variance in the condition from person to person. (It [autism] is a spectrum, after all!) Nevertheless, I suppose that general concepts such as 'simulation,' 'the natural attitude,' 'the phenomenological attitude,' and the like, postulated in these and sim-ilar texts, could be valuable for people, particularly to the extent that they could use them to try to maximize their own social potentialities."

"Okay. Interesting, though I think I'm looking for a more 'personal' kind of response (how neurotypical of me!)," I type. "Earlier you alluded to how studying phenomenology/philosophy of mind had sparked in you an awareness of how 'different' you were from others and a motivation to find out how and why. Can you take me through a quick synopsis of how that process unfolded?"

"Sure, as best as I can recall," Donald offers. "Basically, some kind of connection was forged, or 'lightbulb' went 'off' in my head, after reading so much of that literature, which made me realize that I was indeed quite different than others and that there must have been something 'wrong,' i.e., some kind of theretofore unidentified problem by virtue of which I was quite different and unusual in contrast to mostly everyone who I had known, but the name of which I did not know." I note Donald's placement of the word "wrong" in scare quotes; I hope I haven't bullied him into trying to appease me. "At that point, I was already clinically depressed and was going to counseling for it, and decided to bring up some of these other concerns. I had learned a bit about autism spectrum conditions, and found that I matched the general descriptions and the specific symptomatologies very closely. Eventually, the psychologist introduced to me the fact that no two people diagnosed with an ASD are really the same and that there was a spectrum of severity and problems associated with the condition generally construed. Then came the affirmation and acceptance of the diagnosis, then the self-imposed mantra that this was one of my 'greatest strengths.' Then came the realization, through phenomenology and philosophy, that I was truly quite different from everyone else, and the realization of how other people must see me and what they must think about me. Then came a real sadness over the whole thing."

The sources of that sadness, Donald tells me, were many: family issues, unsparing self-criticism, questionable life choices, financial hardship, and trying situations stemming from difficult circumstances that were beyond his control or anyone else's. He is very candid with me, but requests that I keep the details of this part of his story confidential, which I promise I will.

"So are you moving past that sadness phase at this stage, do you think?" I ask.

"I sure hope so," he replies. "I have work to do and things to accomplish."

It has been a long session. Donald tells me he is getting tired; I am as well.

"I do have one more question I'd like to ask, though," I write, "and then we might want to call it a day for now."

"Sounds good. . . . Sure, ask away!"

"Well, I want to go on a slightly different tack re: the phenomenology-of-self-type question I posed earlier, one that relates specifically to your former musical life. There is literature suggesting that autistic ways of processing music, hearing, etc., are distinctive, that there is a 'cultural' dimension of being autistic that defines a particular kind of musicality and way of engaging with music, [the] individual diversities of autistic/Asperger's folks notwithstanding." I am thinking here of the work of Joseph Straus.[5] "Retrospectively, can you identify any specific features of your 'musicality' that you [would] link to your Asperger's?"

"Hmm," Donald posts. I wait patiently for his more detailed response. "I do feel that the condition may have some bearing on my love of certain melodic and harmonic progressions, matters of orchestration, timbres, etc., that I [find to be] especially pleasing compared to others. Perhaps there is some kind of neurological anomaly attendant to my condition that allows for those kinds of special experiences, but I'm not sure what it is... And as for my work as a musicologist, I think that the condition was somewhat of a boon in that it allowed me to read and write when so many of my classmates (particularly at the undergraduate level) were out partying. They were having fun; I was doing musicology. ☺"

"Well, there is that, but musicology is fun!"

"I know. ☺"

It's time to wrap things up, but I find it impossible to resist one last detour into my proselytizing mode.

"If I might take off my 'scholar's hat' for a moment, Donald, I do want to encourage you to stop thinking about yourself as 'wrong' and about your neurological constitution as 'some kind of anomaly.' You're a cool guy and very likable. The world will catch up; just try to be patient, but most importantly with yourself."

"Thanks for the advice," he replies. "Talk to you later!!"

"Okay. Bye for now. And Happy Thanksgiving!"

"Happy Thanksgiving to you too!"

CONVERSATION 3: JUNE 6, 2014

Almost half a year passes before Donald and I are able to reconnect for our third chat dialogue. It turns out that the intervening months have been very challenging for him.

"How's it going?" I ask once we are both signed on.

"I've been better," he replies, "but overall I'm okay. How are you?"

"I'm doing pretty well, thanks. So I've been doing a lot of these chat sessions with my other collaborators on the book since we last met and I've developed a kind of 'standard repertoire' of questions I pose to pretty much everyone, usually near the beginning of the first session. Some of these were actually inspired by my first session with you way back when—like, 'If you could wave a magic wand and make your autism disappear, would you?'—so thanks for that! Others have come up since then in various contexts, and I'd like to kick things off today by asking you one."

"Okay."

"So, do you consider yourself to be an autistic person, an Autistic person, or a person with autism?"

A minute or two elapses as I wait for Donald's reply.

"I like the capitalization there!" he finally writes back. "I don't think I've seen it signified that way before."

"Okay, tell me why you like that (and then I'll tell you the framework for it afterward)."

"I haven't really given much thought to any substantive differences that those different ways of describing it would entail," Donald begins. "I suppose that, by now, I would describe myself as a person with autism, since I have tried to downplay its prevalence in my life and, frankly, do not want other people to know about it. It is no longer a 'defining' feature of me such that I would refer to myself with the adjective first, with or without capitalization. I've tried to relegate it to a much more ancillary position."

"Ah, okay. So when you said you liked the capitalized version—Autistic person—you meant that in the abstract, not as an identifier for you personally?"

"I suppose abstractly, yes, in the sense that there is yet another way in which people could identify."

At this point I share my framework for the question, as promised. "So there are two basic philosophies," I state. "The 'person with autism' designation uses what's called 'person-first language,' the rationale being that you are a person first and that the autism is just a part of that larger totality. In some circles, that is preferred. But autistic self-advocates (and Autistic self-advocates—more on that momentarily) say that such person-first constructions are demeaning, in that they imply that there is something bad about being autistic, and they don't believe there is. A classic example is a 1999 essay by Jim Sinclair called 'Why I Dislike "Person First" Language,' where Sinclair asserts that 'Saying "person with autism" suggests that autism is something bad—so bad that it isn't even consistent with being a person.'[6] So Sinclair and most others who self-identify as autistic self-advocates prefer statements like 'I am autistic' over ones like 'I am a person with autism,' just as they would say 'I'm left-handed,' not 'I'm a person with left-handedness,' or 'I'm Jewish,' not 'I'm a person with Jewishness.' Re: the capitalization [of Autistic], that takes it a step further. Just as we say 'I'm an American' not 'I'm an american, or 'I'm Jewish' not 'I'm jewish,' if we conceive of autism as a culture, a cultural way of being, it is appropriate to capitalize [Autistic]."

My explanation prompts some lively discussion, including a comment from Donald that initially confuses me. "Come to think of it," he offers, "I remember the singular experience that 'inspired' me to change this designation of myself."

"To change what to what?" I inquire.

"To change the 'autistic person' designation to a 'person with autism'," he clarifies. "Last summer, I was working for a theater company in Pittsburgh. . . . I was out one night and someone leaned over to me and said, 'Has anyone ever told you [that] you seem autistic?' I told him angrily that yes, I [knew] all about it, as well as [saying] some other very unpleasant things that made him bug-eyed and quiet. After that, I really wanted to block this out of my mind. So, I guess for the purposes of these different titles or 'labels,' that has been one way of trying to accomplish that."

Donald's comments jog my memory toward certain writings in the autistic self-advocacy literature, especially chapters in the *Loud Hands* anthology, which I have recommended to him at some point.

"By the way," I ask, "have you found time to check out *Loud Hands* or any of the other autistic self-advocacy stuff I told you about?"

"No, I haven't," he replies after a long pause. There is a sense of shame or at least embarrassment in the "tone" of his response. "I've not [had the energy] to do much of anything. I'm sorry to put it in those somber terms, but that's all I can say."

"Wow. So those personal problems you were having last time we talked, have those gotten worse?"

"A lot. I'm sorry."

Donald offers up a disturbing account of his trials and tribulations in recent months, attributing many of them to his autism. He again requests that I keep the specifics confidential.

"I'm sorry," he repeats at the close.

"No need to apologize!" I assure him. "Certainly not to me, at least! ☺"

"Okay. ☺"

". . . So where are your parents in all this?" I ask, suddenly realizing that for all our conversations I know almost nothing about Donald's family situation.

"My father passed away years ago. My mom is sixty now; she hasn't remarried."

"Does she support you financially?"

"No. I'm completely on my own when it comes to that."

"How do you make ends meet?"

"Well, I've had my TA [teaching assistantship] money in one or even two positions per semester, and I've also been able to make some money as a paid subject for research studies at the local hospital."

"Is that something that pays well?"

"Yes, it is. . . . I was able to eat over winter break because of it."

" . . . But you're going to law school in the fall. Certainly that would bode well for the possibility of a provisional fresh start?"

"Yes. I really do need a fresh start. I'm so sick of music after twenty years, which I never thought I'd say. I haven't even listened to it in a very long time because I'm so disillusioned by the field and, frankly, by [my university's] program in particular."

"Yet you've managed to get through and will graduate, and you've managed to do this despite some potentially overwhelming challenges, right?"

"Yes and yes."

"That's incredible. How do you do it?!"

"I suppose that the knowledge that this stage [of my life] is almost over is the biggest inspiration. For instance, I have to fulfill a music theory requirement this summer, and it's like I can't remember any of it at all. I suppose I've just psychologically 'checked out' so completely that it's just all gone."

I feel bad for Donald. What must it be like to have been so passionate about music before and now regard it almost with disdain? Then again, he is poised to strike out anew in the legal field. Hopefully that will indeed give him the fresh start he needs, and deserves.

I glance at the clock and realize I am on the verge of being late for a family gathering.

"Speaking of 'checking out,' I actually need to get going now," I tell Donald. "Shall we resume Monday at 3:00 p.m.?"

"Sure, 3:00 p.m. Monday would be fine with me."

"OK. See you then. Enjoy the weekend!"

"Thanks! You too."

CONVERSATION 4: JUNE 9, 2014

Monday afternoon at 3:00 sharp, Donald and I are back online together.

"Hi, Donald."

"Hi!"

"How was the weekend?"

"It was okay. How about yours?"

"My weekend was okay too," I reply. "I wanted to follow a thread from the other day re: music. You mentioned, when we were talking about you starting law school in the fall, that you're just really tired of music (I think those were the words). What did you mean by that?"

"Basically, I have found something that I have been enjoying far more, something that is generally more lucrative than music, and something that I want to do after doing something else for twenty years. I've just reached a point where what I used to want/enjoy isn't that anymore."

"So does that mean that you no longer love *music*, or that you no longer love music/musicology as the focus of a professional career. I just want to understand better where you're coming from with that, since it will influence where we might go in these conversations."

"Hmm... I guess in general terms it's music/musicology as the focus of a professional career. Although there are other times that I really have no interest in music and sometimes regret being involved in it for so long. That feeling, however, is fortunately quite rare, and I suppose that it is an example of how we all, at one time or another, question who we are and what we are doing and why, wondering how things might have been if we had gone down a different path."

"Yes, I have experienced similar things myself," I admit, "[but] the truth is, in the final throes of a graduate degree in anything, it's normal to feel burned out on it, even if it is music! Let's try to 'bypass' that situational bump in the road. I want to know more about you as a musician and as someone who thinks deeply about music and all to which it leads (and which leads to it). I define *ethnomusicology* as 'the study of how people make and experience music, and of why it matters to them that they do.' So I ask of you, as a musician, as a music listener/experiencer (however defined), and/or as a musicologist (not in the limited 'professional' sense of the term, but more [philosophically] as one who engages with music as an intellectual endeavor): Can you explain to me how you relate to music, and more specifically how you think that having Asperger's is implicated in that relationship, for better, for worse, or for neither?"

I wait several minutes watching three little dots move across my computer screen; the dots are accompanied by a soft bubbling sound, indicating that Donald is typing. Finally his lengthy response to my question pops onto the screen.

"I think that the way I have best related to music is actually external to my musicological leanings. With [my former musicological] perspective, I of course was able to focus on [music] as, as you have said, an intellectual endeavor, incorporating all kinds of matters philosophical, historical, aesthetic, etc. However, what I have found to be a far more intimate, and perhaps better way of relating to music actually, is on the personal level of the various problems I have been going through. As many others say that music can provide a 'refuge' for them in their times of pain, I think that that is the best purpose I have been able to make of it over the past few years. As of now, it seems like the specifically discipline-related manner of experiencing it is rather ancillary." There are more dots and bubbling sounds as Donald types a second installment. "More specifically, with regard to Asperger's, I don't know if that has anything to do with this, but I had developed a strong interest in the emotional potential of particular harmonic progressions, and had written at least one paper on that subject. Perhaps that was something I found interesting due to some neurocognitive anomaly, but I'm not sure."

"Or as I might prefer to say," I interject with yet another uncalled-for "correction" of Donald's wording, "some special ability related to your neurodiverse framework of cognition. ☺"

I insert the smiley-face emoji to soften the message, but Donald isn't falling for it this time. "Perhaps!" he replies, dubious in spite of the exclamation point, I suspect.

"So I'd love it if you'd take me inside that world, Donald. What specific harmonic progressions? In what repertoire? With what emotional effect on you? And how might an Asperger's way of being in the world reflect, embody, or inform any of the above?"

More dots and bubbling. I wait.

"What I recall are things like descending thirds (I-vi-IV-ii, etc.), use of Neapolitan harmonies, and some [progressions] that are not as unorthodox," he begins. "I suppose that it would depend on the melodic and instrumental contexts as well, so I can't say with certainty that there were one or two different kinds that 'did it' every time. As for the particular experience, I suppose it was kind of the 'goosebumps' feeling of happiness or joy, etc., that they would engender. But as for the Asperger's [way of] being in the world (thanks for the Heideggerean reference!), I really am not sure. I don't know why it is that that particular condition would make me, or anyone else, susceptible to these kinds of responses to compositional details that, on their face, would seem rather trivial."

It occurs to me that we have ventured into quite abstract territory. Donald is politely indulging my line of questioning and offering honest, thoughtful responses. Yet the subtext is clear: try as he or I might, how can either of us ever know whether or not there is *any* specifically "autistic" aspect to his aesthetic-cum-emotional musical preferences where, say, hearing harmonic progressions is concerned? I decide to reorient the inquiry, to put the emphasis where it rightly belongs: on Donald as an individual and musical thinker, not as some card-carrying representative of "Asperger nation."

"So on a more plaintive note (pun intended)," I type, "perhaps you could speak more specifically to the kinds of emotional experiences that music has had on you during difficult times. It may not be productive to try and put this in some autism/Asperger's box, but rather to speak as specifically as possible about what actually *happens* to you when you listen to particular kinds of music. What situations or experiences compelled you or will compel you to seek out music (I'm assuming listening at this point, not playing, since you haven't played for some time now) to ease pain, and how does it accomplish this (and how effectively)? Are there particular kinds of music that do it for you in some situations, others in other situations? I'm really curious to get into the depth of your reflections on music as you experience it."

"I guess that the best way of articulating what 'happens' to me when I am listening to music," Donald writes, "is that I begin to feel that perhaps things will be okay, that I can get through the issues that I have been dealing with, and, perhaps most importantly, I feel at least some sense of personal reassurance; that perhaps I am a decent guy after all that people can and should know and like. I don't really understand, and I wouldn't be able to verbalize, the precise connection between the music and those emotions, but there does seem to be one. Sometimes, also, I begin to feel better and more confident in who and what I am and in what I am all about. And then there are times when I intentionally seek out funny material to listen to, since that makes me feel all-around good!"

Funny material to listen to? I ask Donald if he can tell me what he means by that.

"Okay, I can try," he offers, "though I have found it rather hard to precisely explain it. I suppose that I enter into some kind of spiritual experience while listening to various pieces of music, which is a way of identifying it that I wouldn't often use since I am an atheist and don't have any 'faith based' or 'spiritual' world view of any kind, really. I suppose, however, that when we think of concepts like 'spirituality,' 'reverence,' 'prayer,' etc., maybe even 'meditation,' what I experience under these circumstances is probably as close as I have ever been to attaining the aforementioned states. I think that I had mentioned this a while back, but the music doesn't yell at you, or judge you, or make fun of you for your deficiencies of whatever kind. So, it is a venue, or an aura, if you will, into which I can retreat for some kind of solace or even encouragement."

"That's deep, Donald!" I write, though I'm not sure what all this has to do with the "funny material to listen to" that makes him "feel all-around good."

"So let me ask you," I continue, "what kind of music—and when? Is it always Wagner? Or is it Beethoven for some situations, Brahms for others? Punk rock for this and Persichetti for that? Give me some kind of a road map of your musical choices re: your emotional aspirations."

"Well, and this is going to sound ridiculous... But..."

Radio silence. No dots, no bubbles, nothing. Donald has apparently stopped cold in his tracks. I jump in to encourage him. "Go for it!" I exclaim.

Still nothing. I wonder if Donald has temporarily lost his Internet connection.

"Hey Donald, are you still there?"

Finally the dots start to dance and the bubbles are percolating again. Donald is writing: "Sometimes when I'm in a certain kind of mood, I will listen to absolutely ridiculous songs that are produced by these twelve- or thirteen-year-old girls like Jenna Rose ('My Jeans'), Rebecca Black ('It's Friday! Friday! Gotta get down on Friday!'), Alison Gold ('Chinese Food'), etc. They are just all so terribly bad and are, for that reason, very funny to listen to, especially when you consider that they probably do not even realize that they suck and that everyone watches them for the purpose of having something to laugh at, as mean as that might sound. Then there are other times when I will listen to things that are more on the slow, contemplative side, like music from *Parsifal* and *Lohengrin* in terms of Wagner, or even wind ensemble pieces (a repertoire in which I was heretofore rather uninterested, but one which I have [now] explored more thoroughly). Band pieces like Frank Ticheli's *An American Elegy*, David Holsinger's *Hymnsong of Philip Bliss*, John Mackey's *Hymn to a Blue Hour*, and others serve that purpose rather well. I guess that it depends on the mood, which, I assume, is the experience of the average person anyway." (A list of links to online examples of these and other musical works discussed in the chapter may be found at the companion website [CW 4.1 ▶].)

"Well," I contend, "the average person doesn't go from Rebecca Black to *Parsifal* now, do they?! ☺"

"No, they don't! But I tend not to do that transition in one 'sitting.' I will usually stick with one kind [of music] at a time."

"Hey, I'd say mix 'em up!" I quip.

"Okay!"

The time has flown by, as it always seems to in these conversations.

"I have to go in about five minutes," I tell Donald, "but before we sign off I want to switch course a little bit. Assuming all goes well, you are going to be 'in' this book we're working on with an opportunity to reach a fairly broad audience: people with autism, people without autism, people all along the spectrum and with various kinds of interests in and connections to it.

If there was one thing you could convey to all these people, what would it be? What do you, 'Donald Rindale,' want as many people as possible to know about what really matters?"

This time, Donald is quick in replying.

"Well, I think that, even apart from music in particular, there are so many tragedies and problems that our world faces, but of which we are largely oblivious because of the Yankees, the Red Sox, Justin Bieber, the iPhone, etc. 'What really matters' is a large category of a variety of things that hardly anybody seems to really care about, and that is most unfortunate. You should, of course, care about matters such as these, but you should also be prepared to feel 'different' and 'alienated' and 'out of place.'"

"So when you say we should be prepared to feel different, alienated, and out of place," I ask, "do you mean that you should be *resigned* to such feelings or that you should *embrace* them, or is it something in between?"

"Hmm... Ideally you should 'embrace them,' if that would entail you maintaining your own confidence in yourself and 'not caring' about the [judgments of] others, or perhaps being openly oppositional towards them. 'Resigning' might make you feel saddened and embittered, and may even be used as a pretext to not try to do anything to improve your situation, since 'this is just the way that it is.'"

"I definitely agree," I respond, "and I want to encourage you *personally* to take your own advice on that until we next connect, okay? That's a great prescription for good living. I'm going to work at it too!"

"Sounds good."

"Bye."

"Bye now!"

CONVERSATION 5: JULY 3, 2014

Things are looking up for Donald when we meet one last time to conclude our work on the book. Four weeks have passed since the last session and he begins this one by sharing some new, confidential information that clearly indicates his life situation is improving on several fronts. He also tells me that he is feeling very optimistic about his future prospects, both personally and professionally.

"I'm *delighted* to hear that!" I tell him. "Tell me more."

"Well, I guess it is manifesting most clearly in the change in my thinking about the situation. It seems as though I am returning to a previous mode of thinking from several years ago when I first learned about myself [having Asperger's], where I just didn't seem to care about how this might be perceived by others and focused on how it was actually advantageous to me. After experiencing a lot of the drawbacks of it over the last few years, it seems like I might be turning a corner here."

"That's fantastic!" I exclaim. "It's hard to 'read' body language over the Internet, but even just the tone of our dialogue today feels different than it did in some of our earlier chats. You seem to be much more like, well, the you I imagine you to be: smart, clear-thinking, motivated, committed to making a positive impact on society. It's great to 'see' that, assuming I'm picking up the right vibe."

"Well, I feel this way right now at least!"

I steer the conversation back to music-related topics.

"Last time we talked about [music]," I begin, "you mentioned being quite sick of the whole enterprise. We nuanced it a bit, but still, I'm wondering if now that your self-image and self-regard seem to be on an upward curve, have your feelings about music—and the way music is functioning in your life—been affected at all?"

"I don't think so. I've finished up my last graduate seminar [in musicology] and am eagerly anticipating moving on to my new path [as a law student]. So, I don't think there will be any resurgence of musical interest or activities."

"Fair enough. Are you listening to music at all these days? The wind symphony pieces, Rebecca Black, something else?"

"Oh gosh, Rebecca Black! I haven't listened to music in quite a while, at least not regularly. I've been trying to do as much reading as possible. But, as far as listening goes, there are various political podcasts that I have been enjoying."

"Not ones with musical accompaniment presumably!"

"Nope."

"So I'm curious. In our first couple of sessions, you mentioned that music was kind of the be-all and end-all of your life for many years. Now it seems quite superfluous to you. I *kind* of get that: for me, music's status is constantly in flux and my engagements with it always shifting in substance, intensity, and purpose. Yet imagining a world devoid of music seems kind of awful to me, both personally and because of the value of what I think it contributes to the human condition generally. To what do you attribute the dramatic 'demotion' of music in your life, and what role *do* you see it playing for you in the future?"

"I suppose I could best attribute its demotion in my life to the fact that I am now pursuing something else. Something new has taken hold of me, and what used to do this no longer does. Also, disillusionment and disappointment with the profession and my experience [in grad school] were, I think, contributing factors to that demotion."

"That makes sense. I suspect this is the end of a chapter rather than the end of the story where music's place in your life is concerned, though. My best guess is that it will find a way back into your realms of passionate engagement, though likely in ways neither you nor I can presently imagine."

"I think the way you've described it is pretty accurate."

"Good. Either way, so long as you find happiness and a sense of purpose in life, with or without music really isn't the issue!"

"That's right!"

"So you said it seems like you might be turning a corner here. What's around the bend as far as you can tell?"

"I think that my strongest intention/hope is to try to return to what I once was, albeit without music."

"And what was that?"

"Well, more clear-headed, confident, focused on studying and career prospects, etc."

"How long ago?"

"I think that 2009-2012 was that 'golden period.'"

"So refresh my memory. When did you receive the Asperger's diagnosis?"

"March 2011."

"I'm confused. [You say] 2009–2012 was your 'golden period,' but weren't the years immediately leading up to the time of the diagnosis very trying ones, to the extent that conditions led you to seek the help that ultimately led to your being diagnosed?"

"Well, I guess they were 'trying,' but I was much better able to keep my head and work on my future than I have been for a while."

"Okay. I want to come back to the 'magic wand' question. Any moving of the compass re: whether you'd wave it and have yourself transformed—de-Autized—given the opportunity?"

"No movement on that. I still would de-Autize myself if I could."

"Right. So I think we've reached a pretty good point of closure for this chapter. Would you agree?"

"Yes, I would."

"So share with me your final words on the matter(s), as it were. What can the world (or at least the small portion of it that is likely to read this book) learn from Donald Rindale?"

"Hmm... hold on a sec while I try to convey that clearly."

"Take your time!"

"I think that what people can learn from me is that your life does not always go the way you planned, and that you can experience significant disruptions in your own self-concept, which can in turn disrupt the satisfaction of your goals in a very material way. However, you are the only one who can make any meaningful change, as hard as that might be. But, I hope to be able to look back upon these sad periods with confidence in what can come ahead, notwithstanding the regret of looking behind."

"Beautifully said, Donald, and for what it's worth, I'm pretty sure you are going to achieve just that. This has been a real pleasure, and very enlightening!"

"Thanks a lot!"

"Bye!"

"Bye!"

"GOING ALRIGHT, JUST VERY BUSY"

I can't wait to share the good news with Donald, especially since he's been asking me about this from time to time for well over a year now. "I'm delighted to inform you," I email him on March 6, 2017, "that [our book] has been accepted for publication by Oxford University Press!"

Donald's response comes quickly. "I'm delighted to hear of this news," he writes, and then shares some good news of his own. "I don't remember the last time I wrote, but, barring any catastrophes, I am graduating law school in May, taking the Illinois Bar in July, and then doing a judicial clerkship for a year after law school. I am trying to get back home to Chicago after the clerkship is done to work there, as I miss it very much, and, also, none of us are getting any younger, and I want to be closer to family."

Further details follow as Donald updates me on recent events. Then he sums it all up. "Things generally have been going alright," his email concludes, "just very busy and tiring occasionally."

"I can relate," I assure him, and as I click the "Send" button, I can't help but smile.

NOTES

1. Donald Rindale is a pseudonym. Names of other individuals and of certain locations in this chapter have been changed as well for the sake of preserving anonymity.
2. *Loud Hands* (Bascom 2012a, 10).
3. As described on the home page of its website, Wrong Planet is a "web community designed for individuals (and parents/professionals of those) with Autism, Asperger's Syndrome, ADHD [Attention Deficit Hyperactivity Disorder], PDDs, and other neurological differences. We provide a discussion forum, where members communicate with each other, an article section, with exclusive articles and how-to guides, a blogging feature, and more" ("Wrong Planet" 2017).

4. *Being and Time* (Heidegger 2008). The term *Dasein*, as used by Heidegger, encompasses an immensely complex set of concepts and ideas, but may be generally understood as relating to what it means to be human, that is, to the human experience of being in the world.
5. I was specifically thinking of passages from Straus's book *Extraordinary Measures* (Straus 2011) and his essay "Autism as Culture" (Straus 2013).
6. Sinclair's original 1999 essay, "Why I Dislike 'Person First' Language," is reprinted in *Loud Hands* (Sinclair 2012a).

CHAPTER 5
Elizabeth J. "Ibby" Grace

Music was the nexus between my self and language for a long time... my communicative access. When I relax among myself there are not words going on in my head. There are intervals, tones, it is much more relaxed... sometimes in order to think, I structure the thoughts into more like music, or they do themselves like that. Intravisually, this is close to a screensaver turning from fractals into polygons. So the inbetween is lyrical music or song. I could use it with others to communicate when I was not as good at expression otherwise.

Elizabeth J. "Ibby" Grace (2014)

Saturday, June 28, is a roller coaster ride of a day at the 2013 Society for Disability Studies Conference in Orlando. SDS has been great so far, and today's lineup looks to be the best yet.

I awake energized after a good night's sleep, still basking in the afterglow of the Artism Ensemble's rousing concert two nights prior. I attend some morning papers, enjoy a delicious lunch at a nearby Brazilian restaurant, then head back to the convention center for a session I have been eagerly anticipating: "Intersectionalities in Autistic Culture(s): A Discussion Instigated by This Posse of Autistics and Friends."[1] The name of the panel organizer, Elizabeth J. Grace, is not yet familiar to me, but based on my reading of the session abstract I have little doubt that she and her "posse" are planning to shake things up more than just a bit.

"Elizabeth J. Grace (organizer/moderator) is a flaming disabled Autistic, gay, and butch," the abstract begins. "She is also old (classic?) enough to think the latter carries kind of a cool chivalric code, and to remember when it was a problem because it was then considered 'mimicry' and therefore even worse than 'the dominant paradigm' so thus a failure in appropriate same-hair lesbianism." I re-read that sentence a few times and try to wrap my brain around it, albeit with only partial success.

Next I learn that Elizabeth J. Grace "is fascinated and delighted by the way many folks are currently rejecting the binary and blowing the whole thing up, which is one of the reasons she put together this discussion panel. Another reason," the abstract continues, "is the changing nature of the racial and heritage landscape and discourse in society today. Elizabeth (Ib) is Northern-European American, but not everyone around here is as 'white' as it may at first appear, though (to some people's apparent surprise) that doesn't magically make 'What are you?' the right thing to say. These are some of the intersections that interest her, and as a member of Autistic Culture-much, much more than as a member of Academia, she's discovered to her unending joy she can just flat out talk about this stuff and get other people to talk about it with her."

The abstract's text now shifts attention from the session moderator to the other presenters. Grace, I read, "has assembled the cast of excellently diverse characters below, all associated with Autistic Culture in some way, and all also Intersectional either in Racial or LGTBQIA/Other Space or Both or More in some perhaps surprising ways not even listed, to get the discussion started, inviting everyone in the room to partake freely." I skip down to the bottom of the page and read the list of presenters: Aiyana Bailin, Kassiane Sibley, Zach Richter, Allegra Stout, and Alyssa Z. (Bailin and Sibley, it turns out, have had to cancel and are replaced on the panel by Steven Kapp and Daniel Salomon.)

Returning to the main abstract text, I read through to the end: "It can be argued (as well as clearly seen by joining us, Ib thinks) that in Autistic Culture, wildly honest inquiry is a natural part of the discourse. Welcome, one and all! Our time will be used bringing up the myriad taboo interstitial spaces that are our lived lives and starting startling conversations about them. Note: Ib Grace as an experienced professor/moderator will be responsible for keeping the conversation an emotionally safe space while at the same time being open for some magnificent intellectual danger. This is the opposite of an oxymoron. Flap!"

If "Intersectionalities" lives up to even half of what its abstract portends, I think to myself, then I know I'm in for a wild ride. What I don't know at this point, though, is that the crash course on autistic self-advocacy and neurodiversity I am about to receive is going to change everything, from my understandings of autism and music to my attitude toward life itself.

Four of the five presenters are autistic, as are several members of the audience. The rest of the crowd consists mainly of people who are not autistic but have disabilities of various kinds.[2] As I listen to what everyone has to say, I experience a strange yet welcoming sense of coming home. These people are speaking a language of acceptance, diversity, inclusion, and activism that I have been struggling to formulate in my own writing for years. And it is a language that I have rarely, if ever, encountered in my readings of the autism research literature up to that point.

Following brief and extraordinary opening statements by the five panelists, Ibby opens the floor to a full hour of Q&A and open discussion. I am very curious to know what people thought of the Artism Ensemble concert the other night, especially since this is really the first time I've had a chance to get feedback about the group from autistic adults. I raise my hand, and Elizabeth, who everyone is addressing by her nickname, Ibby (sometimes Ib), calls on me.

"Were any of you at the Artism Ensemble concert the other night?" I ask. Several panelists and audience members indicate that they were. "So I was wondering, you know, we've never had the opportunity to play for members of the autistic community, and I'd be really interested in hearing your honest assessments of the show."

One of the panelists, Zach Richter, virtually leaps from his seat toward the center of the room to speak. "Honestly," he states, "well, I'm going to keep this polite, because you don't want to hear the impolite version—"[3]

"That's OK," I interject, bracing myself for what might follow. "Don't spare my feelings. I really want your honest opinions."

"Well, I'm going to keep it polite. It's better to keep it polite. You know, I've seen you around the conference, Dr. Bakan—"

"Please, call me Michael."

"No, I'll call you Dr. Bakan—and I wanted to say something to you, but I didn't because I didn't want to be rude. But since you brought up the question, honestly, I found [your concert] offensive."

My heart starts to pump up into my throat, but I do my best to maintain my composure. "How so?" I ask, my voice shaking slightly.

Without a moment's pause, Zach launches into an incisive and thoroughgoing critique of the concert: the music was too loud for the autistic people in the audience, many of whom (including him) have sensory issues with loud sounds; for the same reason it was wrong for me to allow the audience to clap rather than instruct them to show their appreciation through "silent applause";[4] there should have been autistic adults as well as autistic children in the ensemble; the program should have featured an explicit agenda of activism in support of autistic and disability rights.

But more troubling for Zach than the problems with the actual performance was its accompanying questionnaire, which had been distributed to the audience to collect evaluation data for Artism's main sponsors, the

National Endowment for the Arts and the Florida Department of State. One item on the questionnaire in particular had fueled Zach's fire: "In terms of promoting autism awareness, this concert was: (1) Excellent, (2) Very Good, (3) Good, (4) Fair, or (5) Poor."

"Why are you asking about autism awareness?" Zach inquires of me; he is visibly upset. "That's wrong. It should be about autism *acceptance*! Have you received funding from Autism Speaks? That's what I think, and I'm angry because SDS told us this was going to be a safe space for autistics, and then they bring in your group and the whole autism awareness thing, and it's like an Autism Speaks agenda and that makes me—us—mad. I've talked to the conference organizers and told them this shouldn't have happened, and I've blogged about it too."

I am stunned. My head reels, for I am truly clueless that invoking the phrase "autism awareness" in present company is akin to waving a Confederate flag at a civil rights rally. For these people, that phrase is inextricable from, to quote Steve Silberman, "the harm inflicted by organizations like Autism Speaks that frame autistic people as a tragedy and a burden to society."[5]

I take a deep breath and collect my thoughts before offering a reply: "First, Zach, let me assure you, we have received no funding or support from Autism Speaks and have no affiliation whatsoever with that organization. Second, I feel absolutely terrible. I didn't know how offensive the phrase 'autism awareness' was until now, nor did I know the history behind it that has contributed to making it so. You are one hundred percent right, and as soon as I leave this session I'm going to remove that phrase from the questionnaire and free myself of any association with it in everything I write or say from now on. I want to do this thing right. I'm really sorry."

A soothing voice enters the soundscape: "We can help you with that."

It's Ibby. I turn toward her and am immediately comforted by her calm presence in what has become a tense environment. "It's easy," she assures me. "If you send me that questionnaire, I can go through and make edits to get rid of that kind of offensive language."

"Thanks, Ibby. I'd really appreciate that, and I'm sorry for taking up so much of your discussion time on this topic."

"That's OK," Ibby assures me, "but we do need to move on now."

After the session, I approach Ibby and ask her for her contact information so I can send her the questionnaire. She gives me a warm smile and hands me her business card:

Elizabeth J. Grace, Assistant Professor
National College of Education

National-Louis University
Wheeling Campus
Wheeling, Illinois

I put Ibby's contact information into my phone and email her the evaluation form as soon as I'm back in Tallahassee. What I don't realize at the time is that Ibby rarely checks her email, or for that matter her office voice mail, on which I leave numerous messages over the course of literally months without any reply. Why isn't Ibby getting back to me, I wonder. Was she insincere about her willingness to assist me when we spoke at the conference?

I'm confused and disappointed, but also tenacious. I open a Twitter account—something I have resisted doing for years—and send my first-ever Tweet to Ibby Grace. Within the 140-character space allotted, I ask her whether she has been receiving my emails or voice mails and if she will help me with the evaluation form—and also whether she might allow me to interview her for a forthcoming book I'm writing on music and autism.

Seconds later, I receive my first Tweet, a reply from Ibby: She's happy to hear from me. No, she never got any of my emails or voice mails—"I'm not good with email or the phone." Yes, resend the evaluation form; she'll be sure to check her email now that she knows it's coming. And yes, she would love to be part of my #AWESOME BOOK!

I literally jump for joy. A few days later, Ibby and I meet for our first chat session.

CONVERSATION 1: JUNE 27, 2014

It's a hot summer day in Tallahassee, just like all the rest. I arrive at my office at the scheduled time and ping Ibby.

"I'm here whenever you're ready," I type.

"So I am here too," she types back immediately.

"Cool. So how are you, Ibby?!"

"Doing a lot better, getting my strength and language back. How are you?"

Doing a lot better? I have no frame of reference for that. What happened? Should I know? I'm not sure how best to proceed.

"I'm well," I write, stalling for time as I consider how to respond to Ibby's "doing a lot better" remark. I decide to go for blunt honesty.

"I don't know the backdrop of your last comment," I confess. "What happened—that made you lose strength/language?!!"

"Oh it's called a TIA [Transient Ischemic Attack]. I guess it means a mini stroke. It was an unpleasant, scary thing at any rate. Sorry. LOL... sometimes I forget to contextualize..."

"Oh gosh. That does sound scary!! I'm sorry, though glad you're doing better!!"

We move on to other subjects, including our mutual friend Andrew Dell'Antonio, a musicologist at the University of Texas at Austin.

"How do you know Andrew?" I ask Ibby.

" . . . I met him because I was keynoting at Syracuse [University] and he [was there at that time]. We got to talking about musicology, which of course is an envy... in college I had wished to study it but when I finally made it to college I got a scholarship for being good at logic, which I also love. So now we are working together on a pretty exciting project."

"Aha. . . . Tell me about the project!!"

"We are theorizing autistic musical phenomenology... I sort of 'think in music' in the same way Temple says she 'thinks in pictures' or... it's the closest analogy," Ibby relates with reference to the famed author, activist, and animal scientist Temple Grandin, and to Grandin's landmark book *Thinking in Pictures: My Life with Autism* specifically.[6] "I had a look at what you are doing and it's going to interest the same people and be different in exciting ways. So this is cool."

"Fascinating! Can you describe that to me in some detail?"

"Thinking in music?"

"Right . . . could you perhaps provide me with an example of how it works? Take me through it step by step?"

"Well... I'm working on it now in some ways, but I can say some things about it that might make rapid sense... Music was the nexus between my self and language for a long time... my communicative access."

"Go on!"

"When I relax among myself there are not words going on in my head. There are intervals, tones, it is much more relaxed... sometimes in order to think, I structure the thoughts into more like music, or they do themselves like that. Intravisually, this is close to a screensaver turning from fractals into polygons. So the inbetween is lyrical music or song. I could use it with others to communicate when I was not as good at expression otherwise."

I am enthralled.

"And I am alexithymic, do you know what that means?" Ibby asks.

"No, I don't. Please explain. Sounds like a variation on the theme of dyslexia?"

"I say a little about this in *Criptiques,*" Ibby says in reference to her chapter "Your Mama Wears Drover Boots" in that anthology, adding, "maybe some in other places, deffo [definitely] on the blog... Lexi is the language and thymia is the feelings. I suck at languaging feelings, but I learned how [to do it] better by studying theater in college."[7]

Later, I do some follow-up research on alexithymia. I find a clear definition in Istvan Molnar-Szakacs and Pamela Heaton's co-authored article "Music: A Unique Window into the World of Autism," in which they explain that alexithymia "is a disorder characterized by reduced or absent affective responses (type I alexithymia) or difficulties in understanding and ascribing affective labels to one's own physiological states of arousal, even when affective arousal is present (type II alexithymia)."[8]

Evidently, Ibby is in the "type II" category. In fact, she seems to be skeptical about the "type I" form of alexithymia altogether.

"Some people suspect alexithymic types of not actually having feelings," Ibby reports, implicitly referencing type I alexithymia, "but no, that's not it. LOL."

"LOL indeed," I jump in.

"Oh, more lingo," Ibby adds. "The a- at the beginning of the lexi and thymia is [like] the a- at the beginning of atheist."

"Right. Got it!"

"No words feelings. Haha. Anyway, I found out when I was in my youth that I could communicate a great deal of emotion in song, to the point where friends with bands had me write for them, to order."

Writing songs to order for friends? Very interesting. I make a note to return to that subject later, but first I want to know more about Ibby's alexithymia vis-à-vis her musical life.

"So you say you suck at languaging feelings," I posit, "but it sounds like you're probably very adept at *musicking* feelings. Am I right?"

"Yes, it seems so. . . . In music, I could create empathetic communication about things I had heard other people talking about, and feel it through myself, even with no experience."

"When you say 'even with no experience,' what exactly do you mean by that?"

"Are you interested in detailed types of examples? Of how I got into writing music?"

"Absolutely!!! The more details the better!"

"So I was a really weird type of kid, but the other kids found out I could do this stuff even before I got kicked out of high school. I was way virginal, I thought I was asexual, which wasn't a thing then. Before I found out I was gay, so. They would say, 'Write us a song that sounds like Manhattan Transfer, but it is funny.' Or, a song that could be done by Ringo [Starr]. . . . This one song [I did] became really popular. It was supposed to be reminiscent of [the Beatles'] *Yesterday*, and be about codependence, and I was like, 'What is that?' And they were like, 'You know how Kristy is totally in love with Gregg and he is, like, mean and that makes her love him more?' And I was like, yeah, OK. . . . At this age I was way too shy and awkward ever to perform, but it was neat seeing people with bands make music out of the inventions I gave them." (A solo vocal rendition by Ibby of her "Codependence Song" may be heard at the companion website [CW 5.1 ▶].)

"Do you remember any lyrics? Could you send me snippets of those? Perhaps from the *Yesterday*/codependence song?"

"Yes, OK, so that one is on my mind now. Minor key sounding of course, cellos in between. That's where most of the emotion comes in how the music actually sounds, and I learned from Arash Babak why that is (more on this later)."

I hope there will be. Who *is* Arash Babak, I wonder.

Ibby posts the lyrics of her "codependence song" for me to view; she has inserted text in square brackets to evoke the sound of the song at key points: "All you ever do is hurt me / Still I beg you don't desert me / I need you like plants need sun and water to survive. [cello bit] [raising crescendo] Ahh, with your ocean colored eyes / shining like a star / how beautiful you are / and with the way your silken voice / dances round my ears / I can't hold back the tears... [back to the slow, downtrend melody] I look back on my life behind me / I thought I would never find me / one like you to whom I'd give my heart in absolute..."

"That is all I remember," Ibby writes, "but the singer should have trouble not crying, like Lana Cantrell, and Nick did a great job."

"That is a beautiful lyric, Ibby!"

"Thank you."

"Who is Nick?"

"Oh, he is the blue-eyed Arabic teenager who commissioned the song. I can't remember his band, it was kind of like ABC. This other guy Nic had the band that wanted jazzy stuff, and funny."

Lots of Nicks and Nics to keep track of, but I think I have it straight. "Ah, okay," I post. "You mentioned the cello part, the minor key. Did you write out parts for the different instruments or teach them by rote?"

"I got on his synthesizer and said, 'It goes like this.' LOL. I can't write [music]."

"Works for me!"

"Nic [he of the jazzy stuff] was more fluent in music, so I could sing stuff to him and he could octave it around."

"Always good to have someone *like* that around!" I type.

I have heard that Ibby is an accomplished Irish music performer. I ask her about that: "So is Irish music the main thing you have been performing lately?"

"Yes, when I perform it is usually Celtic-Irish and Scots stuff—and kid lit music of course, with the kids."

"Kid lit music? Tell me more about what that is—'Mary Had a Little Lamb' and such?"

"'Banana Phone,' 'Señor Don Gato'—kids want more pizzazz these days. LOL."

Ibby and her wife Layenie are raising twin boys—both toddlers at the time of this exchange—so she is clearly up on the kid lit music repertoire. "Yes, they've raised the bar!" I agree, tagging on an LOL of my own for good measure; Ibby likes to LOL.

"There is a wonderful musician around here, Jim Gill, who writes great stuff for kids," Ibby informs me. "They Might Be Giants does great stuff too."

"Yes . . . I don't know their stuff well, but didn't they do an album that was all songs about science?"

"Yes, it is one of my kids' faves."

"I'll have to check it out. Back to the Celtic music, do you sing? Play an instrument? Both?"

"When I did theater improv also, I gained entrée into it by being able to sort of make up songs in [different] genres."

"Let's come back to that—Celtic music first," I suggest, perhaps being a bit more directive of the conversation than I ought to be.

"I really sing, but I learned to do DADGAD guitar [i.e., very basic chord progressions] because playing guitar properly was beyond my multitasking skills while singing. But I can do dulcimer and bodhran [Irish frame drum]... How that got started was [with the] bodhran. There was this amazing a cappella duo of Celtic singers that I loved, and I said: you need a bodhran. And they said: can you sing? And I was like um uh... I didn't think I could perform in public, only sing to communicate what the song was supposed to sound like? But I was like 'uh.' The woman said 'Come to my house for an audition.' She was very beautiful, especially her voice, and I was basically kind of on the homeless side, if not literally homeless. You know, when you busk, you don't have to make eye contact." Once again, I am left to wonder about certain things in the absence of much context from Ibby: How homeless was she? Where was she busking, and how often? Was the "when you busk, you don't have to make eye contact" comment a plain statement of fact or a witty remark? I refrain from asking; I don't want to interrupt her flow.

"So I did [the audition]," Ibby continues, "and they loved my voice, and put me in their band, and we did three-part harmony. Taught me a lot of songs. My 'job' in the band was to sing the randy-sounding lyrics because my voice was a bit church choir. LOL. It was a fun contrast."

"Beautiful," I write. "So let me make sure I understand something. Was this a busking band primarily—street musicians?"

"No no," Ibby quickly corrects. "I was a street musician with no performance skills. This was a real band [that played at] venues around town: pubs and public radio, etc., poetry readings, you know the type of thing?"

"Ah, do you remember what the band was called?"

"Hob Nob. The man who started it was an amazing Welsh storyteller."

" . . . And did you end up singing *and* playing bodhran with them?"

"Yes, and Appalachian dulcimer sometimes. Always singing, though. It turned out I was considered a good singer, but I had to be given red wine to loosen me up at first. LOL."

"Nice! And did you teach yourself to play both bodhran and dulcimer?"

"Yes."

"Impressive! Did you ever learn to read music?"

"I tried to learn how when I was little. I really tried, when learning piano, but I couldn't make myself read it because I could hear it too much. I cheated, like. And didn't know how to stop it? I can parse out the reading of music super slowly. I know how it works."

"In other words, you could play the music you were supposed to be reading by ear?"

"Yes."

"That actually means you're a *good* musician. Many of the best jazz musicians have had that same 'problem' [of not being able to read music well]."

"Really? AWesome!!" Ibby exclaims. I can't tell whether the capital "AW" in "Awesome" is for emphasis or a typo. "I could also know when hearing two songs after each other whether part of them would not harmonize, ahead of time. Gwion loved that."

Gwion? Who is that, I wonder, but I finish my other thread first: "You're not a disabled music reader. You're a highly capable music listener! Being able to translate sounds heard into notes played is actually harder for many musicians—even good ones (especially in the classical world)—than being able to translate notation into musical performance. In many ways, playing by ear is a *higher* skill [than playing from notation]. Yet another twist on the old ability/disability thing, eh?!"

"LOL. Yeah!! I like your style."

"Thanks! ☺"

This time it's Ibby who changes the subject, swinging the conversation back around to the aforementioned Arash Babak. "When I was [about twelve years old], we had a family friend who was an ethnomusicologist from Persia, Arash Babak Bahar Farzin.[9] This is who gave me the knowledge of expressing," she adds.

"So Arash Babak," I inquire, "are he and Gwion the same guy?" I am by now drowning a bit in the sea of unfamiliar names.

"No, Gwion is the Welsh story teller/band leader [of Hob Nob]. Ben [Bahar] Farzin is Arash Babak. He's a Farsi speaker from Iran, but he's Persian because he likes the Shah instead of the Ayatollah."

"Ah, thank you. So Arash is the ethnomusicologist from Persia then, right?

"Yes.

"And Gwion is a man, right?

"Yes, he looks like Dumbledore, but he is younger."

"Hahaha!"

"Arash Babak looks like a walrus."

"Hahahahaha!"

"Actually, I think there is an old pic[ture] of Ben Bahar Farzin on the archive website [of the university where he used to teach]. You will see the walrus thing. Gwion, I can't see him getting anywhere near online; he thinks microwave ovens are Big Brother putting implants in us."

"Haha. Tell me more about how Arash Babak (Ben Farzin) helped you to learn to be expressive through music."

"OK, so this was when they were doing terrible things in Afghanistan that one time (not the subsequent times) and had just got the Ayatollah so there were many Farsi speakers from different countries. Meanwhile my mom was a volunteer English teacher and so she knew a bunch of people, so I got to go to these parties with the cool music."

Now I'm getting really confused. I thought Arash Babak was from Iran. How did Afghanistan come into the picture?

"Wait, Afghanistan or Iran?" I ask Ibby. She is kind enough to clarify.

"See, they speak the same language, Farsi," Ibby explains in reference to the community of immigrants from Iran and Afghanistan she grew up with in the Pacific Northwest, "so they had refugee solidarity in Seattle,[10] like we would if we were washed ashore in China with Aussies and Brits? Unrest caused both countries to have refugees in Seattle."

I have Googled the photograph of Arash Babak. "Just looked up the pic," I tell Ibby. "Definitely walrus, like the actor Wilford Brimley!"

"He played this wonderful thing, this Santur," Ibby writes back. "It's like a hammer dulcimer of ours but infinitely more custom tunable. And I was sort of tortured by [going to] parties and he was really super kind, a Sufi, and I think he noticed this, that I was awkward on the one hand and fascinated by his music and fast hammers on the other, and he invited me over. And he started telling me the modes [in Persian music], about how in [Persian] classical music"

Ibby stops writing mid-sentence. "ZOMG!" she exclaims. "Yes, you're an ethnomusicologist, right? OK, so you also know about the [Persian] modes." I chuckle. "So moving along... he was like, 'OK, so now I will play Isfahan whatever something [mode] and everyone will talk louder, then I will change it so they dance, then I will move this and they will stop and eat: get ready."

"And it all happened that way?!" I ask.

"He was working it, oh yeah," Ibby shoots back.

"Amazing!"

"And making smug walrus faces including me in on the trick. Like, I was in heaven."

"Hahaha! This is turning out to be more of an ethnomusicological story than I could ever have hoped for, Ibby!"

"He is why I wanted to be one, an ethnomusicologist."

"Makes sense! Would have been nice, but now the hot-shot musicologists are all coming to *you* to learn about music, right!?"

"*Nooooo*, not about music, about my experience... and I get to get my musicology lessons for free without paying tuition!"

Ibby returns to the subject of Arash Babak. By now she has mentioned Saudi Arabia, Seattle, Afghanistan, and Iran in chronicling the story of her relationship with him. I want to make sure I have my facts straight, so I ask her to spell it all out for me.

"My best friend when I was little was Saudi," she explains. "We lived in Seattle. Their family helped my dad get a job temporarily in Saudi Arabia, I think, but we stayed behind. Arash Babak sort of protected us at that time. All the people knew each other. I used to get to go to [the] Ramadan Eids [feast][11] and stuff, and was taught to write Arabic, etc. But I have never been to one of these places. Also Musa (pseudonym), he was another guy who hung out—he taught me some Doumbek [drumming] skills, how to play and how to re-head a broken skin, with goat, the traditional twine way."

"Thank you. That helps a lot! What was your dad's job? Something in the oil industry?"

"Environmental engineer, water guy. I think he did the invention of the water works for a new city."

"Nice. Are your parents still alive?"

"Yes, they are, in Pleasant Hill now, which is by Berkeley, retired."

"Did your mom also work? (I mean outside the home. *All* moms work!!)"

"Not usually for money, but she did volunteering and arts a lot, and then became a nurse, just in time to become immune-compromised to where nursing wasn't viable, so she had to immediately retire from it."

"What did she do in the arts? Theater?"

"My mom had been a wedding singer and a set designer and a calligrapher before doing the language teaching with our friend."

"What language teaching? (Did I miss something?)"

"Yes, how we met the Farsi speakers in the first place was, I think, because most of them my mom was organizing to help [learn] their English faster... [For example,] Aarif from Afghanistan [pseudonym] was a great engineer, but my dad would not be able to get him a job unless he could communicate at least somewhat [in English]. This was before my dad became unemployed and went to [Saudi] Arabia for a sec."

"Ah, so [your mother] taught English mainly to native Farsi speakers, right?"

"I think Musa the drummer could speak both Arabic and Farsi and he was the one who introduced us around, and was Arash Babak's friend. That's how we all met. [In answer to your question,] yes, I think so, but I was a kid. Plus I was even more of a space case than the average kid. LOL. With the Saudis, my mom didn't teach them English at all; the relationship was way more about us kids being friends and everyone cooking and dancing."

"Let's talk more about you and your musical experiences.... How do you think being autistic influences the way you sing, play, and listen to music? I guess that's actually three questions in one!"

". . . Oh, so there is this thing that I know I do on purpose. I know that music can help me be in the world more, even when [I'm] in doubt. I know a lot about what people mean in identification when they say they like and dislike various genres, and I know ways to find this out and use it to help connect. I can help people get along with each other's music when they thought they could not."

I wait for more from Ibby as dots dance across the screen with bubble sound accompaniment. "I can hear the genres in each other easily and it is fun to do this," she continues. "Sometimes I immerse myself in music and sometimes I play with it analytically. This enables me socially in ways I would have no chance of access to without it. I learned this around the same age [I was spending time with the] Farsi speakers, actually. Now this is going to sound really out there: I think I can hear people's own music sometimes, but it's how I classify what their soul sounds like to me. I think this is what people mean by aura or feeling? But I can use this facility to predict if people will be liable to get along with one another."

Fascinating, I think to myself. What a talent: to hear people *as* music, to hear what their souls sound like. It puts a whole new spin on the idea of "soul music." And there is more. "Well, here is an autistic thing that might be sort of impairmenty," Ibby suggests. "I do not listen to music and do anything else at the same time, except driving. The music will win."

Later in the dialogue, Ibby and I return to the subject of Irish music. She writes, "I love Irish songs where the words and the rest of it don't match perfectly." I ask her to explain what she means by that. "Like if the music is soaring with sadness and the lyrics are a bit hilarious," she responds, "or the thing is a pro-war march, clearly, in the music, with antiwar lyrics." She gives the song "Johnny I Hardly Knew Ya" as an example and follows up by recording herself singing it for the companion website (CW 5.2 ▶).

"Or my job in our band," Ibby continues, "to sing like an angel about 'Me Husband Has No Courage in Him.' Haha." The reference is to a bawdy old Irish folk song that I know well. I can't help but chuckle imagining a singing-like-an-angel delivery of lines like "Every night when I goes to bed, I lie and throw me leg right o'er him, and me hand I clamp between his thighs, but I can't put any courage in him."

As our conversation continues, Ibby shares one fascinating story after another about her life in music.

"OK. So music is also how I got remediated in math," she states at one point.

This piques my curiosity. "Oh, that's interesting! Tell me about that!" I exclaim.

"In college I could not do math because I had been kicked out of class so much.[12] Anyway, so I found out how bad my math was—grade school level—but this woman doing her Ph.D. (and I wish I could remember her name) got me in her study group of making a new type of remedial class, like, creative people who suck at math. LOL. She assessed me and my anxiety + foundational lacks + other abilities and said this: Math is the lovechild of logic and music. And I was like, 'Well ok then, I can learn that.' I could, too. She told me, 'Don't bother doing calculations and algorithms; in fact, I won't even tell you how until you feel the answer.' Feel it the way I feel the music in my inside, you know? This is the truth: I can feel the math like music, especially geometric math. But a shocking amount of regular math and algebra is geometric and musical... I can feel it the way I feel my inner music. Some stuff I may never get, like what time [of day] it is. I just don't feel that. I guess the time is Kenny G. Snerf."

"What? Joke, right?" I ask. I want to be sure we're on the same page vis-à-vis the talented yet oft-maligned smooth jazz saxophonist. "Because you don't 'get' Kenny G's music? (Now who's the literal, autistic one here?!)"

"LOLOL! Yep."

"Thanks!"

"Just not feelin' him," Ibby adds.

"Me neither!" I admit.

"But oh... there [are people who say that] all autistic people have perfect pitch. Speaking of world music... that pisses me off," she complains. "Perfect pitch makes assumptions I dislike. Part of my relation to music is I can recontextualize myself, get heuristic. . . . All perfect pitch is perfect relative pitch and the difference is whether the referent is in your imagination or in your actual outer ear. That's what I mean to say."

I am impressed by the sophistication of Ibby's critique. From an ethnomusicological perspective, it strikes me as spot on.[13]

We turn now to the subject of autism, music, and emotion. I ask Ibby to describe the kinds of emotional experiences she tends to have while performing, listening to, or otherwise experiencing music.

"OK. It is hard to explain, but," she begins. She pauses for a long time before proceeding. "In music land, I am not alexithymic. I'm almost like the opposite: psychic, sensitive, etc. LOL. Say, like the people, I hear them in my mind's ear being, and [I think,] would I put them together in the same chamber band? And sometimes I don't believe myself. I am like 'Shut up Ib,' and then it turns out cacophony: I was right. 'Here is a person who would be best played as a harpsichord; honestly too much exposure to the friend of mine who takes pride in the fuzziness of her amp turned to eleven on the Les Paul [electric guitar] is not going to end well'... Am I explaining it?"

"Yes, keep going!" I say. Again, Ibby's descriptions of perceiving what people are like—and beyond that whether they are likely to get along—by essentially *hearing* them as music fascinates me. I imagine what it would be like to relate to people as different kinds of music, musical instruments, and timbres; and beyond that to be able to build from such perceptions toward "harmonizing" social relationships.

Now Ibby takes the idea a step further.

"Or there is another thing," she writes, "and I almost never used to listen to this, at my own peril. In Irish music it is funny and they do it on purpose. But: Beware of a person who takes great pains to present [their] opposing self to their actual music. The harpsichord should not be wearing a T-shirt saying Slut City Disco, and if she is, worry why. Hahaha!" Ibby provides a second example. This one, in contrast to the first, is not meant to bring laughs. "I mean, often people lie in the other direction, but that's just that they are caught [within themselves] more. I don't know why this is. This music of people—hearing it—it is a site of great potential for compassion because a non hinky type of hiding of music people do is just not lying, but turning down their volume a lot."

"Non hinky? What does that mean?" I ask.

"Non hinky means relatively less morally blameworthy, or not indicative of the idea that I should be wary of trusting the person," she explains. "Sometimes sad, modest people do this and nobody sees their pain. But those of us who can hear it [their inner music] can be gentle for them, and there when they are ready to emerge. Actually, if I know people closely in life to where I have them nearby, I can help those who are like this to talk by playing real life music that resembles what I hear."

What an extraordinary ability, I think to myself again.

"So, sometimes," Ibby continues, "people make their souls inaudible but it causes me to feel for them because rather than them being shady liars masking themselves, I find they have honest music played very quietly as if their being is squelched. I trust such people, and take extra time and [use] imaginary ears trying to hear them, and hope they will amplify themselves. I suspect that is still a weird statement, but I hope it is better articulated. The reason I think it is important is that muted music is one of my chief ways of knowing if someone is fragile in some way, like being abused or having PTSD. I think the ears with which I hear people's soul music are figurative instead of my regular ears, but I am not entirely certain of this, and have no idea how to find out."

My mind does a 180-degree turn as I try to wrap it around Ibby's novel concept of what "soul music" is. This is not the soul of Ray Charles, Aretha Franklin, and James Brown that I know and love. No, it is the muted music hidden deep inside of other people's souls, people who are rarely if ever heard from by anyone but themselves.

Ibby can hear that music. I wish I could too.

CONVERSATION 2: JULY 1, 2014

Ibby is feeling poorly when we reconvene five days later.

"I am migraining out," she concedes. "Do you have time tomorrow or the next day?"

"Oh, sorry to hear that" I reply. "Let's do it tomorrow."

We reschedule, but before signing off Ibby asks if I would like to read a poem she wrote.

"I wrote it for my wife, Layenie," she tells me. "It's called 'You,' and it includes a reference to my musical thinking."

"Yes, I would love to read it."

The poem appears on my computer screen moments later:

You

by Elizabeth J. (Ibby) Grace—for Layenie

"If thine eye be single," she said
And I knew it was holy; yet holy mackerel
You know what I'm like: I laughed
And could not stop. My mind made
The green guy from Monsters the movie
With the M on his hat and so then,
Of course, my mind made you
Making me laugh some more.

You are the one beyond imagining,
Even though my mind makes kaleidoscopes
And waterfalls, and dreams of helix
Soundscapes of refracting light I can fly on,
Shimmering dapples dance color and float
In ways I can't even sing so much less say,
And I live in a great haze of spacey joy sometimes:
None of that compares
To the beauty, the paradise you are.

But it is holy. The Greek word, here "single,"
Is haplous, which usually means 'simple.'
And the rest of the verse has your body full
Of light. So I am simple, and blessed. I thought
I would be alone, and this was fine with me,
Because I had not met you yet then.
Now that I know you, I will never be
Without you, and this is why
My mind makes you hear what I hear,
See what I notice, knowing
Your magical laughter will move my merriment

Forevermore.

"It is a beautiful poem," I tell Ibby. "I love the line 'My mind makes you hear what I hear,' and what we talked about the other day gives me extra insight into the importance of that line. Layenie is a very lucky woman to be so loved, and clearly so too are you to have Layenie in your life!! Talk to you tomorrow!"

The next day finds Ibby in better spirits.

"How are you today?" I ask her. "Migraine gone?"

"Almost," she replies. "I am more postdrome now but not in big pain, so yay."

"So I really liked your poem for Leyanie (spelling?). Beautiful!"

As I suspected, I have misspelled the name.

"Awww thanks," Ibby replies. "Layenie made up the spelling with her sister because they wanted it to be unique. It's pronounced Lainie though. Jenn at that time went by Jeffy, to also have it be unique, but dropped that."

"Jenn being Layenie's sister?"

"Yep... in a very very small place in Scotland where school can be disrupted because someone's sheep get out and all the kids need to help get them back where they belong."

"Cool, so their family is from rural Scotland? Have you spent much time over there?"

"Yes, we get over there at least every other year; it's awesome!"

" . . . Does Layenie play music? Or sing?"

"She used to play sax but I have never heard her... plays some recorder... sings beautifully; also, she can make up songs."

"Do you do things together musically?"

"All the time at home... as I quip in *Criptiques*... the boys are going to be disappointed when they get into real life and notice that real life isn't structured like musical theater.[14] LOL. (Something like that I said [in *Criptiques*]... haven't read it back in a while.) Sometimes we make up songs and sometimes we topically use extant songs... like they do in these new Aussie films called jukebox genre, such as *Happy Feet* and *Moulin Rouge*."

"Have you and Layenie ever played out together—i.e., does she sit in when you play with Hob Nob or other bands?"

"Oh, the performance times in my life were before. I don't really have that kind of time now because my children are two years old. . . . So now I sing for the boys and they sing too! Also they are really into dancing, which: there is not much more adorable than toddler-dancing."

"That's beautiful! Are they adopted or is Layenie the biological mom? (Twin boys, right?)"

"Twins, yes, she's bio-mom and she tried to pick out the donor whose account of himself reminded her most of me. He is willing to meet them when they are eighteen and also he is a music engineer."

"How sweet! Is he autistic (the donor)?"

"He did not declare, but then, they probably wouldn't have accepted his sperm... his interview sounded mighty Aut [Autistic] though."

"How so?"

"He went into graphic detail about music engineering and why his family was cool because everyone in it knows how to do different things, such as bookbinding and making furniture and studying particle physics. Layenie was like: 'Bingo! They sound like Graces.'"

"Haha! May I ask an awkward question?"

"Yes."

"Let's assume the donor is autistic. Would you prefer, not prefer, or not care if the boys were too?"

"I don't care if they are in terms of them; I love however they are neurologically. They are getting some Aut culture along with some Scots culture... and also though... In terms of there being a certain number of Aut kids in the world, I can't think of a better mother for some—a better non Aut mom—than Layenie, and it would be good to have an Aut parent... So hence why we might foster/adopt some kids later on too."

"Indeed! Question: How to deal linguistically with the whole Pandora's Box of high/low functioning autism?"

"I wrote a thing about that, if you want to see?"

"Yes!"

"OK, let me find it," Ibby writes. She sends me a link to a 2012 exchange between her and a woman named Tina, which appears on Ibby's blog, "Tiny Grace Notes (Ask an Autistic)."[15]

Tina identifies herself in the piece as the mother of "a severely disabled son" named Eric who "is nonverbal, is still in diapers, has self harming behaviors, hits himself in the face repeatedly and eats with his hands."

"I doubt he will ever progress to the point of living independently," Tina laments. "I get really tired of people saying how labels are bad. I mean when anyone sees him they get how tough it is and they use words like severe and low functioning, and they're right to, because he is. I don't see how that's a bad thing, it's an honest thing, from my perspective. Also people who seem so dead set against labeling are either able to write down their views (something my son cannot do) or they are parents of kids who are much farther along than my son. Truthfully I don't really care about the labels, but I do feel upset when people make such a big deal about labels, when it's really clear the severe label isn't one that fits them. Also I'd like to see something that would make him able to go to the bathroom and not have to wear a diaper, use a utensil to eat his food and speak. If that's a cure, then I'll take it, if it's something else, great I'll take that. But I'm sick of everyone arguing about this stuff when they can WRITE and TALK! You seem like a reasonable person. I'd love your views on all this. Thanks."

Ibby is sympathetic in her response to Tina, and she is clearly sensitive to Tina's difficulties. In the end, though, she comes down against the use of labels like "severe" and "low functioning," and mainly for simple, pragmatic reasons.

"So apart from the 'severe' and 'low' and 'high' labels being inaccurate sometimes because they change during context changes," Ibby writes to Tina, "I also don't love that they reduce people to 'functioning'[,] like a human is a human doing rather than a human being. We are meant to BE. That is what makes us worthy, not high or low. But the A Number One thing I dislike is that people might overhear and feel heinous about themselves. This has happened to a lot of people I know, and it is just not worth it."

"Sometimes it seems like No Way Can He Hear And Understand Anything," Ibby continues. "Or maybe you didn't think that but some doctor or speech pathologist or psychologist or psychiatrist told it to you for an alleged fact, and you were like, well, guess they are the Expert. But I don't think the risk is worth it."

"So," Ibby suggests to Tina, "my way of thinking about this is based on an idea made up by philosopher and mathematician Blaise Pascal, called Pascal's Wager, to see if it would be a good idea to believe in God. You can see in the article if you click on it (it's a good one) that the idea is controversial, but it is still useful as a framework. Basically it is that you picture all four scenarios, and here it is[,] filled out for positive and negative language and the kid understanding you or not, with the outcomes."

Ibby has laid out her four Pascal's Wager scenarios in the format of a table. They boil down to the following:

- If you (parent/adult) say "positive stuff" and the child *does* understand words/language, then that child "feels supported by you and gets that you are in their corner no matter what. When others say negative stuff they know they can come home and not have to hear that."
- If you say positive stuff and the child *doesn't* understand words/language, then it "doesn't matter, they can't hear you."
- If you say "negative stuff" and the child *does* understand words/language, then that child "hears that they are 'low functioning' or 'severe' or etc. and either A) just feels bad about self or B) develops Learned Helplessness and Low Motivation to Succeed."
- If you say negative stuff and the child *doesn't* understand words/language, then it "doesn't matter, they can't hear you."

From these four scenarios, it stands to reason that, first, saying "positive stuff" is always a better option than saying "negative stuff," and, second, applying negative functioning labels to people never serves any particularly useful purpose.

"Thanks for sharing that link with me, Ibby," I write. "It's an illuminating exchange."

"I am supposedly 'medium functioning,'" she types back, "so I am in a perfect position to deconstruct that stuff."

"So you mentioned earlier that you and Layenie hope to adopt or foster parent some kids on the spectrum in the future. Do you already have a notion of where along the spectrum the kids you bring into your family might be?" It's a struggle to avoid using "high-functioning" and "low-functioning" in my phrasing of the question, but I manage. Later I will learn alternative forms of language for use in such contexts—for example, "individuals with higher-support needs" versus "individuals with lower-support needs"—but for now those arguably preferable designations are not yet known to me.

"I will probably try to rescue people who need help fighting for the right for their communication to be respected," Ibby writes back, "because that is such a huge issue, and I can talk most of the time. And Layenie, being a pediatric nurse, is good with kids who have medical fragility, which often coincides with [their communication challenges]. But we are both pretty religious, so it will end up being whoever is the next one who needs us. We'd be called, I'm sure."

I ask Ibby what religion she and Layenie practice.

"We have Catholic tendencies and baptism and enculturation, but the church itself doesn't dig it when we are us, so we practice Episcopalian, high church," she explains.

"May I ask you about your love poem for Layenie, 'You'?" I ask. "Well, actually, not about the poem, but the little narrative bio of you below it."

"Sure."

"I'm going to paste the bio here and then ask you about it," I tell Ibby. "Here it is":

Elizabeth J. (Ibby) Grace is an Autistic writer who lives in the suburbs of Chicago with her family. Writing has been very hard for her because until recently she thought the fact that she thinks mostly musically was an insurmountable barrier instead of a potential springboard there for the taking if only she would willingly make the first running jump. Springboards are bouncy and founded on twirling helix towers of secret strength. Ibby is grateful forever to the ones who made this knowledge known, and will show this by writing, and ever newly spring-ing. She blogs at Tiny Grace Notes and curates NeuroQueer [neuroqueer. blogspot.com].

"So can you elaborate a bit on the epiphany that enabled you to see music as something to *facilitate* your process as a writer, as opposed to feel-ing hindered and paralyzed as a writer since you 'thought in music'?" I ask.

That epiphany, Ibby writes back, occurred largely thanks to the mentor-ship of three friends of hers who were writers: Eli Claire, Terry Jo Smith, and Phil Smith ("no relation to Terry," Ibby specifies).

"All of them told me to use my music in my voice like I do when I talk. [The writer] Ariane Zurcher helped too because she explained what they meant. Of course at first I was like 'what? huh?'—she [Ariane] translates well. Haha. And poetry," Ibby continues. "Gerard Manley Hopkins is my guy. He invented sprung rhythm to make poetry back through real ear music closer to real talking. He said read it out loud, broke the unfree verse. But I had to let go, because without melody, the way the words tumble works differently. Melodic music gave me a reason not to itch about the structures, not to be afraid of the writing."

FOOL'S SONNET

By this point, Ibby and I have been chatting for a very long time. I'm start-ing to wear down a bit, and I'm guessing she is too, but this latest episode of the conversation has my curiosity very much piqued, especially with the whole idea of sprung rhythm. I ask Ibby if she'll indulge me for just a while longer, in particular to share more of her insights on sprung rhythm vis-à-vis poetry, ear music, and real talking.

There is no reply for several minutes. I wonder if our connection has failed or if, worse, Ibby has reached a point of total exhaustion and just shut down. I'm about to post a "Never mind, some other time" note when a splash of words covers my screen.

"Here, look at this," Ibby has written, and below that she has posted another of her poems, this one apparently forming her response to my question about sprung rhythm. The poem is titled "Fool's Sonnet":

To write a sonnet is a vintage skill
That should be stranger than it is for me,
But I have lived conforming to the will
Of structure. I have done this seamlessly,

Beset by force. Now, when it is my choice,
Then suddenly the feeling of it moves
Into a game I really like. My voice
Is surefooted and frolicsome, and proves
This life is funny. Anarchism reigns
Inside my secret mind, and when I sing,
My single-minded eye can focus, feign
And fool and foil and skip and spring and wing:
When it's coerced, I can't abide a day;
But, if I choose, the self-same thing is play.

"Fabulous sonnet!" I exclaim. "May I have your permission to include it in the book?"

"Yes, sure. Thanks."

"Thank *you!*"

"My brain is getting hazy," Ibby tells me. It's time to call it a day.

"OK. Bye for now! Unhaze well!"

NOTES

1. The abstract was published in the SDS conference program booklet (Grace et al. 2013).
2. "Very few of us [autistics] typically went to SDS at that time," Ibby Grace explained to me several years after the fact via a March 17, 2017, email, "and one of the reasons so many people came to that particular session is because the other disabled people had been wanting to support more autistic involvement and were showing support. Very supportive and cool of them, and they kept it up [throughout the conference and beyond] as well."
3. This conversation was not recorded, so the version of it presented here is my attempt at a reconstruction of what was actually said based on what I recalled, notes I took during the session, and journal entries I composed in its immediate aftermath.
4. The practice of silent applause, which typically involves holding one's hands high in the air and twisting quickly from the forearms to make the hands rotate back and forth, originally developed as the American Sign Language symbol for "Deaf applause" and is now a standard feature of Deaf culture. It has in recent years been adopted widely throughout the autistic community as well, this as a show of solidarity with Deaf culture and out of respect for the auditory sensitivities of many autistic people. It is also known as the "ASL Deaf clap" or as "jazz hands."
5. *NeuroTribes* (Silberman 2015, 464).
6. *Thinking in Pictures* (Grandin 2006).
7. Grace's chapter in *Criptiques* is titled "Your Mama Wears Drover Boots" (Grace 2014). Regarding the blog references, she blogs at both *Tiny Grace Notes* and *NeuroQueer: Queering Our Neurodivergence, Neurodiversifying Our Queer*, as well as curating *Neuroqueer*. These sites are located at tinygracenotes.blogspot.com

and neuroqueer.blogspot.com, respectively. The specific entry she is referencing here is called "'It Hurts My Ears' Part One" (Grace 2012b).

8. "Music: A Unique View into the World of Autism" (Molnar-Szakacs and Heaton 2012).
9. Arash Babak Bahar Farzin is a pseudonym used to ensure the anonymity of the musician described. Ibby was insistent that his actual identity not be disclosed.
10. Seattle is a fictional location, used here at Ibby's request to protect the anonymity of certain individuals discussed in the chapter.
11. Eid al-Fitr is an Islamic holy day culminating in a feast to break the fast at the conclusion of Ramadan.
12. Ibby discusses this issue in greater detail in her autobiographical chapter "Autistethnography" (Grace 2013), which appears in Phil Smith's edited volume *Both Sides of the Table* (Smith 2013).
13. Absolute pitch (perfect pitch) in autism has been the subject of several articles (Brown et al. 2003; Dohn et al. 2012; Mottron et al. 1999).
14. "Your Mama Wears Drover Boots" (Grace 2014, 20–21).
15. "Labels" (Grace 2012a).

CHAPTER 6
Dotan Nitzberg

. . . the most important thing I want you to know is that Asperger's Syndrome is something
rather fragile and complicated, sometimes even beyond our own grasp, since it's very individ-
ual in its ways of expression and it has several ranks of functioning within it; briefly, it's like a
theme with endless variations. The theme remains consistent but the variations always evolve.
Dotan Nitzberg (2012)

February 7, 2014

My Name is Dotan Nitzberg. I am twenty-seven, originally from
Israel. I am a Pianist, and at the moment I pursue my DMA in Piano
Performance at the University of North Texas under the guidance of Mr.
Joseph Banowetz.

I watched your [TED Talk] presentation about Ethnomusicology and
the way you fuse it with the Autistic aspect, and it left me fascinated and
created a stimulus to do something similar also evolving my piano playing and additional skills.

As a matter of fact, two years ago I traveled to Novi Sad, Serbia, where
I delivered a lecture about how to teach piano efficiently to people with
Asperger Syndrome, considering my own personal experiences as a per-
son who also has to cope with it day by day.

My main question is if it's possible to fuse piano playing studies with
research in the field of Music and Autism at FSU?

Please let me know as soon as possible and in the meantime you can
watch my presentation on YouTube by typing my name.

I first became acquainted with the Israeli concert pianist Dotan Nitzberg
through the above email. We would eventually come to know each other
well, initially via the chat dialogues of 2014 that form the basis of this
chapter, then later on in Tallahassee, where Dotan came to continue his
graduate studies in piano at FSU from 2015 to 2017.

After reading his email of introduction, I take Dotan's prompt to watch the YouTube video of his lecture in Serbia. The title: "How to Teach Piano to People with Asperger"; the venue: the 2012 World Piano Teachers Association international conference; the format: a lecture-demonstration in which Dotan moves between speaking at the podium and performing virtuosic illustrative examples at the piano. It is an extraordinary presentation, and one that essentially lays the foundation for all that will follow between us. The lecture may be viewed in its entirety at the companion website (CW 6.1 ▶).

"Hello everyone. Thanks for coming," Dotan begins. "My subject today is how to teach piano to people with Asperger more efficiently. Since I have it myself, the best way for me to introduce myself is playing for you. Therefore, I'm heading to the piano. I'll play for you two sonatas by Scarlatti."

He plays the Scarlatti pieces brilliantly. I am especially impressed by his sure rhythmic command, the precision of his articulation, his effortless virtuosity, and the almost conversational quality he manages to capture through the complex melodic interplay of the right- and left-hand parts.

Dotan now returns to the podium as the audience applauds. He sports an endearing smile. "So, as I said, my name is Dotan Nitzberg. I'm twenty-five years old; I'm originally from Israel. I currently pursue my master's degree in Lynn University in Boca Raton, Florida, USA, under supervision of Dr. Roberta Rust. Before that I earned my Artist Certificate at the College of Charleston in South Carolina under guidance of Mr. Enrique Graf, and back home I studied with Ms. Yanina Kudlik, with whom I remained under supervision for twelve years (both at the conservatory and at the academy) and... In addition to all of that... I consider myself a challenged person since I have Asperger's Syndrome!"

Dotan asks the audience whether they have ever heard of Asperger's, then provides an explanation of what it is.

"So, for those of you who would like to know some more, Asperger's syndrome is a neurological disorder that causes shortages at the normal life path. It's considered as a relative of the autism spectrum, [a] rather close one; let's say, they're very much like cousins, one lives in Novi Sad and the other lives in Belgrade. Alright?"

There is polite laughter from the audience.

"Yet, the most important thing I want you to know is that Asperger's syndrome is something rather fragile and complicated, sometimes even beyond *our own* grasp, since it's very individual in its ways of expression and it has several ranks of functioning within it; briefly, it's like a theme with endless variations. The theme remains consistent but the variations always evolve."

To illustrate his point, Dotan again goes to the piano, this time to perform Franz Liszt's *Gnomenreigen* Etude. "Through Liszt and his little gnomes," he promises the audience, "you'll be able to figure out my inner mechanism." But as I listen on YouTube to Dotan's flawless performance of the Liszt, I am not able make the connection. It is a subject to which we will return in our dialogues at several points in the future.

Dotan is back at the podium: "So, as I said earlier, Asperger's syndrome is something very dual. It has its luminous points and it has its dark points: people with Asperger are usually very unusual; hence, those points can be referred to as 'Idiosyncrasies.'"

"Before going on," Dotan inserts, "let me put something in brackets. Although the subject is how to teach piano to people with Asperger, I can [really only] talk about *my* own experience; hence I ask you to see the generalization, because I have no other way to talk about it but through my own eyes. In *my* particular case, those idiosyncrasies can be subdivided in three sectors: Musical, Social, and Intellectual."

Dotan identifies an ability to play by ear (including classical pieces), an ability to improvise, and a keen interest in "musical peculiarities (for example: when I was about twelve or thirteen years old I was a groupie of Percy Grainger's music)" as specific musical idiosyncrasies linked to his having Asperger's. His principal Asperger's-related social idiosyncrasy, he professes, is body language, which "can be considered awkward and make people wonder what I'm all about. For instance, I bow on stage in a very unique way, somewhat old-fashioned. It seems out of context but that's my body language. I mean something and the others get something else. It's very common among all Aspergers."[1] Also idiosyncratic in Dotan's estimation are his customary modes of social interaction. "I like nearness, yet, sometimes I am *too* personal," he explains, adding ". . . I don't always know how to balance formality and informality."

In Dotan's Asperger's-related category of intellectual idiosyncrasies, he lists the following three: an ability to learn foreign languages quickly; an ability to "memorize texts and musical pieces in excessive amounts (back when I was a child, this capacity helped me [in] memorizing not only pieces of music, but also entire children's books and poems by foreign authors)"; and a tendency to "express emotions in a very unique way (either too economic[al] or too extroverted), to such extent that it seems to others as an 'emotional shortage,' 'lack of expression' etc."

"Regarding the last point," Dotan relates, "let me share with you a personal story that repeated itself more than once: Throughout my life I had opportunities to play for fellow musicians, and whenever they were asked to give me their [assessments], many of them didn't manage to absorb my distinct way of expression and said I have an emotional shortage. To tell you frankly, it left me confused since Aspergers have [an] overdose of feelings, not a shortage!"

Dotan returns to the piano to perform Liszt's *Liebestraum (Nocturne) No. 3 in A-flat Major*. He translates "Liebestraum" as "Dream of Love," then prefaces his performance with the following comment: "I hope I can express this image of [a] garden so blossoming and full of... love." This he most certainly does, giving full rein to the lush romanticism and unrepentant pathos of this exquisite piece of music. I am struck by the extreme stylistic contrast between Dotan's Liszt and his earlier Scarlatti, by the disciplined, classical restraint of the one, the unbridled emotional yearning of the other. As I continue to listen, I come to a realization: Dotan Nitzberg is more than a great pianist; he is a true musical artist.

The remaining portion of the lecture is given over specifically to its stated main subject: effective pedagogical methods for teaching piano to students with Asperger's.

"So, after presenting some of my characteristics, considering the fact we deal with pedagogy, let me introduce to you two groups of teaching methods I've experienced and endure," Dotan says by way of introduction. "Group A: Teaching methods that were doomed to failure; and Group B: Successful teaching methods that serve me to this very day. Let's begin with the bad group."

The "bad" methods of Group A fall into three categories in Dotan's typology: overflow, demonstrating too much, and inaccessibility of the teacher outside the classroom or studio. Regarding the problem of overflow, he relates that many of his teachers have "had [a] tendency to overflow the head with too many details while working on [a] certain piece. No wonder when I came to class the day after, I remembered only *half* of the details."

The solution? "Never overload the student's head with so many details at once; most likely, he will not remember anything the day after."

On the subject of excessive demonstration, Dotan notes that "Aspergers like me" do not benefit from an abundance of musical demonstrations during lessons. It "confuses and leads only to mental overflow," he contends. ". . . One significant example that lodged in my memory is from my early childhood... my first teacher wasted half of the lesson on demonstrating fragments of pieces and singing the notes out loud simultaneously. No wonder when *I* was asked to do so, I couldn't read a single note! Hence, those who teach Aspergers, no matter what level they are: Don't demonstrate too much, show only the specific passages that require special treatment; otherwise the student will not get the main point."

Finally, Dotan shares his views on problems that are likely to arise if the piano student lacks access to his or her teacher outside the studio: "Sometimes, Aspergers have to cope with obsessive-compulsive thoughts, particularly when bits and pieces within the pieces don't come along the way they want [them] to." In such instances, he insists, it is crucial to be able to discuss such matters with one's teacher, even if the need to do so comes up between scheduled lessons. In his own experience, no one has benefited when such channels of communication have been closed, "neither me nor the teacher. It didn't bring any good result and only deepened the frustration. So always remember, Aspergers usually think beyond the box. Think that way too!"

Dotan now moves on to the "good" pedagogical methods of Group B. Here again, he recognizes three main categories: using parallel examples, using humor, and what he calls "domestic treatment." On the use of parallel examples, he explains that the piano literature "is full of analogies," by which he means "pieces from different periods that share at least one thing in common, like character, tempo, or pianistic texture." Identifying and working with these analogies across pieces "can be very useful for Aspergers."

Dotan returns to the piano to provide an example. "For instance," he says, "let's take the third movement of Schubert's 'Wanderer' Fantasy." He plays an excerpt of the piece then suggests using it as a stylistic model for teaching a second piece: the "German Waltz" from Schumann's *Carnaval*, Opus 9. Now he performs a passage from the Schumann in a style closely related to his Schubert rendition of moments before.

"Keep it in mind!" he states enthusiastically.

The value of a sense of humor in teaching piano to students with Asperger's is Dotan's next topic. "Aspergers most likely will not understand all sorts of humor," he claims, "especially not sarcastic or vulgar [forms]. As for double meaning and puns, well... It depends! Yet, musical humor is crystal clear for us, particularly if one uses it for pedagogical purposes."

Dotan gives an example. While studying with Roberta Rust, he worked with her on Brahms's *Paganini Variations, Vol. II*, which he describes as "a work known for being notoriously difficult." He played her the sixth variation. She listened, then suggested he try it again, but this time with more "lilt." Dotan did not know what this meant, so he asked Dr. Rust. She did her best to explain and demonstrate, but he was still left unsure of the meaning.

Later, Dotan happened upon a recording of "the signature song of the Swedish Chef from *The Muppets*." Hearing the song's playful, gently swinging rhythm, he suddenly understood precisely what "lilt" meant. He applied this newfound knowledge to the Brahms at his next lesson. The results were excellent. Dr. Rust was satisfied with the interpretation, Dotan was pleased, and they shared a good laugh about how this comical song had elevated Dotan's performance of such a difficult piece.

"So one essential lesson," Dotan summarizes. "When you teach, ease up!"

The third and last item in the "good" pedagogy set of Group B is Dotan's category of so-called domestic treatment. "It is very important for us to have a teacher that conveys [a] warm sense of familiarity and domestic treatment," he begins, adding, "after all, that's the key that brings us to brilliant achievements." He again offers an example. "For instance, once I worked with a Colombian virtuoso pianist. I told her I need some help bringing a piece to utmost brilliance. She wasn't only kind and extremely helpful, she even treated me as if I were her own grandson. How sweet!"

Dotan completes this portion of his lecture with a poignant remark: "So, if being welcoming to other people is obvious, for us it's a necessity!"

The last portion of the lecture is dedicated to a self-reflexive case study of Dotan's own learning process, which he demonstrates using illustrations from Debussy's *Prelude no. 12, Vol.1: Minstrels.* He concludes the lecture at the podium: "So, to finish it all, I can summarize my entire presentation with one phrase. Teaching Aspergers piano rises and falls on Janusz Korczak's principle: *'Educate the boy in his way!'* I hope you've enjoyed the show. Thank You!"[2]

CONVERSATION 1: JUNE 9, 2014

"I am here," Dotan announces at 10:00 a.m. on the dot.

"So how are you today?" I ask him.

"Excellent, how about you?"

"Very well, thank you. I usually like to begin these chats with a few kind of standard questions and then we can open up the 'conversation' from there. Okay?"

"Alright, go ahead!"

"So first, do you consider yourself to be an autistic person, an Autistic person, or a person with autism?"

"I consider myself as a person coping with Asperger Syndrome," he replies assuredly. "I prefer using that term rather than 'autistic.' At times it [autism] can sound very rough to hear. . . . I feel odd with the term 'Autistic,' mainly due to past experiences that lodged in my memory."

"I understand," I affirm, then share a terminological pet peeve of my own. "[For similar reasons,] I don't like the word 'disorder' at all. I prefer 'condition,' so that we could talk about people with Autism Spectrum Conditions (ASC) rather than Autism Spectrum Disorders (ASD)."

"I approve the word 'condition,'" Dotan types back in support. "In fact, I am more in favor of that word, rather than 'disorder' or 'disease' as many other uninformed people describe it."

"Remind me, how old are you now," I inquire, "and how old were you when you were diagnosed with Asperger's?"

"Tomorrow I'll turn twenty-seven, and I was diagnosed at the age of sixteen, more than a decade ago."

"Happy birthday!!!"

"Thanks."

"So I assume that you ended up being diagnosed originally because you were facing challenges and difficulties earlier in your life, before you were sixteen. Is that true?"

"Correct. It's not the entire story but that is true!"

"Right, in fact that was my next question! Can you give me 'the entire story,' or at least a relatively brief summary of it?"

"Let me try," Dotan writes. There is a lengthy pause as he collects his thoughts, then dancing dots and bubbling sounds emerge as he types. "To begin with, I started talking fluently [in Hebrew] at the age of nine months, and the first complete sentence I said was: 'That's what I want... Music! Music!' [Shortly] afterwards I was rushed to hospital due to an unknown cause, but my condition improved drastically when my father placed a toy keyboard next to my pillow, and I was fascinated to discover that when I pressed a row of keys it produced a very pleasant sound. That's Part 1."

"Great. Continue to Part 2 then!"

"I could read and write both Hebrew and English at the age of three. I remembered by heart dozens of stories, fairy tales, songs, trademarks, and even license plaques [plates] of different cars. Socially speaking, I found no interest in childhood games. I didn't like to spend time among other peers my age and preferred to socialize with grown-up people or to listen to music all alone in a quieter corner... I showed a very keen interest (and still do) in Music, History, Cultures, Languages and other subjects[,] to such an extent that I refused to move onward to another subject before finishing my 'research' about the previous one, and many other people saw it as a peculiarity or an obsession. At the elementary school I was very sociable but at the same time I didn't have so many friends; moreover, I wasn't particularly athletic and didn't excel in math, and due to that I was subject to scorn by pupils and teachers alike. Only when I moved to a better Junior-High School [did things improve, and since then] the condition has gradually changed for good."

"This was in Israel? (Jerusalem? Tel Aviv?)"

"Yes, in Ashkelon, where I'm originally from. It's in the South of Israel, near Gaza Strip."

"Right. OK. Carry on then."

"What else would you like to know?"

"Can you continue the story up to where you received the Asperger's diagnosis?"

"I started to play the piano at the age of five, but for a very long period I didn't have a competent teacher. Only at the age of ten [did I start] my formal training with Yanina Kudlik, with whom I remained under supervision for twelve years. She gave me excellent rudiments. I was swallowing material and making quick progress, but at some point I started to slow down a bit due to panic attacks [that] originated from rough experiences and fears I kept within myself, [along] with constant feeling[s] of low self-esteem. At the moment I was diagnosed I felt relieved, that finally I have answers to all of those unsolved questions I carried within myself."

I want to continue the conversation, but our allotted time has expired and I have another session scheduled for right after.

"Dotan, I actually have to move to another interview at 1:30, so we'll need to wrap up for now in a couple of minutes," I write apologetically. "Would you like to do this again on Wednesday at the same time?"

Wednesday will not work, he informs me, but Thursday is possible.

"Okay. Thursday it is then," I type. "Same start time as today?"

"Yes!" Dotan confirms.

"Great. Bye til then."

"Take care."

CONVERSATION 2: JUNE 12, 2014

Dotan is already waiting for me online when I arrive at my office for our second scheduled session.

"Hello, Dr. Bakan," I read in the dialogue box after signing on at about two minutes past the hour.

"Hi Dotan. . . . How are you today?"

"Doing alright."

"Glad to hear it. I want to start off with a question that may strike you as kind of weird: If you could wave a magic wand and your Asperger's would disappear, would you do that or not?"

Dotan's reply appears almost instantly. "Not at all. With all difficulties I live in peace with it; moreover, it enables me to do many positive things!"

"That is a fabulous answer!!!" I exclaim, praising Dotan for providing the "right" response as surely as I condemned Donald Rindale (Chapter 4) for having furnished the "wrong" one half a year earlier. There is clearly much more of the interventionist in me than I care to admit, my "value-neutral" aspirations for the project and all notwithstanding.

"Could you provide me with a somewhat detailed listing of the positive things you can do that you attribute to your Asperger's?" I ask Dotan.

"It enables me to absorb languages, cultures and music of many kinds," he replies, "and to organize that information in my head in a very unusual way, I guess."

"Take me inside the way your mind works in terms of those kinds of things. Can you describe how your thought process works when dealing with languages, or cultures, or types of music?"

"Well, as for music and piano playing, it's a riddle also for me; hence the more concrete information I can give you is about languages: I pick languages that I am attracted to [by] their sonority. I listen to songs, and in parallel I learn the alphabet, vocabulary, and exact pronunciation [of words]."

"So you learn languages in a very musical way, it seems. Is that accurate?"

"Yes, exactly."

"That's fascinating, Dotan! May I ask you a few questions about things you said during your lecture in Serbia?"

"Alright, with pleasure."

"Let me copy and paste the relevant part from your script here. Then I'll have a couple of questions for you. Give me just a sec."

Dotan waits patiently.

"OK, here's the part I'm talking about," I post. "It's where you say, 'the most important thing I want you to know is that Asperger's Syndrome is something rather fragile and complicated, sometimes even beyond *our own* grasp, since it's very individual in its ways of expression and it has several ranks of functioning within it; briefly, it's like a theme with endless variations, the theme remains consistent but the variations always evolve. The best way to epitomize this aspect is through Liszt's *Gnomenreigen* Etude, because through Liszt and his little gnomes you'll be able to figure out my inner mechanism.'"

"I see," Dotan responds, perhaps wondering where I plan to go with this.

"So that inspires several questions actually," I say, "but the first is this: I don't know that everyone would find your link between the Liszt etude and your description of Asperger's as self-evident. Could you articulate fairly precisely, to someone who might not get it immediately, what the connection is, and how you arrived at recognizing that connection?"

"Well, I chose Liszt's etude, which is very brisk-paced, to describe what actually happens inside an Asperger's mind in real time: everything is well organized on the one hand, and on the other hand tiny pieces of information are mixed altogether. . . . [T]he way my brain organizes material, or any kind of information correlating to my fields of interest, is very meticulous [on the] one hand. I usually collect details, I often check if they are accurate; if not I revise it, and I don't leave it until I pick the last gem of information, and very often I make analogies between two diverse subjects while trying in parallel to find analogies and similarities."

"Can you expand on how that analogy emerged in your mind in the first place?" I inquire, hoping to coax Dotan into a deeper exploration of his process. I ask him to explain "how it took shape, how it inspired your decision to program that piece at that point in the lecture—these kinds of things."

"As far as I can remember, I had that piece already in my repertoire so I wanted to use it. The analogy emerged naturally while writing the script for the [Novi Sad] presentation."

"Okay. Can you expand at all from what you said earlier about what the analogy is, or was that the whole story?"

"No, I cannot expand. I told you a firm fact."

I resist the urge to continue my line of inquiry, at least for now. Dotan has drawn his line in the sand: he has nothing more to say on the subject. But almost exactly two years later, on May 13, 2016, he and I are sitting together in my office at FSU, preparing for an upcoming joint lecture on teaching piano to students with autism spectrum conditions, when the topic of *Gnomenreigen* comes up again.

Dotan surprises me, stating, "I am now prepared to answer your question [from 2014] in more detail." I urge him to do so. "Liszt's etude, 'Dance of the Gnomes' [*Gnomenreigen*], is a fast paced piece," he begins, much like before, but what follows goes deeper. "It is very mercurial and sparkling. It correlates since my brain is so mercurial; ideas come and go in a spark, it is very upbeat, and all of the myriad of notes to be played in that piece are equal to the zillions of thoughts and ideas running below my digits. It is very picturesque, but it's true. . . . Within my brain, [those] zillions of thoughts are traveling at the speed of light and sometimes it causes confusion, procrastination, stress, etc. . . . [If] I am trying to absorb and classify [all this] information at once, it's not going to work. The brain I possess can record a huge amount of knowledge; the absorption is quick but the classification process is slower, [and] this gap is hampering. . . . The pianist in me and the person in me are two different types. The pianist in me is someone that does [things] almost immediately and instinctively (and quickly); the person is not always as nimble as at the keyboard. That's the main difference."[3] A complete recital performance of *Gnomenreigen* by Dotan may be viewed at the companion website, which additionally includes examples of his performances of solo piano works by Grieg and Schubert (CW 6.2, 6.3, and 6.4 ▶).

Back to June 12, 2014, our chat continues with further analysis of Dotan's 2012 lecture in Serbia. "Let's go to one of the other Asperger/piano piece analogies you present," I suggest. "In writing about what you describe in the lecture as your social idiosyncrasies, you state, 'I have certain difficulty to detect someone else's will to finish [a] conversation; it often leads me to overload the other person with more material. Like Mussorgsky's *Pictures at an Exhibition*, where there's no time to breathe, and all of a sudden a new musical idea appears.' At that point you play a brief illustrative example from *Pictures*, then you tell the audience, 'This fragment [of the piece] reflects this situation perfectly because it seems as if the subject is closed, but not really, and that's the deceiving point.' So let's imagine that I am only reading the text of your lecture and don't have access to your piano demonstration. How would you *describe* in words what happens in [the piece] so that I could understand what you mean, in particular about how Asperger's affects your social performance in a conversation?"

"In a few words: interruptions and clashes," Dotan responds matter-of-factly. "I mean, Mussorgsky's *Pictures at an Exhibition* is a piece that progresses very quickly; there is almost no interval to breathe and then a new [section of] material begins. It happens to me in conversations. Sometimes I am very eager to state an idea while other people are talking and it can be interpreted as a rude interruption of their thoughts."

"Great. Thank you. I want to ask some more questions related to your lecture. This will take a minute [to type]."

"OK."

I return to the lecture script and attempt a brief summary of Dotan's principal pedagogical suggestions.

"In trying to summarize your main recommendations for teaching piano to people with Asperger's," I begin, "this is what I come up with: *Don't* overwhelm the student with too many details, *don't* do too much demonstration; *do* be available to the student beyond the context of the actual piano lesson, *do* use parallel examples, *do* use humor, *do* be warm and welcoming. Is that an accurate brief summary?"

"Correct."

"Okay, so let me follow up on some of those points individually, first of all saying that these sound like excellent pedagogical strategies for people on the autism spectrum certainly, and maybe for people in general!"

"Yes, the main difference is the dosage."

"Aha. Well said! Speaking of dosages, then, why do you think Asperger's piano students have a lower threshold (quantity-wise) for processing musical details [given by] a teacher than non-autistic piano students?"

"You've actually answered that question yourself: because they have to bisect those details to the tiniest units at times, in order to comprehend and use them cleverly. They are not the 'monkey see, monkey do' type."

"Okay, and that actually leads to (maybe answers) my next question, which has to do with teacher demonstrations. In many music cultures outside of Western art (classical) music, music is taught almost entirely by demonstration. I remember studying with a famous Indonesian gamelan musician. I said I wanted to learn a particular xylophone called the *gambang*. He asked me to sit down next to the instrument and started to play it. He played for about five minutes straight as I sat there watching and listening to him. Then he said 'Now you do it.' 'Do what?' I asked. 'The same thing I just did!' he said. I was totally overwhelmed and disheartened. There was no way I could even begin to recall, let alone reproduce, what he had played. There was simply *way* too much information. Is that something like how it feels to you when a teacher demonstrates lots of things in long segments rather than breaking a piece down into more manageable chunks in a linear, systematic fashion?"

I am about to press "Enter" but decide to add an additional sentence before doing so. By now, I have learned that Dotan's habitual mode of response in these dialogues is to be short and to the point. I am hoping for more out of this one: "If possible, don't just answer yes or no, but respond with your own story to illustrate!"

"Yes, I oppose it," Dotan shoots back regarding teachers who demonstrate too much without breaking the music down into discrete segments. "As you can tell, it can be very embarrassing. When I was five, I had a horrible teacher who wasted half of the lesson time playing pieces and singing the notes out loud simultaneously, and then she even complained to my parents that I [could] not read music. That was totally stupid; how she could expect me to read music while she actually taught me to be a parrot?!"

I check the time and realize that I need to be at another appointment in ten minutes.

"I have time for just one last question, Dotan. The question is this: you mention in your lecture that 'if being welcoming to other people is obvious, to us it's a necessity!' That's a beautiful sentence. I think I do understand the reasoning behind your statement, but for someone who is not familiar with the workings of the Asperger's mind, or who has not had the opportunity to get to know someone on the spectrum well, could you elaborate on why that welcoming attitude is so important, especially since most people assume that people on the spectrum tend not to appear as 'welcoming' to other people as they 'should' be much of the time? For many people (I hasten to note, not for me!), this would seem to be a strange paradox."

"It is a necessity because people with Asperger very often can be somewhat timid and shy when they meet a true master or a foreign teacher they don't work with on a regular basis, and if the teacher delivers that feeling of hospitality it can relieve their embarrassment, as if to say: 'I accept you as you are, and I'm here to assist you.'"

"Right!" I affirm. "And once again, maybe this is a matter of dosage more than anything. All of us relish that feeling of being accepted as we are and feeling supported, but I concur that is especially important for people on the spectrum, since you are so often *not* accepted for who you are and *not* supported in the ways that you'd like to be by non-autistic people. Does this align with the way you think about that issue?"

"Yes, totally!"

"Excellent. So I need to go now, but I look forward to continuing the conversation. During our next chat, let's talk about your family. My sense is that you have excellent support from them and come from a loving family. I want to know about how they have supported you throughout your life and how this support has helped you to be the successful, accepting, and mostly happy person that you are." Later, when I read back through the transcript, I cringe a bit at this last part. What gave me the right to make such assumptions about Dotan's family, let alone to share them with him? And would I have made the same assumptions if he had expressed a less positive attitude about having Asperger's?

"We shall keep in touch and talk about it at the next session," Dotan replies diplomatically. "Take Care."

"OK. Bye for now. Thanks!"

CONVERSATION 3 (PART I): JUNE 19, 2014

I arrive at my office five minutes late for my next session with Dotan. He has signed in early as usual, four minutes early to be precise.

"I am here, ready to begin the session in a few minutes," Dotan has typed into the dialogue box.

"Sorry I'm a few minutes late," I respond. "Parking problems. You still there?"

"I'm here, and I'm doing fine. How do you do?"

"Doing great, thanks! May we pick up where we left off? I was going to ask you about your family."

"Yes, of course. I remember that was the topic we were talking about [in] our last session, and I'd be delighted to answer if there is something specific you would like to know about my family circle."

"Okay," I begin, "tell me first then about how your parents have supported you as a person with Asperger's."

"They were involved at every stage of my treatments, they traveled with me back and forth ([from] home [to] piano lessons [to] treatments [and] back home [again]) and briefly speaking... shared every moment with me."

"That's wonderful, and very fortunate. What kinds of treatments did you receive?"

"Cognitive-behavioral, biofeedback, and another very unique treatment called 'the Sandpit.' I was given a small Sandpit with toys and gadgets where I could present problematic situations I faced and through improvised dialogues I could figure out creative ways of solving those conflicts in years to come. It was very much like a puppet-theater."

"That's very interesting, the Sandpit. Did you find it beneficial?"

"Definitely."

"Can you give me a couple of examples of ways it has helped you?"

"Yes, it made me comprehend that most of those [problematic] situations were [isolated] incidents and I should stop blaming myself all day long. Moreover, it taught me that there isn't such a major difference between real life and onstage life; they are all full of parallel lines."

"That's a great insight. Real life is a 'performance' much of the time."

"Correct, or maybe 'a performance sketch' that is necessary in order to master a piece."

"Did the kind of Sandpit Therapy you received give you tools for dealing with a situation like this online conversation we're having? If so, can you give me one or two specific strategies from that therapy that you have been applying in our exchanges?"

Dotan dismisses my question.

"It has nothing to do with this current session, because it is a very pleasant and fluid conversation. The Sandpit helped me [in] coping mainly with rough encounters. For example: Two years ago I visited the Basilica of Annunciation in Nazareth, and at the main hall near the confession deck stood a priest, a Franciscan Friar. I know many of them; many of them [have been] very kind to me. I approached him in Croatian (his native language) and asked him for help. He started cursing and yelling at me. At the beginning I was somewhat terrified, but right afterwards I shook myself up and told myself: 'what a poor guy, if that's his way to welcome guests.' I attribute that virtue also to those Sandpit treatments, among other things."

"That is fantastic, Dotan. Not many people would have the inner strength and self-control to manage that situation so well. I am very impressed!"

"We all learn!"

"How many languages do you speak?"

"Officially eight, and soon I'll add an extra one."

"What are they? And what's the new one to be added?"

"Hebrew, English, Spanish, French, German, Italian, Portuguese, Russian, and soon... Croatian."

"Ah-ha! Good tie in to your last story."

"Well, I [am] usually [on] good terms with Croats. Almost a week ago I visited a monastery in Jerusalem and was welcomed by a Croatian Friar. That was a lovely encounter."

"That's great. You've spoken several times of visits to monasteries and other Christian houses of worship. Are you Christian? Jewish? Your last name led me to assume you were Jewish (which I am, by the way), but now I'm wondering if that was an incorrect assumption."

"I am Jewish, 100%, but I have an affinity to Christianity as well."

"Makes sense. . . . Did you have a Bar Mitzvah?"

"Of course."

"I assumed so, but wanted to check before asking more about it. As an event, the Bar Mitzvah is, for lack of a better term, an intensely social occasion. I could imagine that some of the social demands and pressures would be challenging for someone on the autism spectrum. Was that the case for you? Please describe your recollections of your Bar Mitzvah and what it was like for you."

"That was a very special event," Dotan recalls. "I was extremely moved. Socially, there was no problem of recruiting people. Many of my faithful friends arrived, my family and its circle were all present, even people I hadn't seen for years. Sadly, many people who attended are no longer alive. There was a band playing a mixture of classical and popular music, but the peak was when I played with them on my newly purchased electric keyboard. The day afterward was the religious ceremony at the Synagogue. There were split-moments [sic] when I burst [into] tears, and I'll never forget that moment I had to sing and recite the Haftarah.[4] Both my father and grandfather stood next to me. It was very symbolic not only for my father and for me, but also for my paternal grandparents, who survived the Holocaust, seeing their eldest grandson celebrating his Bar Mitzvah."

"Wow. That sounds like a *very* special moment!"

We shift the conversation from the past to the present to discuss Dotan's current living situation in Texas. He lives on his own in an apartment near campus in Denton. I ask him how that is going for him.

"I manage," he replies. "Slowly but surely I make progress, yet the concern [about my ability to live self-sufficiently] is always in the background, both for me and my parents."

What about traveling, I ask, especially internationally, like between Israel and the U.S., or when attending conferences in faraway places like Serbia?

"I started traveling on my own only recently," Dotan explains, adding that on his one trip to Serbia, in 2012, his parents went with him.

"How do you support yourself financially?" I ask.

"I have a scholarship, but I am mostly held [in support] by my family. Hopefully I'll find an employment very soon."

"What kind of employment do you plan to seek once you have completed your studies?"

"I would like to live mainly on being a performer in public (Classical mostly, but also other genres I can play well). I would like to deliver presentations on subjects related to piano and music in general, and I would like to take up pedagogical work."

"What other genres besides classical [music] do you play well?" I ask him.

"Pop, Tango, French Chansons, Folk Songs, Jewish Music, Christian Music, etc."

"Fabulous. That's quite a range. You mentioned improvisation in your lecture, that you had good skills in that. Is much of your playing in these various genres improvised? Also, do you mainly play solo or do you also do chamber music and ensemble playing?"

Dotan addresses the second question first.

"Mainly solo, but I also play within ensembles from time to time. Depends on the partners, yet my favorite chamber activity is to play piano or keyboards in Jazz/Pop Groups. It is a leisure activity as well."

"Aha. So you do play jazz as well. Are you a skilled jazz improviser?"

"I play Jazz for fun. I mostly improvise in other genres, not necessarily Jazz."

The conversation turns to ensemble playing and to accompanying and chamber music specifically. I ask Dotan what he looks for in a musical partner.

"I want him to be flexible, alert, balancing, and with [a] keen ear and sharp rhythm," he replies without pause. " . . . When I play with other people, I don't want to feel as if I overshadow them, but [on] the other hand I wouldn't like to feel as if I'm dragged after them."

"Do you think that having Asperger's is advantageous, disadvantageous, or irrelevant to you in terms of your abilities as an ensemble player?"

"It is all [of those things] together, and that is what makes it very intricate. . . . It is an advantage because I know how to mend conflicts between people and to take initiatives, it is a disadvantage because I can't tolerate when ensemble players take too many liberties at the expense of rhythm, and [it is] irrelevant because I do it as it is."

"I'm clear on the first two points, less so on the last," I interject. "What do you mean by 'I do it as it is'?"

"I still do it regardless of the Asperger and its social consequences." From this statement I infer that Dotan is uncompromising in his commitment to playing the music 'the right way,' even if that means refusing to make compromises for the sake of social/musical cohesion: he would sooner fall out of sync with his fellow players, I surmise, than sacrifice, say, the rhythmic integrity of the performance.

"Aha. So the music is always first then, yes?" I ask, seeking confirmation for my inference.

"Yes indeed," Dotan states, though his follow-up remarks go in an unanticipated direction. "Music requires showmanship, because we show ourselves and our capabilities, and we show the piece to the public. Many people [have] told me, 'You are showing off.' Well, fine, if the music dictates it..."

The more I hear about Dotan's ensemble playing philosophy, the more interested I become in what it might be like to actually play in an ensemble with him. As luck would have it, I get to do precisely that about a year later when Dotan comes to study at FSU and joins the Balinese gamelan I direct there.

MUSICAL INTERLUDE: PLAYING GAMELAN WITH DOTAN

Playing in a gamelan is a very different kind of ensemble performance than playing, say, in a piano trio; and playing with Dotan the neophyte gamelan musician is surely a far cry from playing with Dotan the virtuoso pianist. Still, music is music, and reflecting on my experiences playing gamelan with Dotan has been revealing, especially in terms of contextualizing some of his comments about ensemble playing generally in our 2014 chat dialogues.

As a member of FSU's Balinese gamelan in the fall semester of 2015, Dotan always played with unyielding rhythmic precision. This was a real asset, since rhythmic accuracy of the highest order is required to make the music's intricate interlocking melodic patterns, or *kotekan*, come off effectively. His rhythmic talent, and even more so his abiding commitment to rhythmic rightness, presented challenges as well, however. When less talented players in his section would get wobbly in their rhythmic execution, Dotan was reluctant to bend; going with the flow did not come naturally to him, sometimes for better and sometimes for worse. Moreover, consistent with his "showing off . . . if the music dictates it" remarks, Dotan played gamelan with an exhibitionistic flair not matched by the other players in the group, especially in passages that he had mastered to the point of flawlessness. This, too, had its pros and cons. On the one hand, the styles of gamelan music we played call for showy virtuosity, even outright bravura, in their native Balinese context. Dotan seemed to intuitively grasp that aspect of the musical/visual aesthetic right from the start, even before having ever viewed or listened to actual performances by Balinese groups: in a very real sense, he played like a Balinese musician instinctively. But the rest of the ensemble generally did not, and as a result Dotan's "appropriately Balinese" physical gestures and musical flourishes often appeared *out* of place in the milieu of a student gamelan group at an American university.

For all his rhythmic sturdiness and tendencies toward showmanship, though, Dotan was unfailingly kind, considerate, and, in his own way, sensitive to the wants and needs of the other members of the FSU gamelan. He may have been "idiosyncratic" (to use his own term), appearing at times rather oblivious to the impressions he made on his fellow students in the class and to their expectations of him, but he ultimately proved to be an excellent team player and a fine ensemble musician nevertheless.

CONVERSATION 3 REDUX (PART II): JUNE 19, 2014

"I want to follow up on your earlier comment that when it comes to ensemble playing, having Asperger's is an advantage because you 'know how to mend conflicts between people and to take initiatives,' " I write to Dotan. "Having spent a good deal of time with—and playing music with—people on the [autism] spectrum, this actually makes very good sense to me. However, for many people, this would be the *last* thing they would expect: in other words, they would assume that [having] Asperger's would create *disadvantages* when it comes to mending social conflicts or taking initiative [precisely] because of the so-called 'social deficits' of the condition. How would you explain the ways that Asperger's helps you to mend conflicts and take initiatives [if speaking] to neurotypical people whose bias is to assume exactly the opposite? Please be detailed in your answer!"

"It is a matter of awareness," Dotan replies. "In my particular case, my Asperger serves me well because I want to be kind to other people. When it works, the results speak by themselves. It means: There is a pleasant feeling of agreement, [of] understanding, and humor is flowing all over."

"So to you," I inquire, wanting to make sure I am understanding Dotan correctly, "heightened awareness and the desire to treat other people with kindness are characteristics of Asperger's, at least in your case personally?"

"Exactly."

"Very interesting, and I must say that this makes a lot of sense in light of my own relationships with people on the spectrum. . . . I usually find them to be much more polite and concerned for the feelings of others than neurotypicals. It goes against all the stereotypes."

"Absolutely," Dotan agrees.

" . . . What about other musicians? Have you known, or are you familiar with the work of, other pianists who are either known to be on the autism spectrum or that you think are, or were?"

"Yes, of course!" he replies. "One of the vivid examples that comes to mind is John Ogdon. He died in 1989. He was misdiagnosed as suffering [from] schizophrenia or manic depression. It ruined half of his life."[5]

"But you believe it was actually autism, or Asperger's?"

"Yes."

"Is that something you figured out or is it something others have suggested?"

"After hearing of his life story and his individual skills, I figured out he might have been an Asperger."

"Ah, okay, but you have not read accounts of others who make that claim, right?"

"I have heard personal testimonials of other fellow pianists who were acquainted with him."

"Okay. So here's a question: when you listen to Ogdon playing on recordings, do you 'hear' that he's autistic in his playing? In a broader sense, does being on the spectrum make you *sound* different than people who aren't?"

"There isn't such a thing as 'Autistic Playing,'" Dotan states unequivocally. "It is rather derogatory to name it like that. But, he could be very mercurial, skittish, unpredictable, and very idiosyncratic."

I wince at the realization that I have likely offended Dotan with my "autistic playing" reference. I attempt a rephrasing of the question.

"Right, I agree with you, Dotan. There isn't such a thing as 'Autistic Playing,' but, from what I'm inferring from your response, there *are* qualities of playing that reflect the preferences and orientations of the ways that someone like you or Ogdon might think about, or might approach interpreting, a particular piece of music. In that sense, such preferences and orientations might be 'hearable' in the performance itself. Does this seem accurate?"

"That's more intact, yes."

"Still off the mark a bit? Please help me understand better if so."

"I meant to say that your last statement was more intact than the previous one," Dotan offers by way of clarification. "You can still hear [Ogdon's] originality. It cannot always be verbalized. One has to hear and sense it. If it's possible, that's enough."

"What, though, is 'it' in that context," I pry, "the 'it' that cannot always be verbalized, that has to be heard and sensed? I'm a little bit confused."

"His interpretation, his personality and the way it projects."

"Okay, so let me approach this same matter from a somewhat different angle. There's a well-known music theorist, Joseph Straus, who's written quite a bit on music and autism. He argues that the autism spectrum is not so much marked by disability or disorder as by a distinctive 'autistic cognitive style,' a way of thinking about and being in the world.[6] I tend to agree with Straus. Let's get away from Ogdon and focus on you, since that's a clearer subject for this inquiry. Do you believe that your 'cognitive style' as a pianist—as a musician and musical thinker generally—is reflective of having Asperger's?"

"I tend to agree with that statement [of Straus's], and my cognitive style has something to do with Asperger's."

"Okay, and so how does that influence the way you play the piano? Can you identify characteristics in your own playing that you'd identify with that part of who you are? If so, what might those be?"

"I am highly influenced by the old-fashioned virtuosi; I polish each passage in a piece until it sounds just the way I like it, sometimes at the expense of [working on] other pieces [assigned to me by my teachers]; I like to investigate the subject of Piano Technique with all of its mysteries; and I have my own ways of defining tone qualities."

"Okay, so let me try to extend on that a bit. In being highly influenced by the old-fashioned virtuosi, perhaps you imply that you are no slave to current trends and fashion—that you are committed to substance and tradition without regard to what others might think of that (or you). In your commitment to polishing a particular piece bit by bit, even if this 'slows you down' in terms of amassing a larger repertoire, you demonstrate a dedication to precision and depth of inquiry that many other pianists might be willing to sacrifice, either for lack of patience or due to greater concerns with career advancement than with the music itself. In your intellectual curiosity about piano technique and its mysteries, and your related passion for exploring and defining tone qualities, there is a level of focus and fixation that exceeds that of the 'average' pianist. In these various ways—preference for substance/tradition over trends/fashions, great attention to detail, deep curiosity regarding finer musical points that are often glossed over or disregarded altogether—you are unique, or at least distinctive, in your approach to your music; and that distinctiveness, on these levels at least, is partially attributable to the presence of an Asperger's-influenced cognitive style you bring to your work as a pianist. Does this interpretation seem accurate? If not, please clarify or correct any inaccuracies regarding what I've written here."

"Golden words."

"Ah, thank you!! I wasn't necessarily expecting such a positive review of them!"

"Although I think nowadays it's on the contrary: people want tradition rather than an individual *façon* of playing."

My French is rusty at best, but I think I correctly remember the meaning of that word. "Do you mean fashion of playing?" I ask.

"Yes, in French, '*façon*,'" Dotan confirms.

Dotan's ringing approval of my last interpretive foray emboldens me to attempt something similar on the "*façon*" theme.

"Okay," I type. "So let me refine my understanding a bit more: people nowadays want tradition, but you are providing something else? Am I to understand, then, that the influence of the old-fashioned virtuosi on your approach does not reflect a dedication to 'tradition' so much as a preference for that individualistic, maverick spirit of daring that the old masters (Who are we talking about here—Rubinstein, Horowitz... Liszt?) exhibited, but which players nowadays are less likely to?"

"Correct."

"Wow. I'm on a roll here!" I exclaim. I decide to push a little further. "So in more summary fashion, distilling the above: as a pianist, you have great patience, persistence, attention to detail (and to particular *details* that other pianists may largely ignore), intellectual curiosity, and, well, bravado, daring—a maverick spirit that honors tradition but isn't beholden to it. How am I doing now?"

"You are right," he affirms, adding with humility, but without false modesty, that "I have those, and I am still learning how to hone them."

"And looking at that list, it seems to me consistent with the kind of attributes that would indeed issue from the cognitive style of Asperger's generally. The cool thing here, though, is that they're really working for you, not against you. Do you agree?"

"I agree."

Suddenly I feel embarrassed. I am getting carried away with this whole interpret-what-Dotan-says-and-make-it-sound-fancier-than-he-does strategy, which has effectively taken over the conversation through our past several exchanges. I ask Dotan a point-blank question: "Do you find it funny how I take your rather concise descriptions of things and make them wordy and verbose?"

"Yes, you expand them," he replies earnestly.

"And it's funny when I do?"

"No, it is a virtue."

I appreciate the compliment, though I am not sure I have earned it.

It's getting very late, especially for Dotan in Ashkelon where it's almost midnight, and we've been at this for hours.

"May I ask you one last question?" I request. "This one has to do with 'emotion.'"

"Certainly," Dotan replies.

"There has been much research and writing suggesting that people on the spectrum may be very 'technically skilled' in, say, playing piano, or painting or drawing, but that they are nonetheless 'deficient' as 'artists' due to a lack or absence of emotional substance in the ways they create and produce their art. To me, this is yet another fallacious stereotype that is egregiously misleading. I assume you agree [with me], but I'd be very interested in your counterargument to the [other] position. You've made several references in these conversations to the fact that, if anything, people like yourself feel emotions *more*, not less, deeply than neurotypicals. Why is that so terribly misunderstood by so many people, and what do you think can be done about it?"

"I tackled that subject more than once in my life and I will not spare it from you," Dotan asserts. "Many musicians offended me by saying [that I was] 'emotionally handicapped,' 'playing like an autist,' and other derogatory comments as such. People who claim that are ignorant and should be ignored. They do not comprehend that at the moment Aspergers tackle a piece they recognize the character and 'emotion' right away. It's instilled there. Their intensity, concentration, and involvement [are] so high that it seems as if they are [just] 'doing their own thing,' [but that's a wrong impression]. . . . [O]nly people with [a] sixth sense—that is, endowed with sensitivity beyond the average—can catch it."[7]

"That is an excellent response, Dotan. Let's take it a step further yet. Yes, those people perhaps *should* be ignored, and their statements are stupid, but in this forum you have an opportunity to help at least some people (perhaps not the entirely stupid and offensive ones, alas) to grasp what they have been blinded (deafened) to by too many stereotypes and too little curiosity. How can people who may *not* grasp the intensity and the emotion, who don't have that sixth sense innately, get a handle on what is special about these performances, what is *good* about them? Dotan, now's your chance—teach us how to listen and how to think better!"

"Listen to them more frequently and try to 'fish' at least five things you like about them in particular. That's my recipe. There is no other choice but to educate people. They can agree with our grasp or disagree, but they have no right to condemn us just because we are Aspergers and we act/think differently."

"Well said, and thank you! Bye for now!"

"Keep in touch!"

"NOT HANDICAPPED AT ALL"

Getting to know Dotan Nitzberg—in chat dialogues and face-to-face conversations, playing gamelan together, as an audience member at his recitals, socializing over a dish of *gado-gado* at a neighborhood Indonesian restaurant in Tallahassee—has inspired me to think about music and teach music in new ways. I believe Dotan has grown from the relationship as well, and that his overall experience in Tallahassee was a positive one. But Dotan's time at FSU was not without its challenges. He struggled with anxiety and painful self-consciousness at times, some insensitive classmates and instructors, and the day-to-day problems of just knowing what to do when, whether in academic contexts, dealing with the campus bureaucracy, or negotiating the finer points of social decorum from the classroom to the concert hall. Granted, university music students often struggle with these kinds of challenges, but there can be no denying that doing so while living with Asperger's syndrome ups the ante considerably.

Yet in the face of any and all obstacles, Dotan perseveres, and he thrives. As he wrote to me in an email on July 2, 2016:

> I finally realized I am not handicapped AT ALL! I just need some extra help in certain things; otherwise I'm good! Those who claimed I am unable of accomplishing a task due to my "DISABILITY" deserve my mercy because they are so full of prejudices. And those who said "I AM NOT SUFFICIENTLY MATURE," woe to them as well, since I grow up and develop, and I do it my way, with my own pace, and I do it with so much fun, pleasure, and grace. Every instant!

NOTES

1. It is notable that Dotan consistently uses the word "Aspergers" as a noun to describe people diagnosed with Asperger's syndrome. For example, he states, "It's very common among all Aspergers" rather than using a more conventional formulation such as "It's very common among all people with Asperger's" or "It's very common among all people diagnosed with Asperger's syndrome."
2. See also "How to Teach Piano to People with Asperger" (Nitzberg 2012).
3. Dotan's quoted remarks are drawn from a live interview I conducted with him at Florida State University on May 13, 2016.
4. The Haftarah is a portion from the books of the Prophets that is recited after reading from the Torah during religious services on Shabbat, the Jewish Sabbath. The Bar Mitzvah or Bat Mitzvah, that is, the boy or girl being ritually initiated into adulthood, typically chants the Haftarah as part of the ceremony.
5. Another noted pianist who has frequently been linked retrospectively to the autism spectrum (though he was never diagnosed during his lifetime) is Glenn Gould (Maloney 2006).
6. See the book *Extraordinary Measures* (Straus 2011) and the essay "Autism as Culture" (Straus 2013).
7. Dotan's claims are supported by recent scientific research. For example, in their 2012 review article of neuroimaging and behavioral studies that focus on musical ability in individuals with ASD, Molnar-Szakacs and Heaton argue that despite pervasive challenges in interpreting "other people's nonverbal, facial, and bodily expressions of emotion . . . there is evidence to suggest that many individuals with ASD show a strong and early preference for music" and are able to comprehend simple as well as complex emotional content in music both as children and adults (Molnar-Szakacs and Heaton 2012).

CHAPTER 7

Graeme Gibson

Graeme: . . . both music and math are tied together [but for] some reason my math is nowhere as good as my music. I leave the math to a friend of mine who is an engineer. He can do calculus on paper without the aid of a calculator. So I trust him with the math. ☺

Michael: That sounds like a good mix of talents. Is your friend also autistic?

Graeme: No, but he is very bright in his own way.

Graeme Gibson (with M. Bakan) (2014)

June 9, 2014

Hello Dr. Michael Bakan. My name is Graeme Gibson. I am the participant in the interview you wish to engage with me.

If you would not mind I would prefer conducting the interview in email because I can think, and carefully reply to each question, whereas in chat there is a lot more personal pressure I have to respond to, which in living with autism that is not always easy to cope with. I like the use of email because I can participate in your interview and go on about my daily activities in between. I have a very busy week which is quite packed and I'm not known to be a morning person even with a good cup of coffee.

This would make things a lot easier for me in return, and give the best answers to your questions in our interview.

Sincerely
Graeme

Graeme Gibson has finally reached out to me. It has been a long time coming, some seven months to be precise.

It all traces back to November 14, 2013. On that day, I'm at a conference in Indianapolis and encounter an old friend: the composer, instrument collector, multi-instrumentalist, and ethnomusicologist Randy Raine-Reusch. We haven't seen each other in many years.

Randy and I strike up a conversation and the subject quickly turns to music and autism. He tells me that he has been following my work, which is especially interesting to him because he has an autistic student, Graeme Gibson, whom he has been teaching for more than twenty years now.

Graeme and Randy both live in Vancouver, where I also grew up. Randy tells me that Graeme was diagnosed with "classic autism" as a young child. From a very early age, he showed a passionate interest in music and musical instruments. Since then, he has amassed a large and diverse instrument collection, which he now curates and shares with the world via his personal website. Graeme plays most of the many instruments he owns. He taught himself to play a number of them and studied the others with either Randy or his other teacher of long standing, the Peruvian-Canadian musician Rene Hugo Sanchez.

Graeme is now in his mid-thirties, Randy reports. He has been living on his own for a number of years, though he maintains a very close relationship with his parents, Deborah and Bill. Randy describes Deborah and Bill as "really nice folks" who have avidly supported Graeme's musical pursuits throughout his life. Moreover, he informs me that Deborah's Ph.D. dissertation was on autism and early childhood language development, with Graeme as her principal case study.[1]

The more Randy tells me about him, the more excited I become by the prospect of including Graeme in my current music-and-autism project. "He's into some pretty amazing things," Randy says with pride: composing original pieces, recording in his home studio, building musical instruments, and doing wildlife photography and volunteer work as a data entry specialist at both a museum and a local radio station.

"You should get in touch with him," Randy encourages me. "Go through his mom. That's your best bet. Here's her contact information." He takes out one of his business cards, writes Deborah's email address on the back, and hands it to me.

"Great seeing you, Mike!"

I email Deborah as soon as I'm back in Tallahassee, sharing some information about myself and the project and asking whether she thinks Graeme might be interested in participating. She replies promptly, telling me that Randy has already given her a heads-up that I might be contacting her. She thinks Graeme will be interested in taking part, though she is skeptical about using chat for our exchanges. Email will work better, she suggests, especially if I begin by sending Graeme a list of questions to work with, which she'll then help him to go through. That way he can spend as much time as he wants to with each question and address them one at a time on his own schedule.

Deborah promises me that she will speak to Graeme on my behalf and that I should expect to hear from him by email soon. She is true to her word, though "soon" ends up being a relative term, and on June 9, 2014, the email included at the beginning of this chapter shows up in my inbox. I quickly get to work preparing a list of questions for Graeme—too quickly, in fact—emailing it to him the next day and inviting him to answer all of the questions, or just whichever ones he is comfortable with. "Feel free to add further thoughts or comments as you see fit as well," I tack on at the end.

The only catch is that my questions list for Graeme is a disaster. There are far too many questions (more than twenty in all), they are not presented in a particularly logical order, they cover an overly eclectic range of topics, and many of them are unnecessarily long and complex: Which of the many instruments that you own do you actually play, and what is/ are your main instrument(s)? Do you play mainly as a soloist or also in ensembles? Do you compose music, and if so what kind? Have you ever recorded any of your music (your performances and/or compositions)? In what year were you born and how old are you now? When were you diagnosed with autism? What was the specific diagnosis? Do you prefer to be referred to as an autistic person, an Autistic person, a person with autism, or in some other way (specify what that would be)? Re: the preceding question, why? What are your favorite kinds of music to listen to? To play? Do you think that being autistic has much to do with how you play music or think about musical instruments? If you could wave a magic wand and not be autistic anymore, would you? Have your experiences with music therapy (described on your website) been beneficial? Problematic? How? Have you received other kinds of therapies/interventions (which ones and with what outcomes)? What kinds of changes would you like to see in how you (and autistic people generally) are treated by non-autistic people? What do you think music can do for people in general? What do you think music can do for autistic people in particular?

And if all this were not enough, I additionally ask Graeme to give me a brief personal history of his life as a musician *and* a brief personal history of his life as a music instrument collector.

Not surprisingly, Graeme is overwhelmed; I have definitely gotten off on the wrong foot here. Fortunately for me, Deborah sees fit to intervene on my behalf.

"Hi Michael: Graeme didn't follow your very clear format, but gives a general description, below," she writes to me in a June 10 email, granting me far more credit than I deserve. "If you'd like more specific answers, such as what instruments out of his 400+ he plays, and answers to your many other questions he didn't get to, I'd suggest emailing him one question at a time and he'll get into a dialogue about it."

"If you scroll down," Deborah continues, "you'll see the answers that I provided about [Graeme's] early history. I asked him to edit but I'm pretty sure he didn't even read them or the rest of the questions you asked. He's easily overwhelmed. Thanks for your patience!"

Deborah has pasted Graeme's response to my list of questions immediately below. I read through it and am impressed by how much information it contains. Judging by Deborah's preamble, I had expected much less. Graeme may not have answered every one of my questions, but he has clearly devoted a great deal of time and energy to the exercise.

"My best answer to give to Dr. Michael Bakan is that I play a range of different stringed instruments, particularly lutes and some zithers," Graeme begins. "My specialty though is stringed instruments. I may play whatever it is I feel like, which the particular instrument may convey the sound of the mood. Or I may play something I learn from my music teachers, Randy Raine-Reusch, who you may know, and my second teacher, Rene Hugo Sanchez, who is from Peru. As to my personal relationships with my teachers I share both interests, and in turn I continue to learn a great deal from them. I currently study with my teacher Rene Hugo Sanchez while Randy and his wife Mei Han are in Ohio. I'm also involved in documenting the repertoire I learn by recording or writing it down in tablature or staff notation on my computer. In learning music I'm a visual learner; instructions I do learn from listening to my CDs, [or] what may be on my iPod or on youtube (depending on [the] performance I like best). I feel the best [with] simply something spontaneous. While I enjoy learning different repertoires, genres and traditions, coming from a personal opinion I don't really play too much in mainstream pop or anything trending because most people are performing that right now. I like to explore things that are off the beaten track, be it in music or in daily life. In my childhood I enjoyed classical music, particularly Schubert's 'the trout,' Chopin, Bach, Vivaldi. As of late in listening to music I have been exploring a lot in Asian music, particularly the classical music from India (both North Indian or Hindustani [and] South Indian) to Far and South East Asia."

"I do play classical guitar, acoustic and electric," Graeme adds, "and recently electric bass which I built with the help of a close friend of mine who is an engineer. You may know my teacher Randy Raine-Reusch, as he and I have a strong friendship in music, [through] which we share similar tastes in music and in particular musical instruments. I also study with a music teacher from Peru, Rene Hugo Sanchez."

The email concludes with quick answers to three questions on the list not yet covered. "Your date is correct. I am thirty-six, born in 1977," Graeme writes. As for recording, "I do record music mainly for documentation and sometimes I may give my music to those who are interested, friends and family." Finally, regarding his diagnosis, "I was diagnosed quite early in childhood around the age you mentioned, but my mother is best to answer the last question. I hope this helps. Sincerely, Graeme."

I scroll down to the final portion of Deborah's email, the part where she—with Graeme's permission—has addressed the questions that he himself did not.

"Deborah here," she announces, explaining first that Graeme—or Gray, as she usually calls him—was diagnosed in 1980 at two-and-a-half years of age: "Because Gray was affectionate with us, his parents, the diagnostic team decided he didn't fit classic autism and diagnosed him with 'aphasia' with autistic features, because he didn't understand or speak any language. When he was six he had language, though he was still delayed and his diagnosis changed to 'PDD-NOS—pervasive developmental delay [disorder] not otherwise specified.' By the time he was nine the definition of autism had broadened enough that ever since he has been diagnosed with classic autism. He's also been described as having high-functioning autism, but not Asperger's because he does have some cognitive deficits in executive functioning, particularly numbers and scheduling."

Graeme started playing music when he was just one year old. "A toy piano was his favorite Christmas present that year," Deborah recalls. "Graeme was always strongly drawn to sounds, especially musical sounds, and would choose an object that produced a sound or tone over any conventional toy. When he was about six years old, we tried him in a music group for children but he wouldn't leave the drum and was asked to leave the class. At that point we were very fortunate to meet Dr. Johanne Brodeur, a music therapist who recognised Graeme's gift of absolute pitch and his ability to discriminate ten different notes played simultaneously on the piano. She taught him to read and even write music before he could read or write English, when his language was still fairly limited for his age, and worked with him weekly on many Western instruments until he was thirteen. He had an electric keyboard that he played constantly. Then he was put on a medication for his anxiety and disruptive behavior that reduced his creativity and his fine motor skills for a few years, during which time he listened to music but didn't play it."

In his later teens, Graeme began to develop an interest in instruments from different parts of the world. "For his seventeenth birthday, he astonished us by asking for a balalaika," Deborah remembers. "I still have no idea where that desire originated." For my part, Graeme's interest in the bala-laika comes as no surprise at all: what musically curious seventeen-year-old would *not* be intrigued by a guitar-like instrument from Russia in the shape of a triangle? "When we found one for him he researched teachers in the area and began lessons with [the Vancouver-based balalaika player] Bibs Ekkel."

"When Gray was in his late teens," recounts Deborah, "our friend[,] the musicologist Jarron Lanier[,] came to visit and through him Gray met Randy Raine-Reusch, and began lessons with him, which have continued for around twenty years. Graeme will tell you about his work with Randy and his other teacher Rene Hugo-Sanchez."

Finally, Deborah tackles the question from my list about the types of therapy Graeme has received, specifically those outside of music ther-apy: "Graeme was born before there were any therapies available for chil-dren with autism. He attended a wonderful preschool for special needs children, which exposed him to musical instruments and sign language, and increased his language. Because I studied and taught at the Linguistics Department at UBC [the University of British Columbia] we had connec-tions to researchers and practitioners in speech and audiology who were able to provide him with early language and social therapy. He was the first child with autism to be integrated into the regular school system in Vancouver and had a full-time aide. Graeme will add how he felt about that and other school experiences."

The pieces of the puzzle are coming together nicely. Despite my hav-ing overwhelmed Graeme with more questions than he was ready to han-dle, the collaboration is nevertheless working out, this thanks both to his patience and Deborah's welcome assistance. They have set me up well to move on to the next stage of our process.

To that end, I take Deborah's advice and narrow the focus of my next round of questions for Graeme to Indian classical musics exclusively: the Hindustani traditions of North India and the Karnatak (Carnatic) tradi-tions of the South. These are clearly areas of strong interest for Graeme based on his response to my first set of questions.

"What is it about North Indian and South Indian music that you like and that you find so interesting?" I ask Graeme in a June 11 email.

"In regards to my fascinations with musics from South Asia, particularly in North and South Indian classical music, I found their use [of] raagas quite fascinating," Graeme replies, using an archaic spelling of the more common *ragas*. "Aside from simply calling a raaga a scale, which is true, there [are] more components to it. In the North Indian or Hindustani sys-tem, in each raaga there is a thaat [thāt] (assigned mode, or some raags [raagas] may not have an assigned mode). Raags use a wide range of scales from pentatonic, six note scales or seven note scales and so on. Some of the thaats do correspond to what we know as modes, but the notation in music from India, be it north or south, is based on a non-fixed solfeggio, so in other words while we use fixed notes, harmonic structures in chords, scales and melodies[,] over there it's more about the use of singular notes, and based on an aural tradition; training is taught from teacher to student through singing and vocalization. The use of rhythm there is cyclical and it's a whole other ball game. The use of microtones does differ [between the North and the South]. . . . [I]n both systems the rules are similar [though] they do differ in some ways. In turn [Indian] microtones differ from quarter tones found in Turkish, Arabic and Persian music."

I am impressed by the knowledge Graeme displays on these topics. His descriptions of the raga and thāt systems are as good as or better than some I have seen in music textbooks and graduate student research papers, and he is just getting warmed up.

"Many other cultures including in Myanmar (Burma) and in Vietnam also use a similar system," Graeme continues, moving further into the challenging terrain of cross-cultural musical comparison. "In Myanmar their classical system, while developed a bit differently than [in] neighbouring India[,] they share some things in common. Similar use of modes is found in Vietnam as well. Randy and I use whatever musical instrument comes to mind, be it a stringed instrument or percussion, depending on what lesson we feel like covering. In the end a large part in music is to have fun. I'm also very passionate towards the musics of South America. As for my [Turkish] saz, I do have others from this region [i.e., other stringed instruments of related types] including a Greek bouzouki, Cretian Laouto and a Joura (a medium length of bouzouki). There is something of a family [of these instruments in my collection]."

Emboldened by how well things are going in my email correspondence with Graeme, I reach out to Deborah with a new request. "Now that there is a bit of a track record and hopefully some growing rapport between Graeme and me," I begin, "do you think he might be willing to give a Google Hangouts chat session with me a try? It's been going really well with the other participants in this project, who have all actually expressed that they find [the chat format] to be very enjoyable and not pressure-filled. I do suspect that Graeme and I may be able to explore his musical passions and talents a bit more efficiently and productively, at least vis-à-vis the way I'm doing this project, if we give Hangouts a try. Of course, if it doesn't work out—if Graeme is uncomfortable or dissatisfied with that process in any way—we can revert back to the email exchanges; one way or the other, though, I think doing at least one Hangouts chat would help Graeme and me get to know each other a little better. Would you mind checking with him to see what he thinks of this idea? Then we can take it from there, depending what he says. Thanks!"

"I'm sure he'll be willing," Deborah replies, "but I need to organize it for him. . . . Hope your project is going well!"

"Great. Let's do it!"

"We're on. That is, you and I are on, and I'll be gently and firmly cajoling Gray into accepting this new experience, always subject to extreme resistance!"

CONVERSATION 1: JULY 4, 2014

Graeme is new to Google Hangouts. We experience some difficulties getting connected. On top of that, he's a late riser and it's still pretty early in the morning out on the west coast in Vancouver.

Then there's the fact that Graeme hasn't had his morning coffee yet, and Graeme does *not* do well without his morning coffee. He gets agitated and a bit out of sorts, but following a brief troubleshooting phone conversation with Deborah, him, and me all on the line—and after that a couple more false starts—we finally connect and Graeme starts to feel better.

"Hello Michael. I see your contact in my google chat," I read as the words pop onto the screen. Graeme's first Hangouts post; I breathe a sigh of relief.

"Hello Gray. Nice talking with you for a minute there on the phone, and I'm glad you got your coffee," I reply, adding a smiley-face emoji for good measure.

"Yes, apologies for being grumpy this morning."

"No problem at all."

"I'm also getting my coffee in now so we may proceed with this chat," Graeme states, tagging on a smiley-face emoji of his own.

I start by asking Graeme what it is that excites him about music the most: "the sounds, the structures, the instruments?" I am hoping to orient the conversation toward topics he is most eager to discuss and to keep the focus clear.

"I love the theory component in music altogether," Graeme writes back, "no matter the tradition behind it. And also the exploration [of] seeing who and what is out there. That is what drew me to 'world music' to begin with."

I take note of the fact that Graeme has placed the phrase "world music" in scare quotes. Ethnomusicologists, including me, frequently do this to emphasize the thorny nature of the construct of "world music" itself, [2] but that rarely happens outside of the scholarly realm, which makes me curious about Graeme's usage. I decide to delay asking him about it until after we have followed through on the music theory topic, though.

"So it seems that the systems behind the music are what interest you the most, right?" I type.

"Yes, that is a huge part of it," he replies, "but also just listening to the music gives me a calming sensation that nothing else at the moment can do so."

As the conversation unfolds, Graeme shares with me his interests in areas extending well beyond music per se: hiking, wildlife photography, and DIY projects involving the building of electric circuits and musical instruments.

"I built an electric [guitar] and bass guitar thanks in huge part to my friend's wood workshop. I did the wiring for both projects," Graeme tells me proudly, following up by emailing me a photograph of the bass guitar. (This photo [CW 7.1], along with galleries of Graeme's bird photography [CW 7.2] and world music instrument collection [CW 7.3], may be viewed at the companion website ▶).

"Wow!" I exclaim. "That must have been a big project. You must be a very talented builder *and* electrician!"

"The electronics is self-taught pretty much, and both were huge projects. If you saw them from a distance you might think that Gibson or Fender made them. But there are unique features in the wood work and pick guard, for example, [which] these two companies often do not do with their products. I looked on the Internet and saw some similar examples but none quite like my projects. They blend the best of both worlds for features in their wiring, volume and tone controls."

"Fantastic! Do you play those instruments very often?"

"My two guitars I play most often, and secondly I have been focusing a lot on my Greek bouzouki and Laouto from Crete, particularly with Dromoi (which means roads), the Greek equivalent to Maqam [Arabic modes] found in old Rebetika music, particularly from [the] 1900s to 1930s. Depends on mood. I love having the freedom and flexibility of choosing what instrument I feel like playing. Sometimes it is at the spur of the music."

"The spur of the *music* or the spur of the *moment*?" I ask.

"Right now not much of the spur of the moment," Graeme quips. "When waking up I do like the quiet now and then. ☺"

I appreciate the joke, though am still hoping for clarification of Graeme's spur of the music remark.

"So you did mean to write 'the spur of the music' then? OK. Please tell me what you mean by that. It's an interesting phrase!"

"Oh, I meant spur of the moment."

"Ah, OK. ☺"

"Again, just the lack of thought process when waking up. I'm in zombie state right now."

"I understand, and we all make those kinds of mistakes. Still, though—spur of the music; I kind of like that idea. It's like the music kicks you in the side and gets your attention. ☺"

"Yes," Graeme agrees. "That is what happens in composition often."

The conversation has taken an interesting and unexpected turn.

"Yes, that's true!!" I exclaim. "Tell me about how you compose."

" . . . To answer your question, I first learned standard five bar [i.e., five-line staff] notation when studying in music therapy. This was way before meeting up with Randy [Raine-Reusch]. But for a long time I forgot much of the basics in this composition. It's coming back to me now because I use tablature a lot, especially for guitar or similar stringed instruments."

"Do you draw upon the different theoretical systems you have studied—raga, maqam, dromoi—in your own compositions?"

"Oh yes, I have books on these subjects too. Which I enjoy consulting now and then."

"What are the titles of a couple of those books? I'm an ethnomusicologist, so I'm always interested in good sources of information."

"Ah, one of the titles for the books I have for the raaga is a reprint of the 'The Raagas of North Indian music' [*The Ragas of Northern Indian Music*] by Alain Danielou (1968). When it comes to theory, I have always loved 'the heavier in knowledge the better.' ☺"

"Ah, yes, Danielou," I comment. "That is a very important book. I'm glad you have consulted it."

"It's a great read too," Graeme adds.

"Yes, it certainly is!" I agree, experiencing a rush of ethno-geek camaraderie.

Judging by Graeme's enthusiasm for high-grade studies of Indian music theory, I speculate that his sphere of interest probably extends to math as well.

"Are you also interested in mathematics?" I ask him. "Music theory and math have so much in common. Those interests often go together for people."

"Yes, I am; both music and math are tied together," Graeme affirms. "But I'm also an audio-orientated learner. For some reason my math is nowhere as good as my music. I leave the math to a friend of mine who is an engineer. He can do calculus on paper without the aid of a calculator. So I trust him with the math. ☺"

"That sounds like a good mix of talents. Is your friend also autistic?" I inquire.

"No, but he is very bright in his own way."

What a great line! I highlight it in the transcript.

"Do you have friends that are autistic?" I ask Graeme.

"Yes, but we [have] different taste[s] and things in life that interest us. I have a couple friends with autism, but my social circle is often with those who don't have autism. It is just how it came to be. My friend Daniel Ouellet, who does the math, is a mechanical engineer."

"I see. Now in one of your earlier emails, you mentioned Randy and one other teacher, who I think was from Peru. Please remind me of his name."

"Yes, that is my teacher Rene Hugo Sanchez. . . . He is a very good teacher and friend, one I draw a lot of knowledge from."

"When you have lessons with him, does he mainly teach you to play instruments, or does he teach you music theory too?"

"He teaches both. We are in the process of collecting songs right now from all the regions in Peru. It's a small country compared to others like Brazil in South America, but that part of the world is a treasure chest for music. In Peru the departments (similar to a state or province) are so small, but each one has several different regional styles of music. This is what drew me to studying and appreciating Peruvian music."

"Yes, Peruvian music is wonderful. I actually play regularly in bands with two Peruvian guitarists: Carlos Odria and Carlos Silva. They are amazingly talented. I especially love the Afro-Peruvian *festejo* genre. Are you familiar with that?"

"Yes, my teacher knows quite a fair bit of African Peruvian music and [music] from around the coast as well. I love studying the alternate tuning systems for guitar, charango or mandolin. They are very inventive. Some involve using capos partially set to bass strings only."

"You are quite knowledgeable, Graeme. I can see that you practice what you preach re: 'the heavier in knowledge the better.' You must be an excellent student, and scholar!"

"It's an addiction of mine I must confess. ☺"

"Hey, there are worse addictions, to be sure! ☺"

"That is true."

"It's an addiction of mine, too," I admit, "but it's also my job, so that's worked out pretty well. ☺"

"That's always great to have a passion that works as a job," Graeme wisely observes. "For me [music] is a hobby and powerful stress relief when needed. I volunteer for a museum, and a radio station, assisting in their data entry through computers. Similar description in job but very different in procedure while at each. Both are quite casual and I enjoy the routine in life."

"That's good. It sounds like you have lots of interesting areas of interest, both vocationally and avocationally."

"Anyhow, I do have to have my lunch if you don't mind. But please do keep in touch. Mom also mentioned that [you should] feel free to keep in touch with her as well. You have our email addresses? My stomach is talking to me right now and I came to believe it has its own will when it wants its food. ☺"

I chuckle along with Graeme's emoji.

"OK, I look forward to continuing this another time, perhaps next week," I propose. "I'll talk to your mom about trying to set up a time that works for everyone. Bye for now, and thanks!"

"You're welcome. Please keep in touch. We can work out a time that works for all. I'm always updating my web site, [it] being a work in progress. Cheers."

"Adios!"

"Adios."

CONVERSATION 2: JULY 7, 2014

Based on the success of our first chat session, Graeme and I (with Deborah's assistance) schedule a follow-up for three days later.

"Hi Gray, I'm here now," I type in after logging on.

"Hi Michael. Good morning. I'm waking up still."

"Ah, here it's already 2:00 in the afternoon, so I've been up for a while. Good morning to you!"

"It's around 11:00 a.m. [here] so I'm not quite there in the afternoon yet," Graeme responds. "By the time my afternoon rolls around you will be in the evening. Fascinating things time zones are."

"Indeed! I wanted to follow up on a couple of things you said last time, OK?"

"Sure, of course. And they are?"

"You talked about the 'calming sensation' that music had on you, and that that was something 'that nothing else at the moment can do.' Could you tell me more about what that feels like, how it helps you, and also what *kinds* of music have that effect?"

"Ah yes, the only way I can describe that to you is it's sort of narcotic. I mean to say [that] as soon as I pick up a musical instrument to play it, or as soon as I put my headphones on and select something I want to listen

[to], something quite different comes over me. However the effect when listening [to] or playing the music lasts for a while it does not last for a whole day. Experience and mood-wise it does change my outlook on the day; it makes it a lot better. There are times if I'm too stressed out, when I take a break from everything and just simply declutter the thoughts in my brain and take the time to organize them. There is not a specific time limit as to how long this experience lasts; each experience in playing or listening to music is different from one to the next."

"So do different types of music affect your emotions in different ways?" I inquire. "I know you have done research on the ragas and [the Arab] maqamat [modes]. In such systems, say, with ragas, they have associations with specific mood-states, seasons, times of day, etc. I'm wondering whether you have any kind of music/emotion system like that personally, whether related to existing systems of different musics or otherwise. Please enlighten me on this!"

"Yes, when I was young (childhood to youth) much of my exposure to music was European classical music. In particular my favorites went from Schubert, Chopin, Bach, Vivaldi and so on. At the time I did not know what this music was. I just knew I enjoyed listening to it. To this day I cannot stand music that is too loud, or something too commercial (stuff in the Top 40 or what's played on the radio these days). But I do enjoy a wide range from traditional to some contemporary, which includes some experimental (free improvisation, avant-garde, and so on). I have noted that each raag may be connected with an emotion or several emotions, but I like to think that is the behavior of music in general. Depends on the mood of the listener: the music here is a lens that amplifies the person's state of mind."

"So when you seek that calming effect as a listener, you still mainly go to the classics: Schubert, Chopin, Bach, etc.?"

"It may depend on the mood I'm in, but usually I seek happiness, joy, relaxation, calming. From another experience, I found in music [that] I enjoy following and learning to play by ear when listening to some pieces. I have a lot of old African guitar music, particularly from the 1940s through the 1970s, found on CD and LP (Record). I enjoy the challenge of music, which it presents in both playing and theory as well."

"Excellent. Thank you! On to other questions then!"

"And what are your other questions then?" Graeme asks me. I take the opportunity to pose the "world music" question I have held in reserve until now.

"I noted in our last chat that you put quotation marks around the phrase 'world music' when I had not. I thought that was very sophisticated of you, and I have my guesses as to why you did it, but I'm interested in your own explanation. Why did you choose to do that?"

"Ah, I often do this as a means to emphasize what world music is. People often have it marked as another genre, but because world music involves numerous traditions [up] to contemporary musics, it's really not just a single genre of music. I prefer to think of it as a spectrum that includes numerous genres. Often when explaining this to most people, usually they are curious and they may not understand what world music is. It is a process of discovery for the person listening to it. Not just a genre. Sometimes boxing things into genres and labels may not work all the time. I found that to be the case with world music, when thinking about this particular aspect of it."

"Excellent answer, and it makes me wonder: do you have similar thoughts about autism and the autism spectrum?"

"Yes," Graeme affirms, "because in autism, I also found that everyone is different from their case, to my case and so on. I do agree with the term 'spectrum' but we still have lots to learn; there is a lot of misinformation out there still. I prefer for people to see me for who I am as a person and not judge me based upon what they hear from Hollywood or the media, which is often very inaccurate."

"I have another question, Graeme. This is one I've asked several of the other people I've spoken to for this project as well. Here it is: If you could wave a magic wand and your autism would be gone, would you do that or not?"

"For me, no. Some symptoms I would like to have gone, like stress triggers and so on, but I fear in the end my music may be lost too. Like you want to keep some old software on your computer you may not run in the newer systems but you need to reformat and upgrade as things develop and improve. I worry that if it was the case [that my autism was gone] my music would go [away] along with the symptoms."

"Anything else you would fear losing, other than your music?"

"I'm not so sure, but I'm certain I will find something. For the most part I'm very happy being the individual who I am. A part of life's journey is that it is an ongoing process in my own self-discovery."

"Thanks! So I'd like to continue a little while longer if you're OK with that, but please let me know how much more time you have here today."

"Ah. OK. I'm available 'til 12:00 p.m., because my stomach is impatient when it comes to needing its food. I have tried arguing with it and lost that argument a long time ago."

We exchange emoji chuckles over this remark.

"OK, so just a couple of minutes. One more question then. Here it comes!"

"OK."

"The book in which our correspondence is going to be included will hopefully be read by quite a few people: autistic people, non-autistic people, musicians, non-musicians, scholars, non-scholars. We have an opportunity here to change the way people think about autism and autistic people, both with respect to music and otherwise. With that in mind, what would you most like to express to the world at large, as it were, from your perspective as an autistic musician, a thoughtful person, and a caring individual?"

I wait a couple of minutes as Graeme composes his reply. I meditate on the dancing dots and bubbling sounds coming from the computer. Finally, Graeme's response appears on my screen.

"I would like to express to the rest of the world, that you judge me for who I am as a person not based on what I am. Autism is a part of who I am but I do not allow for it to define me. In conclusion, as you meet us you will find we are just as diverse and different from one to the next [as other people are]. We all have our own life stories. All we ask for is simply to be treated with the same respect as we would be [if we were not autistic] when it comes to interacting with society in general."

"Thank you, Gray. That is beautifully said. I've very much enjoyed these two chats. Do you have any final thoughts to share or questions for me before we sign off?"

"I'm pleased to contribute to this [book] in the end. Mom has written her Ph.D., [in] which I'm pretty much her subject. So I'm somewhat familiar with academia when it comes to sharing my experiences in autism. . . . Specifically the Ph.D. [dissertation] was about my language comprehension or lack thereof when I was very young. If you met me at the age of two, I was delayed and I had my own means of communicating with the outside world. So Mom had the time and dedication to write a diary of this and now this diary is her Ph.D. . . . And there is one more thing. I'm happy to share [with] you my photos when it comes to my bird and wildlife photography. One of my rare experiences was I had a redwing blackbird land on my hand. I had no food, no seed. I was standing in the park, and he checked my camera out first then decided to land on my hand. I got my iPhone out and snapped a photo. I was left stunned in my experience but amazed I was able to keep a photo record of this."

"Oh, yes, great. I'd love to see that—please send it along! Have a great day!"

"You too. Sunny here today, so I'm hoping for some good photos. Cheers. Adios."

"Ditto. Adios!"

Graeme sends along not just one red-winged blackbird photo but a couple of them, as well as a lovely recording of him performing a modal improvisation on his Greek bouzouki. The recording may be heard at the companion website (CW 7.4 ▶).

"The scale," Graeme says, "is something like a minore dromoi (which is Greek for scale[;] the correct translation is road); the closest analogy we know is the natural minor scale as found in numerous genres of music. In traditional Greek music[,] particularly the early rebetika from the early 1910s to 1930s[,] they often used scales that bore the same names as their Turkish and Arabic equivalents although lacking much of the quartertones. Some current bouzouki makers may add custom frets to . . . achieve the quartertones [for modes like] Hijaz, Hijazkiar, Kiurdi, Houseini, Nihavent, Sabah, Segah, Usak and so on. A scale with the same name[,] Segah[,] is also found in Persian music. Some are regional scales like Piraeus[,] which is one of the areas where Rebetika emerged; the other is Smyrna[,] which is Izmir in today's Turkey."

Graeme provides detailed information about his photographs as well. The one that appeals to me the most is of a female red-winged blackbird.

"Here is a favourite pic of mine I took this year in June to July at Jericho Beach, Vancouver, Canada," he writes. "I used my Canon T3i with 18-55 mm starter lens for this photo and this female red wing black bird did not seem frightened or fazed by this experience. Female red wing black birds don't have the red shoulder pads as their male counterparts [do]. They do share the same type of call when communicating."

The female red-winged blackbird photograph is captivating; it may be seen at the companion website (CW 7.5 ▶). Against a backdrop of wild-flowers and lush greenery, the little bird perches contentedly on Graeme's outstretched left hand. Her shoulder pads indeed show no red, and her coloring is more brown than black, except for her tail feathers and a distinctive pattern of black striping across her breast. With head cocked ever so slightly, she registers a bemused curiosity that is as sweet as can be. She looks so calm and trusting as she grips Graeme's fingers with her tiny feet. Her black tail feathers flank outward to the edges of his hand, her wings tucked behind her back as though in an avian yoga pose.

The more I look, the more I am drawn in; and the more I'm drawn in, the more deeply I am moved. Tears come to my eyes, though I'm not quite sure why. Of one thing I am certain, though: Graeme and I need to share this picture with the readers of our book.

NOTES

1. "The Early Lexical Acquisition of a Child with Autism Spectrum Disorder" (Gibson 2011).
2. *World Music: Traditions and Transformations* (Bakan 2012) and *The Cambridge History of World Music* (Bohlman 2013) offer examples.

CHAPTER 8

Maureen Pytlik

I'm very good at interacting with people when there's a room full of people who don't know each other. It's the sustained interactions and knowing someone that's hard for me. I'm excited by "blank slate" kinds of opportunities, which is what the African drumming stuff was for all of us. It's also something that we were all going through and learning together, so that helped. As does having to do some of the dance moves required in the pieces! Allowing someone to grab your waist from behind and not think anything of it doesn't happen in typical classes or other types of musical ensembles!

Maureen Pytlik (2014)

I have not heard from my former graduate student Carolyn Ramzy in years, so I'm pleasantly surprised to discover an email from her waiting in my inbox when I arrive at my office on September 5, 2014.

Hello Michael,

I hope this email finds you well. I'm not sure if you've heard yet, but I've accepted a position as Assistant Professor of Ethnomusicology at Carleton University. After defending my dissertation in January at the University of Toronto, my husband Marcus and our five month-old son Nadim and I moved to Ottawa in July! Needless to say, it has been a busy time.

I have already met an exceptional undergraduate student named Maureen Pytlik who is interested in your work. She is a double major in both math and music and is particularly interested in your ARTISM project.[1] She is interested in getting into academia and would like to get in touch with you. She herself has a very high functioning Asperger syndrome and is keen to investigate how music helps children with autism. I am attaching her CV here.

If it is alright with you, I'd like to connect you both via email. Just let me know.

Looking Forward,
Carolyn

I review the attached CV and write back to Carolyn, encouraging her to share my contact information with Maureen right away; I'd love to hear from her, I add. An email from Maureen arrives minutes later. She is eager to talk with me about different graduate programs and possible career options. Within short order, we have exchanged a series of lengthy emails and scheduled a phone meeting for the coming weekend. I also tell Maureen about the music-and-autism book project I'm working on and ask whether she might be interested in being interviewed for it. Possibly, she writes back, but she needs to know more about it before committing. Let's talk about it on the phone on Sunday, she suggests.

During our Sunday conversation, Maureen is highly inquisitive—about the book project and everything else. It is also immediately evident to me that she is very, very smart, and that she conceives of her Asperger's condition as integral not only to who she is personally but also to the types of professional life options she might pursue. My already formed impressions of her as a thorough, methodical, and detail-oriented thinker from our emails are doubly confirmed over the phone.

And she is careful. Before agreeing to speak to me in connection with my book project, she requests that I send her a sample chapter. I'm surprised by this—no one else has ever made such a request of me—but I agree to her terms. She reviews the materials I send her and a few days later, on September 10, sends me an email with her decision. "As for the book interview/collaboration, I am eager to proceed with this," she informs me. She then asks me to send her the project consent form, which comes back signed about two weeks later.

"Hi, Dr. Bakan," she writes in her covering email. "Here's my signed consent form for you. Just to be clear, the sentence 'Your participation . . . should always be on terms with which you are entirely comfortable' is very important to me. These terms, for me, mean that I consent to being interviewed in written form as long as I am able to collaborate with you throughout the editing phase for the chapter that will feature my thoughts. Particularly because I do wish to use my real name, I need to be able to approve the relevant portions of the manuscript one last time (unless substantial revisions are later requested by a publisher, in which case I should like to have as much say as any contributing author would usually have) before you submit to Oxford. All of this said, I am very happy to participate and am satisfied by the way you intend to use these written interviews and by your desire to respect interviewees' current wishes regarding the disclosure or non-disclosure of specific personal information. . . . I'm looking forward to 'part one' of the interview! Cheers, Maureen"

CONVERSATION 1: SEPTEMBER 25, 2014

"I am not particularly adept at doing the instant chatting bit," Maureen tells me once we are signed on and have exchanged hellos, "but I'm very good at writing conversational emails. I'll try to find a way to write in my usual email style—fairly open and 'wordy' yet still decently to the point."

"Yes, perfect," I reply, "and keep in mind that I will always have on file the original, unedited [transcripts of our dialogues], so if anything gets changed along the way in the revision process that needs revisiting, we can always go back to that. Also, don't feel that you need to 'instant chat.' I am patient and happy for you to compose your thoughts as you see fit." So I say, though Maureen will soon reveal me as considerably less patient than I fashion myself to be.

"OK, sounds good," Maureen types. "Fire away with your first question. Just don't start with a super open-ended one!"

"Fair enough. How old are you now and how old were you when you received your Asperger's diagnosis?"

"I turned twenty-six earlier this year and received my diagnosis of Asperger's almost exactly ten years ago."

"Do you currently live on your own? With family? In a dorm? With roommates?"

"I still live with my family. (That would be my mom and dad, who are both retired. I have an older brother who now lives in Toronto.) I have not yet experienced moving out of the house that I've grown up in my whole life."

"Do you have close friends, either people you grew up with or who you have met at university?"

Seven minutes go by before Maureen's reply appears.

"I have a few good friends: both friends that I've known for a long time and some that are friends from university. Would you like me to describe a bit about how I got to know them and became friends?"

"OK."

This time, it is twenty-four minutes before Maureen posts her reply. I am starting to see that there is more to her "I am not particularly adept at doing the instant chatting bit" remark than I had thought. I want to be patient, and the last thing I wish to do is put undue pressure on Maureen to pick up the pace. At the same time, though, I'm concerned that if we don't, this process is going to take months to complete.

Finally, Maureen posts a paragraph about her friendships.

"When I started university, I had two established friendships that I knew would continue to exist after my high school graduation. These two friends of mine were both girls from my neighborhood whom I knew through Girl Guides[2] and in one case from school as well. One had been in my grade in elementary school, while the other is two years older. My mom played a very active role over a number of years in encouraging me to develop friendships with both of these girls; she also became friends with their mothers, which helped to establish the lines of communication between our households. I became comfortable enough to call either of these two neighborhood friends on the phone, and we would spend time together at each other's houses once in a while."

Having seen firsthand the difficulties that people on the autism spectrum often experience in establishing friendships and maintaining them over long periods of time, I realize what a major accomplishment it is for Maureen to have cultivated these long-standing relationships. I wonder whether she embraces such challenges of living with Asperger's or resents them, which leads me to deliver my standard "magic wand" question.

"Let me ask you a question that I've asked just about everyone else I've interviewed for this project as well: If you could wave a magic wand and make your Asperger's disappear, would you?"

This time, twenty minutes elapses before Maureen offers a response.

"At times when I was younger I'm sure I would have said 'yes,'" she begins, "but not now. I certainly wouldn't want to lose my eligibility for scholarships that are only open to students with disabilities! I have met many very nice people specifically because my differences fit into a category that afforded me the Asperger's diagnosis, so I would have missed out on some social opportunities if I were not the way I am. (Perhaps if I were naturally more socially at ease in interacting with large numbers of people, I wouldn't crave these opportunities that can facilitate social interaction quite as much, though!)."

"I have very few innate instincts guiding me when it comes to interacting socially, but I do like interacting with people," Maureen continues, echoing a theme that has come up often in my conversations with other project collaborators as well. "I just usually need easy situations to help me get used to what to do in each particular style of interaction."

Having asked one of my stock interview questions, I follow up with another. "In terms of how you identify yourself relative to your diagnosis and how other people may refer to you," I ask Maureen, "which of the following seem fine to you (and which, if any, don't): 'person with Asperger's syndrome,' 'person with autism,' 'Autistic person,' 'autistic person,' 'Aspie?'"

"Since I have Asperger's Syndrome (or AS, for short)," Maureen begins in reply, "I tend to think the best way to refer to me *when my AS is relevant* is as 'an individual with Asperger's (Syndrome).' In fact, I have written sentences that begin, 'As an individual with Asperger's Syndrome, I ... (whatever the case may be)' many times in scholarship application essays. Yes, I am a 'person with Asperger's syndrome.' I agree with this 'person-first' phrasing, although I happen to prefer the word 'individual' (since that most accurately describes who I am) to 'person.' I will usually tend away from the 'person(s) with...' terminology because it seems a little too political for everyday use."

Maureen now moves down the list: "As for 'person with autism,' yes, I will sometimes say that I have autism (especially if I think the person I am communicating with may not know what Asperger's is). I'm probably more likely to say 'a form of (high-functioning) autism' than simply 'autism' all by itself, though. This isn't because I don't consider myself autistic, but because I find that other people are very likely to get a very distorted view of who I am if I merely describe myself as 'autistic.'"

"As for 'Autistic' vs. 'autistic,'" Maureen continues, "I'm not sure I have a preference. I like the idea of fitting in with the Autistic community, but I'm not quite sure what the 'political' undertones or overtones are if I were to refer to myself as an Autistic person. I am sometimes aware of feeling 'autistic' in what I believe to be the true sense of the word, but in those instances I would never refer to myself as an 'autistic person,' as I would not be speaking to another person in moments when I really feel that way!"

I smile at the cleverness of the last remark, though I'm not sure whether or not it has been delivered with humorous intent. Finally, Maureen comes to the slang term "Aspie." "I happen to quite like it," she admits, "but of course its use implies a level of informality that sometimes isn't quite appropriate (i.e., when writing a formal scholarship application. You can begin to see a bit of a trend with me here in the way that I often return to the scholarship theme, can't you?!)."

I chuckle at the parenthetical quip. This time I'm pretty sure that the humor *is* intentional.

We are almost out of time. I decide to close with a third stock question. "The book in which this material appears will hopefully be read by quite a large number of people from various walks of life: people with and without autism, musicians and non-musicians, scholars and non-scholars, parents of autistic children, etc. If there was one thing that you could share with people across this broad demographic landscape—one idea, one suggestion, one principle—what would that be?"

Maureen resists my seeming desire for a pat, sound-bite response.

"Any message I try to impart in a single suggestion may not exactly be what someone else takes out of reading this conversation," she insists. "Perhaps I'll simply share something that one of [the Carleton] psychology professors . . . discussed with me regarding a class she taught on autism in which her students watched one of Temple Grandin's lectures about her life on the spectrum. The students were by and large in agreement that they had learned quite a bit about females with autism from Temple Grandin's talk, even though (unlike some other speakers and experts they had heard) Temple didn't try to speak specifically about women's issues. This was because the perspective she shared was that of a woman with autism, so by the very manner in which she communicated about the matters she chose to speak about they were able to learn something about the topic of females with AS by contrasting her style with [those of] other speakers with AS that they had heard who were male. I believe that some people will find the very manner in which I communicate my thoughts to be intriguing enough." I am certain Maureen is right about that. "Let me just add that I feel a bit of an analogy between myself and Achilles (of Hofstadter's GEB)[3] in having this conversation with you! I'm particularly thinking of the 'dialogues' in which Achilles receives a visit from the 'Author' and they discuss the authorship and origin of their own words!"

It is a wonderful insight and the irony is not lost on me. Maureen has hit on a basic tension of this project, one with which I have been struggling from the outset: how to write in a way that honors the words, voices, and ideas of my collaborators in the context of a book that never escapes the fact of my being its principal author. I find strange comfort in Maureen's recognition and articulation of this vexing paradox.

CONVERSATION 2: SEPTEMBER 26, 2014

Maureen and I reconvene for our second chat session a day later, but before we get started, we talk briefly on the phone. I have requested the call. I want Maureen to know that while I wish for her to be as comfortable as possible during our chats, and while I realize that her comfort may well depend on our maintaining a very leisurely pace akin to that of our first session, it would be great if we could move things along just a *bit* faster.

Maureen points out that this request contradicts my earlier position. After all, wasn't it just yesterday that I told her she should not feel the need to rush, that "I am patient and happy for you to compose your thoughts as you see fit"? I acknowledge the inconsistency and assure Maureen that her comfort and integrity still come first. I promise to do my best to live up to my pledge of patience.

Ultimately we reach a compromise: Maureen will experiment with a less strictly controlled (and thus somewhat quicker-paced) approach to writing and I will work hard to accept the flow of dialogue that emerges, regardless of what that flow turns out to be. With that established, we are ready to resume our conversation online.

"OK. Let's continue!" Maureen types once we are both logged on.

"Yes, very good. Me first," I request. "Yesterday I had wanted to ask about how you think having Asperger's affects the way you approach being a musician, but we ran out of time. Are you prepared to chat about that a bit today?"

"I can try."

"Great. Please do," I write, adding a smiley-face emoji for encouragement.

"Where do I start? Somehow, I'm thinking less about my clarinet playing and performing than about my experiences in my first- and second-year West African drumming/dancing/singing courses, as well as with the [Carleton University] West African Rhythm Ensemble." I am already somewhat familiar with these topics from our first telephone conversation three weeks ago. "University for me was a much-anticipated 'new beginning,'" Maureen continues. "I saw it as an opportunity to be social in ways that I was unable to be in high school (due to struggles with mental health, [mis]diagnoses, and falling a year behind my age group). Taking those African music and dance courses proved to be central to that new way of being."

"Great. Let's go there!"

"Naturally, the ethnomusicology topic being your area set my mind thinking in this direction as well."

"Makes sense."

"I also think that having had to do 'reflection papers' for these courses allowed me time to reflect upon what it even means to be a musician," Maureen shares, adding that she was required to write two such papers for her West African music and dance class. " . . . I found I had a particular liking for and knack for doing these reflection assignments. It seemed like a mix between journaling and writing a more traditional university paper (albeit a very short one)!"

I ask Maureen if she would be willing to send me copies of the reflection papers, and perhaps even allow me to include portions of them in the book.

"I was thinking that (that I could send them to you)!" she replies. "I always keep everything. The hardcopies are filed away in a file folder (I keep a small filing unit for my university coursework over the years—I hold on to everything; I would never throw away an assignment!), and I have the electronic copies meticulously filed away, too."

"Electronic would be best," I write back.

"I still have all of the feedback from my instructor, Kathy Armstrong . . . on the hardcopies."

Kathy Armstrong?! Now this is unexpected!

"I went to the University of Toronto with Kathy Armstrong!" I exclaim. "We both studied percussion there in the early 1980s. We were good friends!"

"Ah! Small world," Maureen interjects, ". . . but I think we know that (it's a small world)!"

"In fact, I just recently reconnected with Kathy via Facebook! And she and I learned West African drumming from the same teacher, Russell Hartenberger—which means that you and I are in the same 'lineage' in a way!"

"I understand the 'lineage' thing," Maureen relates. "My [clarinet] students are using books written by Avrahm Galper—who is my 'great-grandteacher' (via [my 'grandteacher'] James Campbell—who, by the way, happens to be my favorite clarinetist)! Where were we?"

"Ah, getting back to how your experiences playing/dancing West African music provide insight into how having Asperger's influences you as a musician."

"Let me dig up the reflection papers!" Maureen writes. They arrive in my email inbox minutes later. "Just don't consider these [as] necessarily free to quote from—until I 'okay' that—since I haven't read this stuff in ages!"

"Absolutely! You got it," I assure her.

I begin to read through the two papers. As I do, Maureen is compelled to post some contextualizing remarks. Regarding the second paper, she informs me that she wrote it "at a time in my life where I was coming to terms with a mental health crisis [I had] in high school. Some deep reflection going on there." Regarding her general writing approach in both, she states, "I kept the writing 'academic.' But Kathy really liked my reflection style and wanted us to be 'open.'"

The second paper includes two brief poems composed by Maureen. I find them poignant and moving. I ask if I may include them in the book. She replies yes, but only on the condition that, first, I frame the actual poems with the sentences of the paper that appear immediately above and below them, and second, that the poems appear side by side, as follows:

Elaborating on the analogy of call and response patterns as similar to those of speaker and listener I realized that a form of call and response exists in the two poems of mine that follow:

Silent Being	Compassionate Listener
I am the thought that is never expressed;	I am a person who wishes to know;
Silent and lonely, I wait to be heard,	Quietly listening, I hear every word,
By those who will never know my voice.	Of those who had been too afraid to speak.

These two poems were in the back of my mind when I was watching the video footage of *Gahu* being performed in Ghana.

I am very familiar with Gahu, a genre of dance accompanied by music that is associated with certain Ewe-speaking groups in Ghana.[4] Performances of Gahu vary tremendously from one to another, but they are generally characterized by loud, percussive music and highly energetic dancing. I am therefore struck by the association Maureen has drawn between Gahu and the "silent being" and "compassionate listener" of her poems, which at least on the surface seems incongruous.

Deeper reflection on my part leads to a different perspective, however. Effective Gahu performance demands that the musicians and dancers be intimately attuned to one another. For all its volume and exhibitionistic flair, Gahu relies on intricate and nuanced calls and responses among the various players. The lead drummer most of all must *be* a compassionate listener if the entire, complex musical-choreographic matrix is to achieve its desired communal and aesthetic ends. Maureen's poems and their framing commentary have led me to conceptualize Gahu in this entirely new way, which no amount of ethnomusicological reading and study could ever have done.

Maureen's poems are enlightening on another level as well: they complement key concepts and themes that have emerged in my dialogues with other project collaborators. The poems most vividly bring to mind Ibby Grace's comments (Chapter 5) about those quiet people she knows who "make their souls inaudible," causing her to "feel for them because . . . they have honest music played very quietly as if their being is squelched," and to "take extra time and imaginary ears trying to hear them. . . ." Ibby's "quiet people" and Maureen's "silent being," Ibby's "imaginary ears" and Maureen's "compassionate listener," parallel each other. This seems more than coincidental, suggesting shared qualities of perceptiveness and empathy that derive at least in part from shared autistic ways of being in the world.

After sending her two reflection papers to me, Maureen follows up with the assignment description for "Reflection #2" from Kathy, which she wants me to see:

> Describe call and response. Discuss all its forms in *Gahu*. Discuss other applications in music and/or other areas of life. Dig deep. Be creative. Use examples from the video you saw in class.

"That's it," Maureen sums up. "(Oh, and 'two pages.')," she adds in her typically thorough way.

"Perfect," I reply. "And I would echo Kathy's appeal in our dialogues here, [encouraging you] to 'Dig deep' and 'Be creative.' You certainly achieved that in the assignment, by the way!"

"Kathy agreed too. She gave me a rare perfect grade," Maureen states proudly.

"Yay!!"

"And also wrote 'Nice. Thanks for including' about the poems and 'Actually you have a good groove!' about something at the end (amongst other 'well done' comments)."

"Nice. I agree with all of that."

"The 'good groove' remark referred to my dancing, though, I think. It's not possible for you to be able to speak to that! ☺ "

"True, I can't, as I haven't seen you dance," I acknowledge. "I'm ready to ask you questions about the two papers now, if you're ready for that. Let me [copy and paste] a few passages . . . and ask you a thing or two about them."

"Perfect. I like details and specifics."

"This sentence that you wrote captures a 'theme' that comes up in several variant forms in the two assignments: 'I am now far more comfortable with actively participating in all of what we do in class because I no longer impose upon myself the pressure of measuring up to a certain level of accomplishment.' Can you elaborate on how having Asperger's impacts your sense of living up to 'accomplishment,' and how (West African) drumming and dancing help you combat that self-consciousness/self-criticism?"

"Ah, that's true," Maureen notes, referring to the quoted material. "It also probably stems from Kathy's urging us to consider how Ghanaian music-making contrasts with what we've been taught and are learning on our other primary instruments of study."

"Right," I agree, "but let's frame it in terms of the whole Asperger's experience thing, at least as you perceive it in such a frame of reference." Now *that* was a pretty dictatorial prompt, I scold myself while reviewing the transcript later on: a classic case of the Author taking Achilles out at the knees (or is it at the heel?) mid-stride, but Maureen kindly elects not to take me to task this time around.

In learning West African drumming and dances, Maureen tells me that she "was quite happy to open up and be awkwardly uncoordinated, because it was something that created a lot of group bonding in a way. Feeling part of the group was very important to me because having Asperger's means it's not something that I experience easily. . . . It felt nice knowing that somehow my peers felt a slight sense of vulnerability in exposing their 'inexperience.' I just happen to be 'inexperienced' (and especially was in my first year) in the social aspects. None of us (except for one Ghanaian student) came with any experience."

"I'm very good at interacting with people when there's a room full of people who don't know each other," Maureen continues. "It's the sustained interactions and knowing someone that's hard for me. I'm excited by 'blank slate' kinds of opportunities, which is what the African drumming stuff was for all of us. It's also something that we were all going through and learning together, so that helped. As does having to do some of the dance moves required in the pieces! Allowing someone to grab your waist from behind and not think anything of it doesn't happen in typical classes or other types of musical ensembles!"

"Indeed!" I exclaim. "I want to come back to the 'blank slate' idea for a moment. One of the things that I've emphasized in the ARTISM Ensemble is that there is no fixed or desirable musical outcome—or social outcome—to what we do. Whatever comes out of the musical experience, mainly as dictated by what the [participating] children want it to be, is a priori 'the norm' of how it *should* be: these children are assumed to be experts at being who they are; we (neurotypical adults) are not there to teach them, but to learn from and respond to them. Your African drumming/dancing experience is different—there is a set goal of performance—but it appears to be related in the sense that no one (other than the teacher and the Ghanaian guy) really knows how it should be, should sound, should look. This would seem to offer a very liberating opportunity for someone like you who has Asperger's, that is, for an individual like yourself who is chronically pressed to conform to social standards that may be 'obvious' to others but not to you. Does the parallel I'm drawing here make sense? Do you have any comment on it?"

"Yes, I see the parallel and think it's good. Um... I'm having a bit of a hard time figuring out how to comment, though, since I feel that such a question merits a little more thought being invested into answering it."

"That's alright," I respond, "since I need to go in about five minutes anyhow. [But] I do think we've really hit on something good with these reflection essays of yours as a template for developing this conversation, and that this has been a very enlightening session today."

"Yes, I agree," Maureen concurs. "This has been a very useful session."

CONVERSATION 3: OCTOBER 2, 2014

A couple of minutes into my third chat with Maureen, I suggest to her that we experiment with a slightly different approach.

"Rather than me directing traffic," I propose, "perhaps you should tell me how you'd like to get started today."

Maureen likes the idea. "I thought a bit about practice habits and things I enjoy," she types, "particularly in terms of how I approach working on a variety of objectives, like technical aspects of clarinet playing and working on a mix of scales, studies, pieces, etc. . . . I also think we could maybe explore my role as a private music teacher. I love interacting one-on-one with students, but that's because I now have the skills to teach the ones I have effectively and patiently. (I had patience before, but not enough skill when I was only eighteen or so.) I haven't taught for very long, but I still feel it's a very strong part of my musical identity—being a teacher."

"Great topic. Talk about that some. I'd be especially interested in knowing your thoughts on how your Asperger's influences your approach to teaching, and the outcomes of your teaching—both for your students and for yourself."

"Well, one thing is that I've absolutely loved doing workbooks for as long as I could write with a crayon, so I happen to really enjoy selecting appropriate theory books for students to use. This is in large part because I have a go-to standard method book that is suitable for virtually all beginning clarinet students ([they] seem to be a specialty of mine), but there isn't that one go-to theory book that suits a wide variety of students. So selecting books is something I spend quite a bit of time doing. I'm maybe not the most efficient with my time at sheet music stores (as [is true] with me in any book store; I can spend hours!). I also know that teachers generally want something quick for marking [grading] their students' work—which is why teachers' answer keys exist, to save time—yet I enjoy completing the theory workbooks myself as part of my 'down time,' where I can do a lot of thinking (planning my week, letting my mind wander and letting my mind think about teaching approaches, or about my own learning at university). Maybe I'm also aware that it's certainly more cost effective (if the teacher is going to have the resources their students use in their own library) to create one's own answer keys, as long as time is not an issue."

I am reminded of one of my conversations with Graeme Gibson (Chapter 7). Like Graeme, Maureen evidently holds to the conviction that when it comes to music theory, "the heavier the knowledge the better." She understands, though, that her students are not very likely to share that passion.

"My parents tell me that not every student I have is going to enjoy theory like I do, or be a 'theory nerd,' and I'm aware of that. I just invest a lot of energy in assessing the merits of various options in terms of additional resources that will be necessary for each student. I may not start them on theory books right away, depending on their goals (and the parents' intentions) and learning styles; but I certainly want to be able to recommend the most suitable theory book that I can find for each individual student. . . . I need to be sure of my selection (of supplementary resources) so that I can focus on communicating with the student's parent(s)—whenever I decide that the time is right for introducing something new into the student's list of homework items—the necessary information about obtaining the resource rather than being stuck in decision mode (i.e., trying to figure out how best to approach teaching a student, and holding them back because I haven't made up my mind and acted upon something)."

The conversation eventually turns to Maureen's way of interacting with her students during lessons. "I am very focused on each individual student," she claims, "and don't have any preformed thoughts that they should all be doing some of the same stuff or in the same way. Maybe this is my [Aspie] 'lack of generalization' thing, that I don't have only one way (or a select few ways) of teaching as my default." I appreciate how Maureen's position here turns the standard tropes of restricted and repetitive behaviors and lack of cognitive flexibility in ASC on their heads; she is essentially claiming no less than that her flexible and open-minded approaches to teaching are a *product* of her being on the spectrum.

"Maybe, too," Maureen continues, "it has to do in part with the fact that I have not had decades of (teaching) experience and dozens upon dozens of students. I like allowing [my students] to ask questions to see how they are learning new concepts, and I really do want to know what they are thinking. I try to give them space and time to 'digest' the bits of information I'm giving them and want to make sure that they understand what I'm hoping they'll accomplish for each little exercise. I want them to know what type of sound or technique or result I'm after when I ask them to play some-thing (no matter the length) for me. I try to foster an interaction style that allows me to ask them 'How did that sound?' in a very specific way (i.e., 'Did it sound like those notes were smooth and connected to you?' or some-thing like that—always with a goal in mind for work and improvement, of course). I let them know that 'mistakes' (without always calling them that—saying 'fingering blips' or whatever it is) are part of a good learn-ing process, and can be seen as very positive *as long as* one knows how to improve (or 'fix') those areas—which is where my knowledge as a teacher comes in."

The more I read, the more I realize how much I have to learn from Maureen, not just about teaching music, but about effectively interacting with my collaborators in chat dialogues like this one as well. Really wanting to know what they are thinking, giving them the space and time to figure out and express what that is, avoiding the temptation to impose "any pre-formed thoughts that they should all be doing some of the same stuff or in the same way"—these are valuable priorities to have in mind whether you are teaching clarinet or doing ethnomusicology. Maureen is once again helping me to see things that should be obvious all the time but too often are not.

Maureen has more to say on the subject of her teaching approach: "I am very detailed in explaining things, so I have to make sure I do so in a way that is appropriate for the age and level of the student as well. I can't impart way too much detail or a student wouldn't understand me. Or else, it would tax them too much when I'd rather they save their energy for something else I want them to focus on." These comments remind me of Dotan Nitzberg's "dos and don'ts" of teaching piano to students with Asperger's (Chapter 6), particularly the part where Dotan states, "no mat-ter what level they are: Don't demonstrate too much, show only the specific passages that require special treatment; otherwise the student will not get the main point."

Next, Maureen touches on how reading her students' body language affects her teaching method. "I do try to communicate that I can sense to some level how they are feeling—that is, in their bodies, not emotionally—as they're playing for me . . .," she begins.

This catches my attention. "That last sentence is interesting and I'd like to follow up with a question about it when you have a moment to pause," I interject.

"Allow me to finish what I was in the middle of describing first," she volleys back, Achilles style, then picks up where she left off. "I'll comment if I think that they're tired or 'out of air' most likely, and switch gears just temporarily (inserting a bit of casual chit-chat if suitable, perhaps asking about their music class at school or a band they play in to see if there are any commonalities between our experiences or to discover what it is that they notice; again, I like to know what musical things they notice, and can encourage good habits—like how to pay attention to a conductor when faced with difficult passages). That being aware of what is 'taxing' for a student and pacing the exercises I'm having them do during a lesson is probably the one really strong commonality [in how I teach] all of my students. Something I might ask a student (partly to see if I'm interpreting things correctly) would be along the lines of, 'So, was that really easy for you to play or were there some parts that were difficult that time?' I want them to help identify the bits that need to be worked on. It's an either-or question. Beginning students and those without years of lessons need help with the concept of 'breaking a piece down' when working on it at home. I want them to learn, and I try to coach them through that process of identifying areas that they can improve, and how to go about doing that."

Judging from her account of how she teaches, Maureen is as empathetic a teacher as any clarinet student (or parent of a clarinet student) could ever hope to have. Like most every other autistic person I have gotten to know, she defies the commonly held notion that individuals on the spectrum lack empathy, indeed even a capacity for empathy.

I share my opinion that the whole autistic-people-lack-empathy theory is fallacious and invite Maureen to respond. She basically agrees with me, but with qualifications: "Communicating this empathy or 'over-the-top trying to relate and identify with other people' thing is what is very difficult, and I think that's why we're often perceived as lacking something. There *are* autistic people who do simply lack some basic skills in understanding others. It can be learned, but if an individual isn't properly aware of their own weaknesses (or perceived weaknesses due to a communication issue) they aren't exactly going to improve in that area very much. That's why I really see myself very much as a 'one-on-one' person. I can develop a rapport with someone (student, parent, other musician, etc.) and identify any issues that I may have in being understood."

Maureen provides a personal example of her "over-the-top trying to relate and identify with other people" challenges. As a freshman clarinet student at Carleton, she recounts, "I erred (according to my clarinet teacher) on the side of being (or trying to be) too 'expressive' in my performances. I felt comfortable in front of the audiences, but could sense some of my technique slipping because I was focused perhaps a bit too much on the audience, and on making sure I looked comfortable in front of them." The effort required to "make it look effortless" can confound any elite classical music performer, but for those with an ASC the challenge may be especially daunting.

" . . . As you describe the ways you teach—and learn—clarinet, and 'classical' music generally," I observe a few minutes later in the conversation, "you frequently emphasize how you are detail-oriented, committed to breaking down pieces and problems (technical, musical, etc.) into digestible units, and geared toward a focused and analytical way of thinking and communicating about music. Yet the appeal of playing and dancing West African music/dance for you seems to tap into a very different sensibility—holistic, open to diverse possibilities, driven by feelings rather than analytical processes. Both 'modes' (the analytical one of your 'classical' music persona, the holistic/experiential one of your 'African' music/dance persona) are clearly important, valuable, and *enjoyable* for you. What does each do for you, as it were? And again, to what extent does living with Asperger's influence how and to what extent these different modes take on meaning and significance in your (musical) life?"

"Holy cow! That's a great question," Maureen exclaims, but then confesses that she does not yet feel prepared to address it. "This has been a busy conversation! . . . Can you help start this [new] part of the conversation off?"

"How can I help?"

"I need some speculation to agree or disagree with."

"OK, pause and let me think about that and I'll have it to you in a minute or two."

I begin to type. Maureen does pause patiently for a while, but before I am done there is a ping and a dialogue box appears on the screen. She has placed the text in parentheses, as if to say 'Not to interrupt you, but...': "(Relevant aside: 'Thinking and communicating about music' in the two different modes are very different. In one [classical] this is done explicitly, outside of the music, while with the 'in-the-moment'/experiential stuff [African]—even being 'taught' it (by Kathy, and also by a few Ghanaian teachers she has brought in to our classes)—the communicating about music bit happens through the music itself. The repetition is necessary, and musically—I suppose—ability/skill is acquired before understanding. Experience is a huge part of how the learning process even happens for this style of music-making.)"

As it turns out, Maureen's "relevant aside" is kindred in spirit to the "speculation" prompt she has requested, which I am still in the midst of composing. It is rather long by the time I finally complete and post it.

"It seems to me (i.e., it is my speculation)," I begin, "that for people with Asperger's, life has two 'pulls' that are at once compelling and scary: control and freedom. My research and conversations with folks on the spectrum to date have convinced me that the one is related to the other: that Autistics (again, using the term in a broad sense) tend to see a greater range of possibilities, of permutations and combinations, in any given circumstance or situation than most other people do. The world is endlessly fascinating and full of possibilities and opportunities, but when there is *so* much of all that—and maybe the filters don't work to full potential in terms of prioritizing which of the many interesting things to pursue, to what extent, and in what order—it all can get to be rather overwhelming. Thus comes the impetus to control, to limit, to define parameters in ways that shut out the 'noise' and 'static' of too much input and information. In that mode of being, it is a comfort to *just* concentrate all energy and attention on one subject—be that scalar formations in music or parts in vacuum cleaners; ergo the 'restricted and repetitive interests and patterns of behavior' symptomatic profile [of ASC]."

I'm not done yet. "But there is still that impulse to explore those fascinating and open possibilities that the world presents," I continue, "so that in a context that offers its own limits and parameters, but in ways that facilitate free expression and open exploration (as, for example, West African drumming and dancing do), the experience can be very freeing, liberating, agency-inspiring. This is potentially the case, I think, for just about anyone, but because of the intensity of sensory and intellectual experience that characterizes autistic life, it may be especially true, and intensely and urgently so, for folks on the spectrum. So there's my speculation. Your turn! ☺"

"You have learned and observed very well," Maureen responds.

"Why, thank you!" I reply.

"This is definitely a major 'issue' (or part) of what having Asperger's is like for me. I am pulled in these two different directions. My modes of being can fluctuate between the two styles of having control and experiencing freedom, but I have a hard time (as with any polar opposites) hovering in the middle between them without gravitating toward one extreme or the other at any given time. My 'rigid thinking' is not so much of the 'fixed' variety of rigidity nowadays, as opposed to merely sticking within a certain framework. I don't switch gears all that well (especially when I'm not anticipating having to do so), so keeping to primarily one task or mode of being/thought is easier for me than experiencing too much of a mix of contrasting styles. I'd describe this type of thing quite readily as the 'It's either this or that but hard to be both' mentality (which, as I've just explained, I'm rather susceptible to)."

"Right. I can relate actually!"

Maureen reads between the lines: "Whether you have 'splinter traits' of Autism or not, you certainly interact well with someone who is Autistic and needs a certain type of structure and understanding."

"Probably a combination of 'splinter traits' and having been at this kind of work for a while" is the best I can come up with in response to her kind words. "Again, though, thanks!"

"Where are we going with this dialogue presently? Is there anything you'd like to leave me with to think about?"

"Actually, I'd like you to keep going on this question if you're game, going into more detail on the actual clarinet playing vs. West African dancing/drumming examples specifically. If you are still up for that, let's go with this momentum."

"Alright, I can keep going."

"Great!"

"I do sometimes wish I could—and occasionally try to—play clarinet with the sense of exploration and free discovery of my WARE (West African Rhythm Ensemble) experiences. I'm not able to accomplish this in very many ways—other than 'playing quietly' with finger motions that may not be legitimate fingerings, but which can create intriguing resonance and/or key-stroke sounds on the instrument. I can become engrossed by some 'ostinato'-like patterns of clever finger movements that both feel right and are maybe tricky or fun to do and work out—but then I may become aware that I've been 'goofing off' with my instrument in my hands, at which point I would usually begin to wonder what [it was] I [had] intended to practice when I took out my clarinet and set it up in the first place."

"Aha. Interesting," I interject. " 'Goofing off' vs. 'productive exploration and creativity'!" I want to probe that distinction further but Maureen is already on to something else; we will return to the topic in our next session, however.

"I am not exceptionally skilled at improvising," Maureen continues, "but will occasionally do a bit just for pleasure. For example, I bought a Phyllis Tate piece (it's for clarinet and piano, and has four movements: Prelude, Aria, Interlude, and Finale) a few weeks ago and enjoyed casually sight-reading the Interlude [which has no piano part]. Since it was visually appealing to me—lots of sixteenth notes, staccato marks, a huge variety of accidentals hinting at chromaticism and/or atonality—I chose this move-ment as the one that I would dive into first to have some fun with my new sheet music purchase. Afterwards (i.e., after having done some technical work with the notes in various measures and discovering as best I could what it sounded like at a decent tempo), I spontaneously began improvising in the upper registers because I was enjoying the sound of the quasi-atonal

Interlude. I was intrigued by the sounds and technical challenges. I played some made-up 16th-note runs, strung them together in a way that was based (as I was able to deduce, even though I did not explicitly choose this before playing) on chromatically embellished whole-tone scales, and tried to work in notes and/or trills that had some 'clarinet-specific' feature."

Maureen has been going at a feverish clip for quite a while by this point. Now she takes an extended pause. I wait to see if she's going to continue.

"I'm actually starting to get a little tired with all this writing," she posts finally. "I'm just going to sit here and think for a little while."

"OK. If you are tired, do you want to call it quits for today and pick up again tomorrow, say, at 3:00?"

"Yes, that sounds fine."

"Great. I'll talk to you tomorrow at 3:00. Bye!"

"Thanks; I realize I *am* rather tired and need a break now. Bye!"

CONVERSATION 4: OCTOBER 3, 2014

"Good afternoon, Maureen!"

"Hi! I just logged on. I'm ready to start."

"Great. Let's continue with the whole clarinet vs. African drumming discussion, shall we?"

"OK," she agrees, but she wants some help. "I have a hard time launching in dry, but give me some material to get started and I should be fine."

"Could we pick up from the 'freedom and control' thing I wrote toward the end of yesterday's session, which you seemed to think was a pretty good launch pad for this topic?"

"Sure. Anything more specific?"

"What would be great would be to have you dig in more deeply [using] specific examples from your experiences playing/teaching clarinet, as well as drumming/dancing in your West African classes."

"You'll have to guide me a bit to get me started," Maureen appeals, but then a spark ignites.

"Oh, something came to mind!" she exclaims. "What about the tactile stuff (since it's something that is so often talked about in connection with Autism)? I do have some preferences for the feel of certain things that I have to hold in my hands for long periods of time. I could talk about how I preferred certain drumsticks (ones with a particular 'smoothness' to them, for instance—although not necessarily specific sticks) over others, and how there were one or two particular hand drums that I greatly preferred over the others as well. (I wasn't as fussy about the stick drums.)"[5]

"Yes, please keep going! That sounds interesting."

"Well, when I was in my first year of the Bachelor of Music program (2007–08), Kathy was able to get us new Ghanaian drums (made by a Ghanaian drum maker based in New York, I believe) to replace the old, inauthentic drums Carleton music students had been using prior to that point. The hand drums were the first ones we started using in our class, and I was excited to learn a bit about how they had been made. Since they were still brand new, it was really obvious that the animal hair had been scraped off of the skins on the drumheads, since there were often large patches of brown- and white-colored hair around the rims of the heads. Some drums, in particular, had more or less of this."

"I'm interested to know whether you liked or disliked the feel of the animal fur! ☺"

"Yes, I was getting to that. At first, I was not used to having this hair on the drums at all and didn't know what to make of it (so to say, as I always observe these types of details). Then after some experience playing a lot of our instruments I discovered that it was rather more comfortable to rest my hands on the soft patches [of hair] when we were supposed to be listening [to Kathy rather than drumming]. The hair was very smooth on some drums, especially when it was oriented in one direction (like petting a dog or horse backwards, I suppose). So it was easy to sort of stroke the hair back into its flattened, smooth place if it had been 'rumpled.' I also had a favorite drum that didn't have this hair on it; this drum was a bit larger, but was distinctive because it had what seemed to be a large leaf image on the drumhead (just a peculiarity, I guess). The strings (well, cords; there were others with actual thick, white strings) used on it were small red and yellow ones [that were] used together, and so I liked it at first because it looked different (and was individual like me!). It was also a very comfortable size right where I held it between my lower legs and knees, so I tended to want to pick that drum out [to play] if I could (i.e., if I could get it before one of my classmates did). It was the first drum I distinctly remember having a preference for."

"Interesting, and I like the 'and was individual like me!' reference."

"Perhaps I knew that I would want to have a go-to drum back in first year because familiarity and sameness were so important for me. (I also had a favorite *axatse* [gourd rattle], which I liked because of the shape of the gourd and the length and smoothness of the excess string [on the rattle's beaded netting].) In order to be sure that I could identify the drums I was using for the next time (usually class the following week), I suppose I instinctively wanted to pick something that stood out a bit."

Ergonomic factors were also important to Maureen: "I also wanted a drum that I could lift easily with my legs while playing it (to get a nicer, more resonant sound when playing [strokes on the center of the drumhead]), so I tried to get one—if I had to choose in a moment from some rather unidentifiable drums—that was not too heavy or thick at the bottom. After a while, especially in the second year class, it became apparent that some of us were more or less adept at lifting the drum up for individual center-head strokes. Since I was good at this (as long as the drum fit nicely for me when I sat with it) I wanted to be able to show off just a bit that I had developed an admirable skill(!), but in a subtle way, [so as] to avoid being 'annoying'!"

I am intrigued by the depth of detail in Maureen's report. I have played these same types of drums for many years and can honestly say that virtually nothing she's talking about has ever even crossed my mind. Now, though, it all seems quite fascinating.

Maureen has more to say: "I also liked the contrast in textures between the few drums with plenty of hair on their rims (or even still a bit on their heads) and the smooth, almost waxy feel (I really don't know how to describe what it was like) of those particular drumheads. It annoyed me that one drum that had [a] good contrast of textures (again, for me to feel while we were listening to Kathy but not playing) was not level; it had a dent or dimpled area on the rim of the head, so I kept wanting to rotate the entire drum around to find the spot on the head that I liked best for the actual hand-strokes—and also for resting for long periods between playing (i.e., if we were learning new things or listening a lot)."

" . . . One reason I think I really wanted this sameness in drums from week to week so much during my first year [class]," Maureen reasons, "is that I was trying to be, and usually was, very open about so many other aspects [of the class experience]. This is the 'control' vs. 'freedom' thing. I knew I was trying really hard to enjoy being liberated in our African drumming classes, so I needed something [constant] that I could cling to. . . . It took me many months to be able to just grab my water bottle to drink from [during breaks], as casually and at ease as other students. . . . I also had a (mildly) hard time not standing so rigidly when we had moments just standing around. I needed Kathy to be managing and directing the class at all times, or else I would feel a little awkward or unsure of myself. I never let this show to anyone, though, but perhaps they noticed to some extent that I might have been a little bit of a social outsider (or not a social butterfly, anyway; this *was* the music department!)." I chuckle at the parenthetical remark.

"I tried to make up for feeling just a little uneasy before things officially got underway each class by participating a lot and letting Kathy call on me," Maureen recounts, "and by raising my hand and/or shouting out answers without inhibiting myself that way (as that's how these classes functioned). I really enjoyed doing these things, and had no trouble writing an answer on the board if this was needed for any of the rhythmic dictation exercises. I was also very good at understanding directions for things like dance 'choreographies.' I understood what concentric circles were and things like that (which—being a math student, too—I can't quite see how someone doesn't know something as basic as this. Yet, as I've said, this *was* the 'music world' that I was living in at these times; it seems the 'music' and 'math' worlds could hardly be more different!)."

"So, I'm curious." I type. "Did the 'shouting out answers' tend to go over well with the other students in the class? Or did that sometimes seem to be taken by them as a bit annoying?"

"I can absolutely say I fit in with the answers thing. I certainly couldn't do this in other classes (and sometimes had to hold myself back in my music theory classes), but even in Kathy's classes I didn't do it all that often. I just felt comfortable enough to do this when it seemed right. As for annoying, what was annoying was people idly playing on their drums or other instruments while Kathy was explaining something. That or playing really loudly and being way off!"

"Understood!"

"There were a few students that got called [out] by Kathy more than once [for] that, although I never did. I was very good at following those instructions. I had learned from an earlier age that not 'shutting up' when others wanted you to was rude. I also reacted quickly (intellectually and by enacted response) to instructions. I usually heard the instructions correctly, though sometimes I didn't (especially when it was a detailed explanation of what the supporting drum parts were, or which part of the circle [of drummers, bell players, etc.] was supposed to play what next, or possibly [if I was] being distracted by other stuff in the room), but once I heard the instructions clearly I implemented them pretty well and as accurately as I could. The positive feedback I received from Kathy on several occasions affirmed this."

There is a moment's pause before Maureen resumes typing. "It's weird that I was so good at changing things up frequently in these classes," she reflects. "Maybe the music—and having lots of instruments and/or parts to play (Kathy wanted us to be fluent in all aspects of our pieces)—gave me huge motivation to try doing so many things. I was very eager to try things in general when I started university, but doing too much all at once was still something I avoided (except in the musical context—in terms of African drumming and dancing especially, and clarinet to some extent as well)."

Yet despite her concerns about "doing too much all at once," Maureen did ultimately explore many different kinds of opportunities available to her, and not just in the musical arena: "I tried tons of new stuff (although they were normally very structured things like attending workshops and lectures, and signing up for as many leadership or mentorship programs as I could—not really the stuff other students look forward to when heading to university for the first time!). One way that I could make my 'new beginning' mindset concrete was to jump at new opportunities (although nothing too drastically new at first; I still needed sameness—it's the two 'pulls' again, isn't it?)."

Both literally and figuratively, Maureen jumped highest in West African music and dance, and her willingness to push beyond the comfort zone there spilled over into other areas as well, albeit with some peculiar effects: "I was able to let the sensibility or whatever rub off in my clarinet playing (and many other aspects of my life), but I hid the source of this from my teacher (thinking that it was too weird to say that I had learned anything 'musical' from such a different musical arena! Oh, I could acknowledge it, just not out loud. That's also a very autistic thing, having a large discrepancy between what I think and what I can comfortably say)."

"That's really interesting!!" I exclaim.

"Maybe what I learned was a willingness to be open and to learn in a refreshing way!" she adds, and then, "I want to hear what you have to say now."

"Sure," I say, but I'm not quite ready to close the door on the current topic. "I have some thoughts," I assure Maureen, "but I am really keen to hear more about this comment of yours first." I copy and paste the relevant quote from a few lines up the transcript:

> I was able to let the sensibility or whatever rub off in my clarinet playing . . . but
> I hid the source of this from my teacher (thinking that it was too weird to say
> that I had learned anything 'musical' from such a different musical arena!)

"When I was writing that I was wondering what exactly 'it' was that I was hiding," Maureen reflects.

"Me too! And *why* you felt compelled to hide 'it' as well!"

Maureen explains: "It was hard to identify, and at that point (well, for most of first year) I had not yet told my clarinet teacher about being on the Autism Spectrum. I wasn't sure it was appropriate to discuss 'abstract' stuff in lessons that—as I saw them—were supposed to be very specific and practical, with aims in mind and outcomes (performances, juries, and the like) to 'measure' (however subjectively). The 'Asperger' thing with me that was pretty pronounced then was the whole 'this is what we're doing so this is what we're doing (and nothing else)' sort of thing. Yeah, I'm running out of steam on this train of thought! Now I want to 'listen.'"

"OK, though I think we're just getting to the heart of it, so with your indulgence, I will try to stoke the fire while you rest for a bit."

"Absolutely," Maureen replies.

"OK, rest. This will take me a minute to compose," I write while Maureen takes a breather. "That phrase you used, 'this is what we're doing so this is what we're doing (and nothing else),' is, I think, very illuminating. The kind of focus and discipline that comes with the embrace of such a philosophy has great advantages and merits, of course. It enables people, autistic or otherwise, to really focus in on a task and attend to its deep understanding and mastery, which is great. Indeed, were it not for that quality, I'd venture to say that there would not be very many great artists, mathematicians, scientists, surgeons, plumbers, or computer programmers, etc. Yet that same quality can also be counterproductive. It can limit our willingness—and thus our capacity—to think outside the box (sorry for the cliché!) and also to really *play*, which is something all humans need. It is ironic that we still use the phrase 'playing music' when in so many contexts, certainly in the conservatory/classical environment, so much of what is emphasized is done, to quote you, 'with aims in mind and outcomes to "measure."' Problematic, too, is that most 'therapies' and 'interventions'—musical or otherwise—employed in work with autistic people (usually children) proceed from this same assumption that 'what we are doing,' if it is to have value, is necessarily approached 'with aims in mind and outcomes to "measure."' There is a time and a place for everything, including that kind of approach—in music or in music therapy—but when that becomes the presumed 'best practices' model, it is at best limiting, at worst tragic."

I pause for a moment to plan out where all of this is going. "What I found so exciting about your story," I resume, "is how you gleaned, somewhat explicitly and somewhat implicitly, a sense of how what was imparted to you through the freeing experience of drumming and dancing in a West African–derived framework *did* transfer over into how you were thinking about clarinet playing. I suspect that much of what you learned in the African ensemble context has transferred into other spheres as well, and had a strong influence on what you value as a clarinet teacher, and (I would add) as an autistic self-advocate as well. Now I'll sit back and let you either affirm my hunch or knock it down, probably a bit of each, I suspect!! ☺ "

Maureen has gotten her second wind now: "Well, your whole '*play*' idea I totally agree with. That's a huge part of why I'm so impressed by your ARTISM Project—because what you're doing is something that I simply believe in very firmly, and [yet I] couldn't imagine how it could be contextualized within academia. My [university] clarinet teacher—to my great luck (although I wouldn't have put it that way earlier on)—talked a great deal about *play*ing clarinet and having me *relax* (although with good purpose) and *enjoy* my clarinet playing (for less pedagogical reasons, but because he was a great teacher and great person; he has since moved to New Brunswick, which was disappointing for me, but I digress). His standards were sky-high in terms of the 'conservatory' training-type stuff, and he demanded a great deal of me musically, but he was also happy to chitchat about things outside of my lessons (but not during them, only when I was packing up and whatnot). He would chat with my dad (who often drove me to lessons 40-plus minutes away) about whatever new library book my dad was reading and he was genuinely interested in my math courses, or whatever it was I was doing and learning."

Listening to the second movement of Leonard Bernstein's Sonata for Clarinet and Piano performed by Maureen and her collaborative pianist, Nick Rodgerson, during a 2012 recital leaves no doubt in my mind that she has been the beneficiary of outstanding teaching. A video recording of that performance, filmed by Maureen's brother, Tim Pytlik, may be viewed at the companion website (CW 8.1 ⏵).

"I do know that the first thing my teacher would ask me every week was how my week had been," Maureen continues, "and I had a hard time giving a conversational answer. 'Good. Busy.' and the like were typical answers. He would mildly complain that I was always busy (and that the extent of this wasn't healthy for me), but I think I didn't know how (or rather hadn't expected) to have a conversation that would be cut off as soon as I was set up and ready to start."

Maureen's last remark leads me to reflect on the countless times I have found myself in similar situations, getting into conversations knowing full well that they'll never be completed. I then wonder why I've allowed myself to get into those situations as often as I have, and also why it has never occurred to me until right now that it's actually a pretty weird thing to do.

"Anything else you want to talk about before we sign off, Maureen?"

"Well, I do have more to say about what I like about the philosophy behind ARTISM, mostly based on the way I was raised as a young child."

I'm curious to know more.

"I loved being a child and doing-and-exploring-and-learning all sorts of things!" Maureen exclaims, adding parenthetically, "(I got my own library card a few days after I turned four, and everyone I mention this to is bowled over by how apparently unusual this was. Since I knew how to provide all of the information that would be required to obtain a library card [address, postal code, phone number, and even my parents' names—just in case!] I was allowed to get a card of my own.) My mom was heavily involved in shaping my views when I was young. She's excellent with little children and always treats people (no matter how young or little) as 'intelligent.' I just really love the play-based stuff . . . [especially] physical hands-on toys (which unfortunately are less and less common now, especially as technology 'takes over'). I had tons of educational toys and I loved them! My mom liked that I could keep myself occupied when it was 'nap time,' [that is,] when I was old enough not to want a nap (i.e., four or five or six or whatever), yet she still needed a rest from being worn out by what mothers have to do raising busy kids and running a household. I could play with my toys (and do things sequentially, or whatever it was, particularly for things that came with numbered cards or books or something) and simply sit on my floor doing whatever it was I was busy with. I was good at being busy."

Maureen pauses. I wait for the next dialogue box to appear: "Oh! (for the math people), I even had a toy that taught me binary (0 to 15) when I was two!! (I didn't 'master' it until I was four, but it's still pretty cool that I was learning binary at that young an age!) Both of my parents were computer people."

"Aha, that's interesting (your parents being computer people)."

"Yup, bit of a stereotype there," Maureen notes. "Oh, another thing! My very first music teacher (baby and then infant group classes), who became my brother's (and then my) first piano teacher, had a son who at some point allowed his child's calculator to reach my hands in the 'waiting room' area of his mother's home piano studio. Anyway, so I played with this Texas Instruments calculator while my brother had his piano lesson and loved it so much (it had a handle on top for child-sized hands, and rubbery buttons, which I am still really fond of—[I'm] very annoyed that rubber buttons on calculators have been replaced by plastic ones; yes, I know they last longer but the feel of punching in the rubber ones is irreplaceable!) ... and asked for one of these Texas Instruments calculators for my birthday (again, I believe, my fourth)."

The more Maureen tells me about her upbringing, the more it becomes clear that she enjoyed a happy childhood, and in no small measure because her parents not only supported her "unusual" passions, but celebrated and nurtured them. I tell her that at some future point it would be interesting to talk about how her parents have helped (perhaps also challenged?)

her "abilities to thrive and find comfort in a neurotypical-dominated world such as ours."

"Hey—wait! It's my world too," Maureen fires back. "We all just are different people (some more alike than others) living in the SAME world!! ☺"

I match her smiley-face emoji with a genuine smile of my own. She is so right.

"Yes, it is your world, too," I agree, "and what a perfect place that is to end this dialogue (at least for now)."

"I agree that we've arrived at a good place to end," Maureen affirms, then takes it a step further. "Why don't we actually go ahead and end the entire dialogue now, though? I'm just not sure how you'd like to end this conversation. Is there a final question that you have for me?"

"A final question. Hmm. Well, I wonder if we could kind of return to a question I posed during one of our earlier chats, perhaps prematurely at the time. That was the one where I asked you, if there was one idea, thought, or suggestion you could share with readers, what would it be? You gave an interesting answer the first time, but in light of the way things have developed in these dialogues since then, I'm thinking you might have something else to add along those same lines. Yes?"

"Sure. When you posed this question to me earlier I didn't think I had anything all that important to say. I didn't want my words to be misinterpreted if I attempted to share some kind of profound insight into the effect that music can have on the life of someone with an autism spectrum diagnosis. Now that you've brought us back around to this topic, though, I suppose I could share a thought or two for the sake of our readers who might be hoping to learn something insightful from me."

"Great. Please do!"

"I like sharing and I like being helpful, so part of the reason I like music—and specifically playing the clarinet—is that it allows me to do those things, through performing and teaching. There are non-musical ways that I can share and be helpful too—take my willingness to be interviewed for this project as an example. Music is important but it's not the only thing in my life; yet I will always be a musician. So it is with the role that autism plays in my life. Just because I will always have Asperger's Syndrome (regardless of how this diagnostic term is relabeled in the medical community), that's not to say that it's the only thing that directs my thoughts, ambitions, and behavior. I live and grow and change and focus on different things at different points in my life just like anybody else."

"Beautiful, Maureen. Well spoken! This seems look a good point at which to close. Agreed?"

"Yes."

"OK, then. Bye!"
"OK, signing off. Bye. Thanks!"
"Ditto!"

THE AUTHOR MEETS ACHILLES

March 12, 2016. I am in Ottawa giving the keynote address at a musicology conference at Carleton University. Maureen is in the audience. To see her there as I recite passages from dialogues that we shared months before is almost surreal.

The afternoon is segueing to evening by this time. I have had the pleasure of Maureen's company for most of the day. We have breakfast at a nice little spot around the corner from my hotel, where we meet for the first time and get to know each other face to face rather than just computer to computer. We take a circuitous taxi ride to the university (the driver manages to lose his way somehow, but Maureen sets him straight). I get to hear Maureen present an exceptionally creative conference paper based on her own recent music theory research.

Then, finally, there is my talk. After it's over, I open the floor to discussion and something quite magical happens. The majority of the paper has centered on my dialogues with Maureen. The questions and comments from the audience follow suit. Everyone wants to know more about Maureen's story, and the good news is that she is here to tell it, as only she can. The whole dynamic shifts in a very organic way and soon it is Maureen who is fielding the questions, or else it is her and me riffing on them together, call-and-response style and in sync with the audience. We are grooving, Maureen and I. This is our Gahu, and to make it all the more special, Maureen's teacher and my old friend Kathy Armstrong, whom I haven't seen in thirty years, is also on hand to share in our special moment.

It is the Author who has journeyed to the land of Achilles this time around, and at the fusion of their horizons they have found something like common ground.

NOTES

1. More precisely, Maureen's course of study at Carleton involved the completion of two separate four-year undergraduate degree programs, one in mathematics and the other in music.

2. Girl Guides is a Canadian organization founded on the same model as Girl Scouts in the United States. Both organizations are members of the World Association of Girl Guides and Girl Scouts.
3. Maureen's reference is to Douglas Hofstadter's Pulitzer Prize-winning book *Gödel, Escher, Bach: An Eternal Golden Braid* (Hofstadter 1979).
4. For detailed discussion of Gahu, see David Locke's book *Drum Gahu* (Locke 1987).
5. In the West African styles of drumming that Maureen studied, some drums are played with the palms of the hands only and others with a pair of wooden drum sticks. She refers to the former as hand drums and the latter as stick drums.

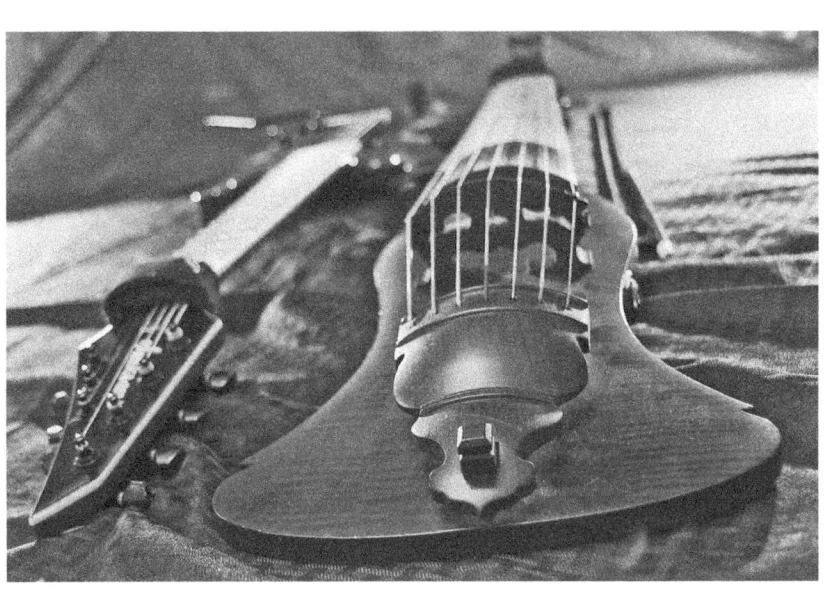

CHAPTER 9
Gordon Peterson

In my mind, there is an impossibly complex web of musical and non-musical cultural connections across time and geographic location. I see a ribbon-like time line in my mind, which curves back and forth, doubling back on itself, curling around at other points, as time is not, in my mind, truly linear, but more like David Tennant's 10th Doctor [Who] says, "wibbly-wobbly, timey-wimey stuff."

Gordon Peterson (2014)

April 22, 2014

Hello, Michael!

It has been such a long time. . . . I just watched your FSU TED Talk on autism and music, and I am thrilled with the work you're doing! Will read your work as soon as time allows (major career change going on right now; was a tenured music professor, but the recession "forced" cuts at my school and I, and four others from the school where we taught, are out on our asses now).

I was diagnosed (finally), at the age of forty-five, with Asperger's. It explains so much, but has been difficult to wrap my head around. It's a correct assessment: I'd been in psychiatric counseling, with disastrous results, for years prior, as Autism Spectrum Conditions (thank you for that change of terminology [from Disorders]) were not even on the radar. This finally has begun to give me the tools I need to cope with my surroundings in a more effective way.

I don't know if you have any interest in applying what you're doing to adults on the Spectrum, but if you [do], I'd love to discuss it with you and see if there might be some way that I would be useful/of assistance. I did what I did, getting a doctorate and spending my life in music, because there is really nothing else I can fixate on like I can with music. It's really all there is... There is so little information, except for Temple Grandin's book [*Thinking in Pictures*] and [a] few other sources, about adults with Autism, especially those like me who are so high-functioning that no-one can tell, until they can and all hell breaks loose. I would love to see what can be done with folks like me, perhaps applying some of the ideas you're using with children...

Anyway, it is so good to see you doing this work (and good to see you on the TED talk!!), and I'd love to keep in touch if you're amenable.

All the best,
Gordon

Talk about out of the blue! An email from Gordon Peterson.[1]

Gordon was part of the first generation of graduate students I ever taught. This was back in my rookie professor days at FSU in the mid-1990s; he may even have been one of the original members of my Balinese gamelan group at the university—I don't recall precisely. Either way, he was there very near the beginning and was one of the best players in the ensemble: a lightning-quick learner, extremely musical, amazing memory and perpetual curiosity.

I liked Gordon a lot. He was funny, smart to the point of brilliant, and self-deprecating. He was also considered a bit odd, not just by me but by pretty much everyone else in the FSU musicology cohort as well. Gordon had a quirky sense of humor and some unusual mannerisms. He could seem fully engaged in a conversation yet "spaced out" at the same time. He was confident and gregarious yet frequently came off as painfully self-conscious. These seeming incongruities were perplexing, at least back then when "Asperger's syndrome" and the "autism spectrum" were not even on my radar.

I get right back to Gordon, explaining that his timing is excellent since my current work is gravitating toward an increased focus on adult autistic musicians like himself. Would he like to be a part of it? Yes, he replies, most definitely. A few weeks later we connect on Hangouts for our first chat.

CONVERSATION 1: JUNE 5, 2014

Gordon is half an hour late for our scheduled 1:00 session. Perhaps he forgot about the appointment. Then, just as I am about to give up and sign off, an email arrives: "I'm just setting [Hangouts] up now, downloading the iPhone app. My computer's in the shop with a bum logic board at the moment, so it's all iPhone for a few days. I'm on now, though! Let's see if this works..."

Moments later, the welcome ping sound chimes and a dialogue box appears on my screen.

"I'm here!" Gordon announces triumphantly.

"Hi Gordon!"

"Hi!"

"So shall we get started?"

"Sure!"

"First, a few questions that may seem odd," I begin, "but which are part of a standard protocol I'm working with."

"Okay. Fire away."

"Do you consider yourself to be an autistic person, an Autistic person, or a person with autism?"

A minute or two passes before Gordon posts a reply: "Hmm. Probably an autistic person."

"OK. Any thought process behind that decision?"

"Well, the capital 'A' indicates a certain dominance in my life, which may be the case, but as I come late to my awareness of my autism, it is not so prominent in my self-identity as of now," he explains. "'A person with autism' takes too long to say," he adds.

"LOL re: 'a person with autism' takes too long to say," I write, only to learn that Gordon wasn't trying to be funny.

"Truth!" Gordon exclaims. "That's what came to mind!"

"Oh, OK." I'm slightly embarrassed. "In a similar vein, do you consider yourself an autistic musician or a musician with autism?"

"A musician with autism," Gordon replies, this time without a moment's hesitation. "That takes too long to say too, but 'autistic musician' indicates to me that my music is directly influenced by my autism, which I'm sure it is. I just don't yet know to what extent... Does that make sense?"

"Absolutely," I affirm. "So, thinking 'out loud,' as it were, what do you think might be some ways in which your music is, or has been, directly influenced by your autism? Feel free to be pretty speculative here!"

"I know for sure that both my total devotion to my study of music, to the exclusion of all other career possibilities, is most likely a product of my autism. My creative process, both in performance (live and in the practice room) and [in] my composition and studio work are strongly influenced both for better *and* worse by it. With live performance, I go into a zone where nothing fazes me. The 'love of my life' broke up with me the morning before a big performance. I was a complete basket case all day... Until I hit the stage and the music started. Then there was nothing else. I played a perfect concert, and then collapsed in a heap when it was over. But I could have gone on all day."

"When I get my momentum going in practice, or composing or mixing in the studio," Gordon continues, "I totally fixate and I'm gone. Don't interrupt me, because it feels like a bomb going off in my head when that concentration gets broken. And it's very upsetting, too, as sometimes, like now, it takes so long to get to the point where I *have* some momentum, that breaking it sets me all the way back to the beginning. My process is too delicate, and requires more consistency . . . than is perhaps appropriate for consistent, reliable creation. When all ducks are in their rows, though, I am definitely in my happy place."

"Wow! Thanks. Another of my 'standard' interview questions, then: If you could wave a magic wand and have your autism be gone—poof, just like that!—would you do that?"

"No," Gordon asserts. "It's my superpower when it's working in my favor. But, if you ever watched the [television] show *Heroes*, every superpower has a 'down side.' I'll take the down side because the good is *so* good..."

I now move gingerly into more personal territory, inquiring about Gordon's parenthetical "was a tenured music professor" reference in his original email. What happened there, I inquire, and was autism a factor?

"Yes. That had everything to do with my autism," Gordon insists. "All the usual stuff: being misunderstood as 'arrogant' (I still don't get that... I try so hard to keep a sense of humility, but people get really pissed at me when I start speaking with any authority) . . . [and being] accused of things I didn't do, which totally sets me off with panic attacks... I had just lost my job and tenure from Whilston College, where I had worked for ten years, bought a house, started a family... It all fell away with the recession. The school cut Music, French, and Religion from the curriculum, and five tenured profs lost their jobs. My wife and I divorced, she took our son, I had to short sell my house, and now this dean in my new job, who had had the job before me and wasn't willing to fully relinquish it, was giving me hell for what my colleagues agreed was nothing. I couldn't handle all that at once. I totally imploded, resigned the post and here I am. Though it was a lot to handle, and even some 'normal' people might have cracked too, I played my situation with a classic autie cut-and-run."

It is a whirlwind of information. I try to process everything that Gordon has just shared but can't quite figure out how to connect the dots. I need more context.

"Double-wow! So clarify the timeline. You taught at Whilston College for ten years, were tenured there, then they cut your entire program so you lost your tenured job? Then you got another teaching position (where?) and that's the one where you think your autism caused problems that led to your dismissal? I'm just trying to get the facts straight here. . . ."

"Yes," Gordon confirms. "I was hired at Whilston in 2001 and taught there until 2011. I was tenured in 2008. The geniuses in Finance had the school's entire endowment in the stock market and we lost it all. They cut programs in 2010, and we were given the 2010–2011 academic year to continue working while we searched for new jobs, or retired. I got hired in early 2011 by Stonehurst University in St. Louis.[2] It is their policy not to hire with tenure, and since they were my only option, I accepted the job and lost my tenure. The new job was tenure track, though, and they put me on a three-year contract to earn it back. And that didn't work out so well. The 2012–2013 school year was mostly spent on disability leave after totally melting down from a completely unnecessary bad evaluation. I had never had a bad evaluation in my career up to that point."

I interject once again to ensure I am getting my facts straight: "Two questions: Were these musicology positions (if not, in what field)? What was the diagnosed condition leading to the disability leave?"

"These were generalist positions. Both [schools] were small liberal arts colleges where I more or less did everything. My terminal degree is a [doctorate in Early Music]. The [ASD] diagnosis definitely played a part in [my] leaving Stonehurst. My autism therapist and my regular counselor were both adamant that I get out of that work environment, and the overwhelming nature of the situation led me to follow pretty much any advice they gave. I wasn't in much of a place to think well for myself."

"Makes sense," I type. "So how did that all go down sequentially? First, the crisis at work, that led you to seek counseling, that led (eventually? quickly?) to the diagnosis of Asperger's?"

"Well, I've been in counseling most of my life, especially during crises. Always the therapists had missed the mark on what they thought was 'wrong' with me, so I was going anyway. It just so happened that, when things started falling apart at Stonehurst, that the counselor I was seeing, trying to cope with this latest crisis, made the diagnosis (Fall 2012). For the first time *ever*, I felt the correctness of the diagnosis. It was confirmed by an autism specialist within a month of the initial diagnosis. And the diagnosis is Asperger's."

"Ah, OK. That all makes sense. So just a little more on this personal history then we'll move on to more fun stuff, OK?"

"Okay! I have to go in about half an hour. I'm squeezing out a living teaching private [music] lessons right now."

"This might be difficult to do, but I'd like for you to retrace the steps of your life back to when you first started having whatever kinds of issues/challenges/problems/skills/gifts/attributes you now attribute to Asperger's, then chronicle the progression of your life through that lens up to the diagnosis and beyond that to the present. That might eat up your half hour right there!"

"Wow! Yeah… That's kind of what I'm doing all the time now as I start to understand the patterns of my life better…"

Gordon takes several minutes to compose his response. "I have always had problems socially. Always," he complains. "People love me one minute and hate me the next and I've never had a clue as to why or wherefore. Always takes me completely by surprise. It takes me a *long* time (and always has) to learn the 'rules' of any social group that I'm in. When I'm interested in something, there is nothing else. I have always sensed that there have been 'two of me…' One that is rational and can objectively observe even myself. Then there's 'Him,' this guy with a brilliant, insightful mind and exciting imagination that does *whatever he wants*, reacts however he wants, and there is almost nothing the other me can do about it. My whole college life: I was just doing what needed to be done, good decision or bad didn't matter. It just had to be done. That's it. That's definitely the Aspie guy. Been that way all my life, never understood until recently why."

"When I get it in mind to do something, though, there's no stopping it," Gordon proclaims. "I also have an ability to see subtle patterns in all sorts of things, though mostly in my chosen field [of music], that very few people I've met pick up on. It made for some great grad papers. There's more, but I'll have to include it later. I'm afraid I'm going to have to [go]… I'm sorry… Gotta make that money…"

"Absolutely! Far be it from me to stand in your way doing that!! Bye! Thanks!"

"Thank you!"

We plan a second session for four days later and sign off.

CONVERSATION 2: JUNE 9, 2014

Today we are right on schedule.

"Hi! I'm here!" Gordon announces at precisely 1:30 p.m.

"Hi, Gordon. So am I!"

"Fine coincidence!" he jokes. "Hope you had a good weekend!"

"I did. You?"

"Yup. Gigs and some moving done. And some relaxing too."

"What kind of gigs?" I inquire.

"Electric viola da gamba in a trio with keyboards and drums, and electric bass in a Country/Rock band. Giggin' for a living… sort of…"

I'm eager to know more—an electric gamba trio is certainly not something one hears about every day—but I resist the urge to ask, at least for now. There is still some unfinished business from our last session.

". . . So I want to dig a bit deeper into the 'autistic' aspects of your musicality/musicianship," I begin. "You've already articulated how the intense focus you have—non-distractibility, singular attention to the particular project you're engaged in—has been a great advantage to you musically, that it's enabled you to achieve much of what you have. But what about the actual way you make music and the ways you think about music? What do you regard as distinctively 'autistic' about those, for better or for worse? You alluded to a couple of things last time, something about attention to patterns within the music that others might not recognize/create, but I'd like a much deeper foray into your auto-ethnographic perspective on how you make and perceive music in a distinctly 'autistic/Aspergersy' way. Just as a frame, I define *ethnomusicology* as 'the study of how people make and experience music, and of why it matters to them that they do.' I'm basically interested in how you conceive of yourself in such terms!"

"I guess I'd have to start with the singular nature that music possesses in my life," Gordon posts about three minutes later; he has been thinking—and typing. "It starts with the way I came to study music and orient myself toward becoming a musician to begin with; it seemed to happen on its own, as I'm discovering that this is the way that the Aspie elements of my personality behave. I believe I indicated last time that I often have the sense that there are 'two of me.' The Aspie-me does what it wants, and there is not much the more rational, 'normal' side of me can do about it, try as I have my entire life. There's just a part of me that will be what it will be, and that is that. For better or for worse, the Aspie-me is the one that holds the reins. The 'normal' me can only advise, sit and watch, and all too often plant its face in its palm. If Aspie-me isn't happy, ain't nobody happy."

"So as I left the safety of childhood/adolescence and had to make the jarring change into choosing a life-path," Gordon recalls, "the only one that made any sense was music: music was the lens through which I had always viewed the world. Each event/period in my life had been marked by the music I was hearing at the time. Music has the same ability to stimulate recall for me that smell has for everyone who can smell. I formed my identity around music—what I liked, what I listened to—far more than anything else."

That cultivated musical identity worked out well, at least for a while. "So when I oriented my life toward music as a vocation," Gordon reminisces, "I blossomed academically and socially for the first time ever. I was totally mediocre in public school, [but] in college, I graduated near the top of my class. I was hyper-focused and lived the study I was doing. The only time I ever got less than an A-minus in a class was in the first semester in a new school. It takes me a good while to adjust to new surroundings, and that adjustment period is very disruptive to everything I'm trying to do. There is a lot of wailing and gnashing of teeth when I have to uproot, even if the move is a good one. So I guess the first way in which my musicianship is affected by my Asperger's is in the total fixation I have on the art form generally. I have no active non-musical hobbies, for instance. I don't do anything else!"

"Next," Gordon adds, "I'd have to say that my music is affected by my Asperger's in that I have my own way of doing things... I mean: electric viola da gamba, eh? I deliberately set out in my education to learn as much about 'the rules' as I could so that I would be able to break those rules with impunity, as I knew I would. I just can't do some things the way others do... I see or hear another way." Gordon's recording of an original song of his, "Sisyphus," offers a striking example of his maverick musical approach. It may be heard at the companion website (CW 9.1 ▶).

Gordon now moves on to an enlightening discussion of the integral links that exist between his musical and intellectual pursuits. He introduces a topic, the "web of connections" that exists in his mind, to which he will later return: "As I was studying musicology, I came to the conclusion that I wanted the concepts I was learning to influence the sound I made; that the scholarship, for me at least, should be practical. From that point, I began to create a web of connections in music through history and around the world, a web that I will try to explain at some point, but it might take a book to do so. It's a web of aural symbols and signifiers, both ancient and new, that I try now to weave into my own compositions and performances. Everything I've heard that I found notable has woven itself into that web. I have a visual picture of it in my head, but I can't draw well enough to replicate it. There's more I can say... am I answering the question?"

"You're starting to," I reply as my fascination grows. "Keep going!"

"If you've ever seen the Temple Grandin film[3]—the way she visualizes the patterns of cattle movement. . . . I have those same kinds of visuals in my head about music through history and as one moves around the world."

I wait, expecting more on the topic, but there is only radio silence—no dancing dots or bubbly sounds. I attempt a motivational prompt: "OK. Please elaborate. This is exactly the kind of thing I'm interested in. I'm tired of hearing about 'how autistic people think about music' from people who aren't autistic. We need people who are [on the spectrum] to speak for themselves, so go at it, man!"

"Wow. Okay. I've never really tried to explain it before, mostly because explaining it seems awfully daunting... but here goes..."

"Great."

"First of all, I 'think' about music with my whole body. I think it and feel it, and there's no difference between thinking and feeling. Next comes the dependence of music on language and vice-versa (a chicken-and-egg thing, I think). Man, this is going to come out so disconnected at first... I'm really sorry..."

No need to apologize, I assure Gordon. To me, it is not coming out disconnected at all. I am intrigued.

"An ah-hah moment for me was in gamelan with you at FSU, when I heard the names of the instruments and realized that the whole Balinese language sounded like gongs," Gordon recalls. Well, not the *whole* language, I am tempted to correct him, but I wisely resist the urge. "No *wonder* metallophones were the instruments of choice! Or did the sound of the music influence the sounds in the language? No matter, they're intimately connected. Even in European musics, French music sounds French, Italian music sounds Italian... etc., because it's connected to the language and speech rhythm."

"That's why serialism never took with the general public," Gordon suggests. "It was too removed from speech patterns to mean anything to average listeners. Hang on a sec... distressed twenty-year-old kitty... gotta see what's up..."

"OK. Let me know when you return."

A few minutes go by as Gordon tends to his cat.

"I'm back," he informs me. "He got out into the hallway (I'm in a duplex) and got disoriented. He's fine now. Poor little guy."

"Oh, glad he's OK and back."

There is another long pause. I wonder if there are more problems with the cat, but it turns out Gordon has just been reading back through the transcript.

"Okay. I just reread what I wrote and it's not yet communicating what I see/hear/feel...," he reports. "It's just barely scratching the surface."

"Well, there are a couple ways we could go with this," I propose. "You could either continue to write now, or we could go on to some other topics and questions, and you could write up the whole thing about how music works for you and vice-versa later, in an email, and send it to me. Also, keep in mind that we can edit whatever we do here, so you needn't be intimidated to think that 'Oh, if I write it in this chat, it will be published exactly that way.' I'll give you the chance to give feedback on the transcript after the fact. How do you want to go?"

"Let's go on to some other questions, and I'd like to take some time to think and really formulate clear thoughts on this. The web is really complex, and I hardly know where to begin. Oh, and by the way, I was going to say earlier (before the cat got out) that I'm known, among those who know me, for accompanying particularly well, as I often seem to know what others are going to do before they do it, and I'm right there with them. Drummers like me because of that..."

"Yes, as a drummer I can say that we would, ☺" I respond. "So, are there ways in which your Asperger's has hindered you as a musician too? So far, it sounds like it's mainly been a plus."

"Yes, there are ways that it's hindered me," Gordon notes. "They are the same ways that it's hindered me in other aspects of my life—social interaction. I've been fired from, or have left, more bands than I can count. I have had to learn to keep my mouth shut, and speak about music only when spoken to, as I usually know more about, or at least have more opinions about, what's going on musically than most others in the room. So often, as with a great blues band I was playing with, I'll be hired very enthusiastically, and then one day (or so it seems to me), all of a sudden, I'm a piece of shit and I'm out of the band. I have no idea why, except that it's just the way it goes when you're wired all funny. . . . Also, because conditions *must be just so* in order for my creativity to flow, I have very long dry spells, creatively. I want very much to compose professionally, for instance, but my life has been so chaotic these last years that I cannot create consistently. *Very* frustrating. I spend more time getting things *just so* than I do getting things done."

"So about the getting fired unexpectedly thing: you say you have no idea why, but since receiving the diagnosis, have you tried retracing your steps, as it were, to see if there are patterns in your behavior that may account for these difficulties?"

"Yes. I am doing a lot of retracing these days. I've only known I'm Aspie for a year and a half. It has totally reframed many events in my life that had previously left me very confused... With regards to Asperger's contributing to what might otherwise appear to be simple writer's block: [I'm] thinking... I italicized the 'things have to be just so' [line] because they do... I can perform [live] under almost any circumstances: I just go into my happy place and there's nothing else. But the creative process in the studio is very different: I have to have long blocks of uninterrupted time, time I *know* is not going to be interrupted. If I even suspect that I might not be able to complete my thought, I can't even get started. I can't *make* myself get started... Maybe that sounds normal . . . but I know that it's the 'Aspie-me' that's active when I can't make myself do things. I don't know how else to explain it... I just know that it's that bit of me that's in charge, and there's no remedy until it decides it's ready to move on. Living in a world that is so hard to understand, where interactions with people are always a crap shoot as I never know if I'm behaving 'correctly' or not, safety, or the perception of being safe, is an overwhelming need. Threat of interruption plays on my sense of not being safe... and interruption can cause a panic attack (and has on many an occasion)."

"That's deep," I say, "and really gets at a core issue of autistic experience re: safety/anxiety. A thread we can continue next time, since today it's I who has to leave. I'm three minutes late for my next appointment. Sorry."

"No problem. I'll be thinking and writing about my 'web' in the meantime."

We arrange to meet again on Friday.

"Bye, and thanks!" I conclude. "Send the 'web' thing along sometime between now and Friday if you get to it. I'm excited to see what's going on in that amazing mind of yours!"

CONVERSATION 3: JUNE 13, 2014

Gordon has completed "a considered response to the questions from last time" and emailed it to me.

"Did you get it?" he inquires.

"I just saw the email and am going to open it, paste it in here, and read it; then we can continue with the conversation, OK? Give me a few minutes while I do all of that."

"Okay!"

I open Gordon's email. The length is impressive at more than 1,500 words, a veritable essay; the writing is even more impressive. Gordon has written a poignant and deeply introspective autobiographical memoir of living with Asperger's, and of living with music.

"I've been thinking a lot about your questions regarding how my ASD affects my music," he begins. "After all this pondering, I have reached the conclusion that I don't think it really does affect it; not the final product, anyway. I don't believe that ASD is at all apparent in the music itself."

"What ASD does affect is my process," Gordon asserts, "and it affects everything, for better, but mostly for worse. And the more I think about how it affects my process, the more I revisit the question you asked at first, which is if there was a magic wand that could make ASD disappear, would I want it gone. My new answer is yes, I would want it gone. I think it may be much more trouble than it's worth." Next, Gordon ventures inward: "In my mind, there is an impossibly complex web of musical and non-musical cultural connections across time and geographic location. I see a ribbon-like time line in my mind, which curves back and forth, doubling back on itself, curling around at other points, as time is not, in my mind, truly linear, but more like David Tennant's 10th Doctor [Who] says, 'wibbly-wobbly, timey-wimey stuff.' The ribbon stretches back from today all the way to the beginning of recorded history, and before. There aren't hash marks to note the dates, but the dates hover above general areas of the line, and the side of the ribbon looks like a window, where I see the movers and shakers of the times (that I know of), the way people looked, their food... everything I know about the culture appears through that window, encompassing a day in the life of that era. Each window (though they're continuous and one blurs into the next) can be entered like a portal to that time, and I can walk around in it, looking at the instruments, hearing the sounds, hearing the language... if I go deep enough, it's like I'm there."

"But that's all in my mind...," Gordon laments. "It means nothing to anyone that can't get inside my head with me. I draw on this time-ribbon all the time... it's where everything musical, creative, or scholarly comes from. The part of my mind that houses it is the ASD portion of me (there is a portion that's not ASD, that's quite normal, in fact. It just has little control over the ASD side. It's more of an observer. I've already told you about it). But it's where my ideas for original music come from, it's where I go when interpreting other music... it's where I live. But what difference does it make? Other non-ASD artists have their places they go to get what they need to create, other ways of organizing their inspiration and knowledge. I guess I say that because I love what's in my head... it's an exciting, magical place that amazes me whenever I think about it or spend time there. The contents of that ribbon are so beautiful and highly detailed, and I can get to feeling kind of 'special' about it all. But the fact of the matter is that it's only special to me. I can't possibly explain it to you in the detail I'd like. Even if I could, turning that vision into words only detracts from the power and beauty that I perceive in it... trying to tell someone else what it's like doesn't measure up, not even close, to what it's really like. And as for the product I produce using it? Well, I live in poverty and obscurity, so I guess it's not translating to the 'real world' very well. So, at least as of today, I don't see that it's a useful or desirable ability outside of keeping my own head entertained. Not quite the superpower I would like it to be."

"ASD is also a major stumbling block in my professional and personal life... oh hell, life in general," Gordon acknowledges. "My inability to maintain good relationships, the way everything *has* to be before anything can be done... if something is done out of 'order' I get disoriented at best, totally panicked at worst... I've spent more time trying to create the necessary conditions for consistent production and creation than I have actually producing or creating. I hate that. When I'm on a roll, there's no stopping me, and I think the product I'm able to produce is unique and very good... I base this on actual feedback. My compositions, what few of them actually have been finished, do, I think, sound as I want them to, and are different than anything else out there... but what's unique about that? Of course they're different. Everyone's music is different from everyone else's, even if there are similarities. I don't play my own stuff out much. Why? I don't know exactly, but I do know that it's something in the ASD brain that keeps me from pursuing it..."

"My biggest ASD-based problem with production of any kind is momentum," Gordon explains. "It takes me FOREVER to get the 'speed' up to write, produce, practice regularly... anything that a good musician should be doing. Once my routine has been broken, I cannot repair it and have to create a new one. I can't tell you how many years I must have lost in this process. Once it's going, though, I experience a usually short-lived bump in creative output until the next external influence comes along to interrupt me and break my stride. Once that happens, practice routines fall away, composition becomes blocked, and I become very depressed. I've set my life up so there is constant musical activity occurring regardless of whether my own routines are in place or not, so I have external motivators that keep me from losing too much time or skill, but I always feel like I'm starting over. This has been a particularly bad problem since the end of my academic career last year.

"Rudderlessness, which is what I'm experiencing right now (I don't know how to be anything other than what I was when I was professor. When I stop and think about it, I have been on one side of the podium or the other since I was five years old... I can't even conceive of anything outside what I was doing... I have NO IDEA where to go from here... totally lost), is just the worst. I need to create routines and 'proper parameters' for my work, but if I have no idea what my goals are, I don't know how to set up the routines... routines for what? To go where? In what time frame? I don't know, so I languish and piss about trying to find SOMETHING to latch onto and get going again.

"But I don't even know what I'm looking for... That's why my bliss was in school, doing my degrees. Such tidy short-term goals (absorb the material and own it, write the paper, get the grade, get an A in the class), and achievable long-term goals (finish all the courses and get the degree). So few variables, and the longest-term goal of employment and work being something that was 'for later.' When I did get my job at Whilston, the nature and culture of the school allowed that kind of safety to continue on. Though I had some terrible experiences with my immediate colleagues, because they'd given other people terrible problems too, no-one paid much attention and I earned tenure anyway, over their objections. I've been very lucky until recently, as I need a more sheltered environment than some, and I got it. It's gone now, but I sure was lucky to have it. My home life sucked, though, and was chock full of stupid interruptions and an uncooperative, insensitive spouse, and I couldn't get my 'routine' together because of that. I got it going a few times, and made huge strides when I did, but it wasn't until she was gone that I was able to get anything rolling creatively."

At the close, Gordon's tone brightens, at least a bit. "I think one of the positive effects of my ASD is my ability to compartmentalize," he writes. "It's why I can go on stage in the midst of a total life crisis and not be affected by it. The second I set foot on a stage, whether it's a literal stage or just standing in front of a lot of people, a switch gets flipped and I'm a different person. I don't even try, it just happens. I'm 'on,' and I do my job. Then, when it's over, all the anxieties and Aspie crap all come back. But for those brief, shining hours I can function without questioning whether I'm doing the right thing... I am confident in and know my work as a performer, and that comes through when I play. I attribute that to the 'superpower' aspect of my ASD. That's as good as it gets, though."

The piece ends on a somewhat ambivalent note. "All the downsides listed above still apply," Gordon concedes, adding, "I'm really not so sure now that ASD is something I'd want to keep if I had a choice..."

I marvel at what Gordon has shared with me.

"That's deep stuff, and beautifully written," I write. "Thank you for your candor and honesty."

"Of course! That's what a proper study needs, eh? ☺" he replies. "I realized upon re-reading that [it] may seem like there are a few contradictions in there... I'm happy to straighten those out if there's any confusion."

"Actually," I note, "I think the contradictions are the exception that makes the rule. The further I go into this work, the more it is evident that contradiction is the new normal of ASC." It's a missed opportunity for me. Why not just leave space for Gordon to unravel his *own* contradictions? But I'm lucky, as Gordon manages to turn my potentially flow-killing remark into a revealing opening.

"Ah! That is interesting!" he comments. "I've kind of felt that, whenever I try to explain and the contradictions appear, that the contradictions aren't really contradictions... they exist because two opposing... things... (stupid, can't-think-of-the-word... stuff...) *can* and *do* exist in my mind, and make perfect sense. It's why I'm a Buddhist... Opposites are just two sides of the same thing, not necessarily contradictory. Does that make sense? I'm meaning to agree with you... ☺."

"It makes great sense, Gordon, and I totally agree. So having said I'm OK with the 'contradictions' you recognize in your own mini-essay, I think I will probe more deeply into some aspects of them. You state forthrightly at the beginning that you've changed your thinking re: my earlier 'magic wand' question and would now be willing to wave it and get rid of the pesky ASC part of you. By the end, though, I'm not so sure you really would, as you do come around to saying that the ASC part of you is where the magic and inspiration lives. This is a fascinating quandary (for anyone not living it!). I have sometimes been of the view that, say, with many artists, or creative types generally, there's a kind of all-or-nothing package deal aspect to what you get—great ideas, imagination, depression, autism, ADHD, great focus and discipline. Some weird combination of any or all of these qualities; you can't take any of them out of your shopping cart and the dark aspects are kind of the price you pay for the magic. [Then there's another part of me that] has no patience or use whatsoever for the whole 'tortured genius' mythology and thinks that giving people the opportunity to be happy and able to function well—whether with the aid of medications, therapy, medical interventions, or what have you—is well worth whatever 'cost' it might carry in terms of diminishing a person's creative brilliance. I must admit that initially I was very skeptical of [the latter] view, but over the past few years I have gravitated more towards it (though I'm not entirely there). I'm not sure that this is exactly a question, but the thought was brought to mind when reading your discussion of your process and feelings about it."

"I've been on some of those medications," Gordon shares, "and have spent the better part of my life trying to mitigate the 'down side.' It doesn't work (for me). Whether it's because of a unique ASD brain chemistry or not, antidepressants make me suicidal. All of 'em. Anti-anxieties are great for short-term, need-to-not-be-freaked-out-right-now situations, but I've been on one Rx for three years now and it is *seriously* messing with my head. I'm stepping down off it now, hoping to find that I'm still here and haven't been too damaged by it, but the step-down is a bitch. They say it's a harder drug to kick than heroin. Never done heroin, but this sucks and I believe it."

"Anyway," Gordon continues in this somber vein, "this is to say that I have found absolutely *no* help from counseling or psychiatry. For Pete's sake, it took them until I was forty-five to even begin to think I might be on the Spectrum!! And then they can only deal with the symptoms, and when I take meds I lose creativity. When I lose creativity, I become more depressed; despondent even, which seems to defeat the purpose. So, to try to make sense of the contradiction, let's see if this works: in my case, I think ASD causes more problems than it solves. The 'superpowers' I gain from it aren't particularly useful ones (if only I could have fixated on software development or finance... but *nooooo*.... I have to fixate on music at a time when it's become so devalued in my culture that the likelihood of making a living at it is lower than at almost any other time in history), and the time I *have* to take to 'prepare' and 'create routines' is much greater than the time I actually get to spend doing what I love to do, and then the routine gets broken all too easily and I have to start all over again. Tortured artist? You bet. Self-torture for sure, and I can't seem to stop it. It just keeps going round and round."

There is that other side, though, and Gordon goes there next. "But I've experienced the *up* side, and it is magnificent!" he exclaims. "So, having experienced it, I want to experience it again... I am compelled to experience it again. I don't want meds to kill it... I don't want the psychiatrist's idea of a 'happy life.' Seems like bullshit to me anyway. Who *really* has a happy life? So I have to deal with this thing. The artificial happy is not an acceptable alternative. So I guess we can consider my relationship with ASD as one of the Love/Hate variety. The good in this, though, is that I've only recently become aware that ASD is the issue, *not* the depression and anxiety, which are only symptoms. I am learning skills to mitigate the down-side, and I may yet prevail. Some positive life-changes are coming soon, including a move into my gf's house, where I should be much 'safer' (living alone does not, I have found, work at all). She knows more about my condition than I do, and does her best to help when the going gets weird."

I ask Gordon to translate "my gf's house." "My girlfriend's house," he clarifies.

By this point, there have been references to several romantic partners and I want to make sure I have the story straight. "So thus far," I write, "you've alluded to three major romantic relationships: the 'love of your life' who dumped you in your time of greatest need, your wife who was an unsupportive partner, and your current girlfriend who sounds great and knows more about your condition than you do. Are those the 'big three' thus far in your life? Could you elaborate a bit on each of the people/relationships; how, if at all, do you feel your ASC contributed to what happened (good or bad), and why does your current gf know so much about autism?"

A couple of minutes pass before Gordon begins typing his reply. "I'm processing what has happened in past relationships these days," he finally posts. "ASC has had everything to do with the failure of every single relationship I've been in up to the current one, even though my relationships have generally lasted no less than a year. The 'Big Three' you mention is probably a good term for the current mode of thought. A marriage is a pretty big deal, and mine lasted for ten years. Well, it lasted for four years and deteriorated for six. My ex-wife is a Japanese national, and very provincial in her attitudes, as I've come to understand from other Japanese who have spoken to me since our divorce. She had very strict, yet unspoken, codes of behavioral expectations for me which I could not live up to. That being said, she didn't live up to mine either. Long before the ASC diagnosis, I've known that I've needed lots of quiet alone time, not to be interrupted when working. I've had panic attacks (that I didn't know were panic attacks at the time), sometimes publicly which is always embarrassing, sudden, explosive reactions I couldn't prevent to things she'd say or do... many of the typical ASC things... and she would come down on me so hard for those. No willingness to even try to understand why I couldn't stop these behaviors, no respect for my needs for privacy (why would she? There *is* no privacy in a Japanese household)... marrying her was just a naïve, bad life choice. Our son... I see him on Skype maybe once a week for 15 minutes, maybe an hour. I haven't seen him in person for over two years, as his mother will not bring him to where I live, and I have no money to travel. She takes him to Japan every year though. Yeah."

Another long pause. I can only imagine how difficult this must be for Gordon to write.

"I don't really want to talk much about the last gf, the 'love of my life...,'" he continues eventually. "She tried, and I never saw the beginning or end coming... it was all a rush and a whirlwind. She was very young (as I am in my mind, so I don't see the importance of such differences) and it just all fell apart. Bygones. Jenna [pseudonym], the lady I'm moving in with, knows more about ASC [than I do] because when we started dating she started reading. She recognizes, embraces, and *wants* to help with ASC-related difficulties. As we talk about the move, she often brings up how such-and-such might affect my ability to do so-and-so with respect to ASC, how we can keep me calm, focused and on task. She is respectful of my personal space and time, doesn't push me in ways she's read ASC folks don't like to be pushed (and she's usually right), and very, very patient. Got me a keeper here, I reckon. I hope so, anyway. I think this relationship stands a better chance than anything previous because I am now aware of my ASC and can deal with issues accordingly. She knows about it and can do the same. Time will tell, but I think this is the winning combination that has been lacking in every other relationship."

"Just one clarification," I request. "'Love of life' gf was before or after the marriage?"

"After the marriage," Gordon tells me.

"Okay, thanks. So Jenna sounds fantastic, and it sounds like you're primed to move into the good neighborhood of life. For a thoughtful person such as yourself, the value of being able to excavate cause-and-effect in your life 'til now through the lens of your (still very new!) diagnosis should provide more peace of mind than anything else imaginable; add to that a supportive partner who seems committed to taking the journey with you and you have a winning situation in the making."

At this point, I shift the topic: "So I want to go back to something you said earlier, the 'tortured artist, you bet—self-torture, to be sure' reference. I think you give yourself too little (or too much?) credit there. You were a tenured professor in a job you loved that had the rug pulled out from under him, you had a serious condition that had been misdiagnosed and misunderstood your whole life, you were being treated for problems that—as you aptly recognize—were symptoms rather than causes of your [real] problems. That's a lot of 'torture' coming from the outside; you can't claim to have done it all on your own. ☺ It's all going to get a lot better. . . ."

"Thank you!!" Gordon exclaims, seemingly glad to have received this vote of confidence. "These last years have been unbelievably difficult and disorienting. I have to remind my own family that I was, at one point, successful (tenure!), and that I haven't been a failure my whole life. In fact, I wasn't a failure at all until the recession hit. I may still not be one, but from childhood my family expected I wouldn't become much. There's some baggage there, and I tend to blame myself."

"Why the low expectations from your family," I ask, "and are they supportive now?"

"The first part of that question is pretty involved. I was born after my parents had already raised four kids. My next sibling up is seventeen years older than I, and in the year after I was born my second-oldest sibling died in a Vietnam-related helicopter crash. He was in the Navy. My siblings do not hold my mother, in particular, in very high regard, and they seem to have had a pretty rough time growing up because of her. She and I are close like crazy, and they see that as her having completely taken control of my life. They figured I wouldn't be able to handle life away from home. The situation I'm in now is 'proving' that to them, as I require financial assistance from my family right now... I'm not making it on my own."

"What they fail (or refuse?) to recognize," Gordon continues, "is the success I *did* have, and they don't see the outside factors as really being factors. They've all been very successful in their lives; my oldest brother invented the magnetic strip on the back of your credit card, and the hard drive in your computer (I saw the prototypes back in the 70's when he took my parents and me on a tour of the company he was working for).

My youngest brother, who refuses to speak to me now because I had a panic attack he didn't like, got amazingly lucky when he rode a chairlift up a mountain with a guy who asked him to do some P.I. [private investigative] work for a ski area law suit. He's made millions in the decades since that and lives in a gorgeous house he built in the Sierra Nevada near Lake Tahoe. My sister hasn't done so well, but still has raised a family, has grandkids, and lives in the very nice house she and her husband built thirty-five years ago."

Gordon's bitterness toward his "very successful" siblings, or at least his two older brothers, ramps up as he fleshes out his story. "Never once did anyone come to visit me while I was successfully pursuing my career," he complains. "Nobody saw it, so it doesn't exist. I was born to fail, and that's what they see happening now. The bro who isn't talking to me gives no credence to my ASC [diagnosis] and thinks I should be locked away in a mental hospital. My oldest brother is kinda catching on now, as my sister is *very* supportive (she worked with Autism Spectrum kids when she ran a Sylvan learning center), and she's been trying to change the general perception of me. My ASC counselor even suggested that, if my mother *did* treat me badly, I am unaware of it possibly due to my ASC and the fact that I wouldn't recognize bad treatment from her if it kicked me in the shins and said so. So many social cues and subtle things people say and do to me get missed completely that this is not out of the question. It's very likely that I turned out just fine, [at least] undamaged in the way they imagine, but they're so convinced that I *have* to be damaged because they are... well, you see where I'm going..."

"But as far as you are concerned," I inquire, "your mother is and always has been loving and supportive (both emotionally and economically)?"

"Yes. Absolutely. She has a very hard time with the ASC 'label,' but she's trying."

"Where's dad in all of this?" I ask. "You haven't mentioned him."

"My dad is probably the genetic wellspring from which my [autism spectrum] condition flows. He is a wonderful, kind, compassionate, and completely uninvolved individual whose sole mission in life since he got married to my mom is to stay the hell out of her way. He has done very well with that, but in so doing has not been very fatherly. He's the nice guy in the recliner watching the news. And the guy I went camping and on day trips with. I love him to death, but hardly know him. That doesn't bother me... I understand, and in 'not knowing him,' I think I know him pretty well. My sibs *are* bothered by that, though... They have very baby-boomer expectations of our parents, if that makes sense. I don't share those expectations at all."

"Acceptance is a virtue," I opine. "Gotta meet people where they are before inviting them over to wherever you think they could or should be."

"My thoughts exactly," Gordon affirms. "The sibs all want our parents to be what *they* want them to be. So [they essentially] do the same to me that they do to my parents, it seems. I accept [my parents] on their own terms, for who they are; the way I like to be treated."

"Good for you, and that might be one of the 'pluses' of your ASC," I speculate, "—being able to do that and recognize the value of doing so."

"Yes. I believe that is true, and it's something that I have thought about," Gordon relates. "I do feel that my own experience has made me much more receptive to others' differences. When I was at Whilston, I was actually known among the students as someone they could talk to about anything and not be judged, merely advised, if they so desired. Otherwise I was happy to simply listen and lend support."

"You mentioned that your parents are helping you out financially now. Are they well off? What do/did they do for a living?"

"My folks are not well off, but they did put some [savings] aside for me. I'm basically using my inheritance now. My dad was a junior high school math and history teacher in . . . California, for thirty years. He then went on to substitute teach in Oregon and the Sacramento area for another twenty-five years. He flew for the Navy in WWII, and is *very* good with woodworking. He built me a bunch of Medieval fiddles that are just *awesome* (the [university where I did my doctorate] asked him to build some for them; he wouldn't—said it sounded too much like work), and the best electric bass I've ever played in my life."

"My mom ran everything else," Gordon acknowledges. "She raised me, was very (overly? I don't know) involved in everything I've done, and they've been so supportive over the years. They bought me my first [viola da] gamba when I stumbled upon one quite by accident but knew I had to play it. They're my best friends (even with the minimal knowledge of my dad), my biggest supporters, and they are going to be leaving soon. My dad is ninety-two, my mom is eighty-eight; they both fell recently, though they weren't injured badly, but it was enough for my sibs to mobilize and get them into a supervised living situation. They're currently in . . . a suburb of Sacramento, but are moving back to Oregon this month to be near my sister in such a facility. Their days are numbered, I know this, but I don't know how okay I am with it all… so much change right now, so much chaos, it's hard to sort out."

"Yes, that's tough," I empathize. "But maybe you have a new best friend in Jenna who will help you navigate these turbulent waters. Let's hope so anyhow!"

"That's what I'm thinking!" Gordon affirms hopefully.

"Have you explored any of the autistic self-advocacy groups, like ASAN, the Autistic Self Advocacy Network?" I ask Gordon.

"At first I was looking around for support and advocacy groups. I will admit to not following up on that search, though. I tend to go inward rather than reach out, and when I do reach out, it's usually only to one person at a time. I'm not sure about the specific groups, but I did a lot of reading on various sites to try to start understanding the condition and re-contextualizing my life as I learned more. The diagnosis, for the first time *ever*, fits like a glove and *sooooo* much of the past is starting to make more sense."

"Let's take a journey into that intriguing mind you describe," I propose. "You mentioned before that compartmentalizing is one of your ASC-related strengths. So... you've got this whole 'time ribbon' thing going on that enables you to travel through time and space and to absorb, transform, and make manifest the various things you discover along the way. That lives in one region of your brain, sharing space—and seemingly in some kind of alternately enabling and dysfunctional way—with your ASC. Anxiety, depression, and low self-esteem appear to be squatters in that same apartment complex. Am I on track so far?"

"Yes, I'd say you most certainly are," Gordon confirms. "Damned squatters..."

"OK, good. That's just for openers. So who's living in the apartment complex next door—shall we call it Normal Acres?"

"Yes! Normal Acres is where the 'other me' lives," Gordon establishes. "And he is who I tried to be growing up. I've *always* known I was 'different,' and growing up I did whatever I could to be 'normal.' Normal Acres is the product of that. Unfortunately, the resident, Norm," Gordon explains, giving his non-ASC alter ego his own nickname, "can't do much about his crazy neighbors. He has a lot to say about them; spends a lot of time on the front porch watching them and trying to figure them out, and he has a lot of opinions about how they could be less obviously crazy (I know I'm not really crazy, but I'm thinking in terms of how neighbors often view each other—those 'others' are 'crazy'), but getting them to listen is really a trick. They try, but don't always succeed. Norm can get pretty upset about that, but he's generally not inclined to get upset. In fact, the [apartment managers] sometimes call on him to balance out someone *else's* crazy when they can't deal with it. (Wow. Never realized how very third-person 'Norm' is to me. That part of my personality really does seem separate and remote.) A case in point is when I'm around a friend or acquaintance that is going off the rails. A switch sometimes flips for me, and Norm appears to balance out and help calm the person who's going off. I've often wondered about that phenomenon... How am I doing on that so far?"

"You're doing great."

"He's kind of a Jiminy Cricket-type," Gordon says of Norm. "I've had panic attacks, ones where 'the bomb' goes off and I'm on the floor writhing and crying. I've probably hurt myself by punching a door or something, but there's always a part of me that is passively observing and critiquing what is going on. I can totally lose it to the point of being completely out of control to the observer, but there is always a small part of my mind that is totally in control, of itself if nothing else. It's the weirdest thing sometimes. It's when I feel the most schizoid (I know that's not the proper term for multiple personality disorder, but it's quicker to write... except for the explanation that followed that I could have left off), and it is a strange sensation indeed to be totally losing it, yet to have this calm, quiet place in my head where maybe a song I heard earlier that day is still playing, yet I'm unable to pick myself up off the floor and stop screaming. WTF..."

"Wow," I respond, "that's pretty deep."

As is so often the case with these sessions, I am by this point fully immersed in the conversation but out of time to continue it. "I need to go now," I tell Gordon, "but I'd like to sign off with another prompt for you, to which you can again respond with an email essay like the last one if you'd be so kind. Let me compose that."

I ask Gordon to give me a couple of minutes, explaining that this is going to be a rather involved prompt. But after about a minute, and while I am still typing, a new post from Gordon pops onto the screen. "One last thought about Normal Acres," he writes as an addendum. "It's that small modicum of control that I still have that keeps me from hurting others when I 'lose it.' I will almost always turn thoughts of harm toward myself. No one is in danger around me but me. I never hit or otherwise abused any of my partners, ever."

"That's good!" I exclaim.

I complete my lengthy prompt and share it with Gordon: "So it sounds to me like ASC/time ribbon brain guy (let's call him Ascot) is very interesting and wonderful, but mercurial, stubborn, and a pain in the ass to deal with. Normal Acres guy (Norm) is nothing if not steady—and basically a good guy—but feels pretty powerless to effect change of any kind, especially in coming up against the assertive/mercurial side of Ascot. Still, Norm fulfills a crucially important function in ensuring that everyone else is safe, even if he and Ascot are not. And Norm—and maybe even the 'artistic' side of Ascot (as opposed to the ASC side) as well—feels pretty powerless to take effective action when Ascot's ASC/crazy side decides to act up. Indeed, what comes through very clearly is that he feels powerless, impotent."

It occurs to me that I may be overstepping my bounds with this metaphorical cadenza, but I decide to take it a step further yet. "You've said on any number of occasions that when that Ascot side takes charge—for better or for worse—there's no stopping him. He's gonna do what he's gonna do (but he's *not* going to physically harm anyone, dammit!). Frankly, I don't believe that powerlessness is as real as you claim it to be. Sounds a lot to me (to paraphrase a quote from you describing your dad) like Norm's sole mission in life since he moved in with Ascot (or since Ascot moved in with him?) is to stay the hell out of Ascot's way. There's your prompt. Enjoy! Bye for now."

"Oooooh... Good stuff!" Gordon alights. "Okay! Thank you! And I look forward to our next talk! Have a great weekend!!"

"You too," I say.

"And yes," Gordon adds, "that is a very good summary!"

Gordon's essay arrives as an email attachment about two weeks later.

"Well, here's the essay...," he writes in the covering email. "I can't say I'm particularly pleased with it as a piece of writing... I'm exploring a part of me I have avoided acknowledging to *anyone* since I was seventeen, so I've never really thought much about it until now. I've just known it was there and thought it something of an unfortunate curiosity. I hope you find this useful. If there are details you'd like further clarification on, just let me know. Thanks!!"

I open the attachment and read what Gordon has written.

"ASCOT AND NORM," BY GORDON PETERSON

The most curious thing to me about my life experience, whether as an ASC person or not (I do not know if others like me experience anything similar), is the sense I have had for the better part of my life that there are "two of me." I'm not sure when I first noticed this. My earliest recollection of feeling somehow internally divided is from when I was about seventeen. An incident I do not wish to specify set off a very strange episode in which I spoke as someone who is me, yet separate from me, and I referred to myself in the third person, by my name. It was kind of a Gollum/Sméagol moment, I guess you could say. But it was very strange indeed. I have not had such an episode since, but I have continued to feel the duality. In all my years of psychiatric counseling, I do not know why I never brought it up... I guess I just figured it was in my imagination; nothing to see here, folks... But there is something to see here, and the more I explore it, the more it seems to be intimately linked to my ASC.

In our interviews I have, for the first time actually, mentioned this duality to someone. I have never spoken of it before. Frankly, I was surprised when it was taken seriously, and we started to define it. Defining it is not something I have ever really tried to do before, for prior to my diagnosis I knew that I did not fully understand what I was dealing with, and like I said, I figured it was just a silly imaginary thing that would just make me sound like I was crazy if I said anything about it. I'm not crazy. I, therefore, let it be and did what I've done throughout my life with my ASC, which is to simply do my best to mitigate the strange feelings and misunderstandings and their resultant behavior, to a greater or (mostly) lesser degree of daily success. Through this interview process, though, I've begun to understand and define these two different "Me's." The first we have dubbed "Ascot," as he is the Me that is the Aspie. He dominates my life... he is Me most of the time. He is the creative one, the one with the ideas, the "Time Ribbon," and all the wonderful benefits that come with my ASC mind. He is also the source of all the trouble that comes with my ASC mind, and since he is the emotional center of my experiences, he is the one that panics, who "'spergs out," as I often call my full-on Aspie moments ('spergin' out" = panic attack/breakdown/freakout). So he is Me in the broadest sense; the best and the worst.

Now Norm is also me, but he is what I might call an opinionated bystander; a Jiminy Cricket type. No matter how bad the freak-out, there is always a calm eye in the storm; a part of me that is not freaking out. It's Norm. In Norm's space, a song I heard earlier that day still plays while the rest of me is curled in a ball sobbing and banging my head on the floor. He speaks to poor little Ascot, telling him that he can stop if he wants (he never seems to be able to, try as I might)... he is a calm, rational, logical persona that seems to have absolutely no say in how Ascot behaves or responds until after the fact, but he knows when things are out of control. He knows when they're about to go out of control, too. Perhaps, then, he does have some useful influence: He has come in very handy with spotting situations that I might be in that could result in unfortunate Asperger's-related events. On more than one occasion I have calmly, rationally recognized a situation that I've been in as one similar to another that turned out badly because of me, and I have been able to preempt the inevitable, excuse myself and get the hell out before any damage was done (damage to relationships, mostly). He also works with Ascot to organize all those "brilliant" ideas into something cohesive, and is the mastermind behind the way I organized my career goals to be as stable as possible (that didn't work out due to circumstances beyond my/our control, but we're trying again).

When I first started thinking about the relationship between these two elements of myself for the purposes of this essay, it was suggested that these personae were reflections of my own parents. It is true that my mother is the dominant parent in my life, the source of the beauty and chaos of my upbringing; all the best and the worst, just like Ascot. My father is, and has always been, the calm, but relatively ineffectual until after the fact, eye of the storm. He has seemed to have made it his life's work at home to stay out of my mother's way, but I realized that, just like Norm, he is a stabilizing element. Sometimes, even most times, like Norm, there really isn't much he can do to calm things down; both my dad and Norm have to patiently ride out the storms generated by both my mom and Ascot, respectively. But sometimes they can organize, advise, and run interference when unfortunately familiar circumstances arise. My dad has been a much-needed level head more than once.

There is another phenomenon in my life that I think I can attribute to the "Norm" side of me. If you meet me on the street, or know me but don't ever really need to engage with me in any kind of personal or professional activity, or if you are a counselor asking me to "tell you what's wrong" (how often I have caught myself altering my narrative to a given counselor to seem more normal... I never knew why I seemed compelled to do that), it will probably never even occur to you that there might be something "different" about me, other than the obvious things like the fact that I'm a musician instead of something "normal." I have always, on a sometimes-conscious, but mostly sub- and unconscious level, worked very hard at appearing "normal." I was obsessed with it through my childhood and youth. I knew I was on the outside looking in, and God, I wanted to be "in" so bad. I used to practice facial expressions and body postures in the mirror, for instance. I still do sometimes. The thing is, though, that I did not do this with the conscious intent of "practicing fitting in," but because I just found myself doing it. I found the expressions of my face fascinating, and would just make faces and look at them. Little did I know that I was practicing "normality." I now recognize that as what I was doing. I think it was Norm, actually, doing it; teaching me to "fit in." I think it may be a testament to the success of my Norm side and practices like this (and there were many and diverse sorts), in that it took so long for anyone in the psychiatric community to even begin to suspect that there was something deeper and more hard-wired going on than mere "depression" or an "anxiety disorder" (the latter I had on a MedAlert bracelet, as it was the closest thing to accurate I had known to that point), even though I have been in psychiatric counseling most of my life.

By mimicking and internalizing the behavior patterns of both of my parents, I've been able to keep myself relatively balanced (until recently when everything fell apart). Norm has helped me appear relatively balanced to the uninitiated bystander. But I am Ascot through and through. It's no wonder that, in high school, I loved The Who's album *Quadrophenia*. I listened to the whole double LP set every week, if not every day, from the time I "discovered" it when I was sixteen through at least my first couple years of college. I didn't understand fully what it all meant, but it resonated within me profoundly. "Can you see the real me? Can ya? CAN YA?" It's Ascot. But thank you, Norm, for helping me get by. We need you, and you are Me too. I'm not "bleedin' quadrophenic," as Jimmy says in the opera. I'm just the product of a rather unusual assimilation of my role models, and a very astute subconscious that is able to act and manifest actual results on its own without me even knowing sometimes. I have to admit, it's really weird when that happens. Up until the loss of my tenured professorship in 2010, my career path met with remarkably little resistance... everything just fell into place. The right things happened at the right time to get me to a pretty close resemblance of where I wanted to be in my life professionally. I know I made that happen, but until I actually "met" Norm though this interview, I did not know how I did it. It all just seemed to happen, and I always just kind of knew what I needed to do next. But it was me, Norm-Me, doing all of that.

It makes sense, though, that there should be a very high-functioning element to my complex psyche. My I.Q. tests put me in the 98th percentile of intellects on the planet, and I've always wondered why all that brain space never seemed totally available. It seems now that it might be used by Norm, and he is very, very busy indeed. It will be interesting, now, to see how I perceive life in general in this new light.

N.B.: That was the past. None of this has been working like I just described since around 2008. All the things Norm had seen to that would keep "us" safe, create a "normal" life for us, provide a steady, predictable and unassailable income for the rest of "our" life have failed, turned out to have been bad choices, or otherwise been taken away by unfortunate, recession-based happenstance. While Norm is still there and his presence is the same as it's always been, he is utterly and completely ineffective at guiding us now. With the onset of this profound crisis and all the other chaos that has erupted simultaneously, Ascot is beyond freaking out and there is not much Norm can do. I am barely functioning now. I need so much help to get through what's happening and what's been going on that it's just humiliating. My family has been helping me with organizing what's left of my finances and taking care of hiring lawyers and such for continued divorce-related bull-shit, as I cannot even comprehend how to deal with either of those things. I cannot manage my money, when I have some. I cannot understand legal things... they're rules that I cannot apprehend. (I use that word on purpose. I can understand the law or rule or regulation as I read it, but only in an "academic" sense. I cannot apply it to myself somehow. There is a huge chasm between theory and practice when it comes to the rules and laws of society, work environments, and many other situations—except the obvious stuff like "don't steal" and "don't kill people..." where the basic laws are clear. But I have had more than one run-in with police just because I "looked suspicious." Damn I hate that. I never know why.) Nothing we taught ourselves over the decades seems at all relevant or useful now. Every day I don't know what to do. This life is so foreign to anything I have experienced in the past, so far outside my needed patterns and predictability that I am literally unable to comprehend what's going on around me every day. I feel like I'm just stumbling through, doing whatever seems most essential for that day, if I even can. Some days are spent in bed, as I just cannot cope with the overwhelming amount of chaos and change. Norm is even at a loss. I thought moving from Portland to Tallahassee back in 1994 was hard. I did it never having even visited the FSU campus, with no idea of what my living circumstances would be... nothing. It was a bold and very un-ASC-like move. I thought I was going to die. I had no idea what was in store.

This essay feels truncated, but I don't know how to describe any more... I've said what there is to say, as far as I can tell. I guess if there are any further questions I might be able to say more about it. Like I said, this is my first time even acknowledging this element of me to anyone other than me.

CONVERSATION 4: JULY 4, 2014

It's the Fourth of July, US Independence Day, and Gordon is on the move. More specifically, he is in the process of moving in with Jenna. It's going to take a good long while, though.

"In the midst of a very difficult and time-consuming move that will probably last the rest of the month," he writes to me via chat while taking a break from his packing, "but the outcome will be worth it."

"Yes, I'm sure it will," I reply. "Exciting change of life moment, moving in with Jenna and all!"

"Yes! So good not to be alone, and so good to be with her! Happy me!"

"Yay!!"

"Even my twenty-year-old cat is settling in quickly," Gordon reports. "He's calmer than he has been in a while, and eating more. Doesn't even mind the dog that much..."

So Jenna has a dog; it's going to be a blended family.

"Animals pick up the vibe," I type. "Must mean *you* are projecting better ones!"

"Could be! The apartment I was in was pretty depressing and confining, though. We're in a house now with a deck and hot tub and lots of windows... much better. And it's quiet. Very few sirens, which drive us both nuts."

"Yes, much better. Can't remember if I asked: What is Jenna's profession?"

"She's an artist and retired cosmetologist. Great art all around and free haircuts! Woohoo! Ka-ching!"

"So you're both 'starving artists'? How are you affording the nice new digs!?"

"Well, Jenna is part owner of an apartment complex and gets rent income. The apartments are about to sell, and she'll receive a nice little chunk of change for that, which we will probably live off of indefinitely. I bring in enough to cover any gaps in the meantime..."

"And the house I'm moving into is hers already, so the basic expenses were covered before I even got here. I'm kind of 'icing on the cake,' as it were, financially.... Which is good, 'cause I ain't got no cake."

"Well, what's a cake without icing anyhow?!"

"Bread," Gordon jokes.

Gordon is clearly in a good mood, light years removed from his depressed *nota bene* self at the end of "Ascot and Norm." The main purpose of this session, which I have requested, is to have some follow-up discussion about that essay. I take the initiative.

"So there's a kind of duality in 'Ascot and Norm,'" I begin, "an interesting one in that it is actually sort of a reversal of the duality I observed in that first essay you wrote for me a couple of weeks before. In this latest one, all the way through until the last paragraph or so, you come across not exactly as upbeat, but as at least maintaining a calm, rational critical distance from your subject. You are writing about yourself (selves) but in a way that kind of keeps them at arm's length, in the third person. Then right at the end, there is a shift. You sound despondent, beaten down, helpless, pretty much all of a sudden. It's interesting, because in your earlier essay, the negative tone dominated the majority of the piece, then at the end you came around and cast (optimistic) doubt on the skeptical, nihilistic projections of what had come before. So first, do you see what I'm recognizing (in either or both essays) and, if so, any theories as to the psychological backdrops of those shifting dualities?"

"Yes, I noticed that too, and let it be," Gordon states. "I think the core of this duality is that I am on such shaky ground in my life right now... I *want* to be upbeat and positive, but that's what I was before everything went to shit. I'm actually afraid of being too positive. This may sound very Eeyore," he writes, invoking Winnie the Pooh's lovably morose donkey friend, "but I have found that hope begets expectation, and expectation sets up disappointment. The more hope I allow myself, the more devastating the disappointment if the resultant expectations are not met. It's a cruel and difficult cycle. My friends in my Buddhist community don't get it... I should be chanting and praying harder the worse things get. But instead I am compelled to withdraw from practice altogether, as prayer begets hope, which begets the rest, and I have to just stop and let things be what they will. They totally don't get that, and the disapproval ratings soar. Yet another reason to pull back into my shell until the danger passes."

"Wait! 'Disapproval ratings soar' from Buddhists? Dude, you must be hanging out with the wrong Buddhists. That should not be part of the paradigm!"

"Heh heh...," Gordon chuckles. "Well, they try to understand, but religion, even lay Buddhism, can get dogmatic... If you don't do the same dance as everyone else, you must be doing it wrong. I probably overstated by using the word 'disapproval,' but when I try to explain why, when this practice teaches and encourages vigorous embracing of life's travails in order to overcome them, I instead turn inward and withdraw in a very not-vigorous way, I get a lot of head-shaking and 'he doesn't get it' kind of responses. Oh, I get it alright... I just can't do it."

Gordon's last remark captures my attention. It seems to cut to the core of a common sentiment I have heard expressed by many of my autistic friends and collaborators: getting it and doing it are entirely different things, especially where the challenges of social interaction and etiquette are concerned, and it is the doing-it part that perpetually mystifies.

"Of course, then, that means I'm not doing it right, or I lack faith, or blahblahblah," Gordon adds to that same train of thought. "The fact of the matter is that no organization of any kind that I have ever belonged to has fit to the extent that I can totally adopt the dogma. Ever. I *always* have to adapt it to my own patterns of thought and feeling. The dogmatists, who are almost always NT [neurotypical], I think, just can't accept that, it seems. I'm talking all the way back to Cub Scouts. Couldn't do that right either."

Our time is up. Gordon needs to get back to packing and loading. Before signing off, we take stock of where we are and determine that we have reached a good point of closure. Besides, Gordon is busy, what with the move, getting his music career back on track, and countless other commitments and activities. We agree that our work together on this project is done, at least for the moment. Then we bid each other farewell and sign off.

"TWINGES OF TENTATIVE OPTIMISM… WEIRD!"

It is October, 2014. The relentless Florida heat is finally abating, though sporadically at best. Much of my time of late has been dedicated to working on the Gordon chapter of the book. I email him a draft and ask for feedback. He gets back to me on October 24 with the following comments: "Although I *did* cringe at some of the things I said, and the way I'm just back and forth with the whole love/hate-my-autism thing, I hesitate to mess with it myself. It's honest… it's a process, and it represents exactly the confusion and push/pull that I felt at the time (still do, but my living context has changed, which has also, at least for the moment, eliminated a lot of negativity). So, while I will cringe a bit, I know my anonymity is fairly safe, so I think just letting it be is fine. It's what I said, and what I meant."

"I just sent you an email with corrections I found," Gordon adds by way of conclusion. "I'll continue to read over it, but I don't think I want to change it… but that may change!"

I promise Gordon I will take care of the corrections and keep him apprised of any new developments. "So, things going well?" I ask.

"Getting better!" he replies. "I actually have twinges of tentative optimism… weird! I reached a critical number of private [music] students this last month and am now able to pick and choose a bit more, cutting down on drive-time. There has been a flood of studio work and composition to do (paid), and I finally got my web-design business back up and running after an epic software fail. So good thing. I'll be moving again in a few months, as Jenna's apartment complex sold and she's bought us a new house and an extra rental property. As much as I hate the chaos and delays of routine that come with moving, the space will be much bigger and more flexible for the work I'm doing. Oh, and I'm playing a concert of Spanish Baroque and Medieval stuff tonight. Should be a great show!"

"Oh, wish I could be there for the concert. Saw that posted on Facebook. Break a leg! Bye for now, and thanks!"

"OK, bye. And you're welcome!"

NOTES

1. Gordon Peterson is a pseudonym. Other names in the chapter, as well as most of the locations, have also been fictionalized at Gordon's request for the sake of preserving anonymity.
2. Stonehurst University, like Whilston College, is a made-up name, and the university where Gordon taught was actually in a city in the US Midwest other than St. Louis.
3. The movie to which Gordon refers here is *Temple Grandin*, starring Claire Danes in the title role. The critically acclaimed 2010 HBO biopic was directed by Mick Jackson. Danes won both Golden Globe and Primetime Emmy best actor awards for her portrayal of Grandin, and the film was also awarded a Primetime Emmy for outstanding made-for-television movie. As an author, Grandin has done much to define public understandings of autism and the autism spectrum (Grandin 2006; Grandin and Panek 2013; Grandin and Scariano 1986). Oliver Sacks's profile of Grandin in his bestselling book *An Anthropologist on Mars* was also highly influential in reshaping modern perceptions of autism (Sacks 1995).

CHAPTER 10

Amy Sequenzia

I am usually not very aware of my body. I don't always know when I am in pain, I can't always feel certain types of pain, I rarely know where it hurts. To simply get up from a chair is sometimes hard, as if my body forgets how to move. I don't always know that I need to go to the bathroom. So when I feel the music inside my body, when I feel my blood running with the music, it is an amazing thing.

Amy Sequenzia (2014)

"I am autistic, non-speaking," proclaims Amy Sequenzia in the opening sentence of her powerful contribution to the anthology *Loud Hands*. "This label is a pre-judgment based on what I cannot do. It makes people look at me with pity instead of trying to get to know me, to listen to my ideas."[1]

The last thing Amy wants is pity. She does want to be heard, to be taken seriously, to speak out on behalf of the mistreated, the muted, the marginalized, and the most vulnerable among us. She wants to compel others to do the same as well, and she has little time or patience for those who would ignore her calls to action. Yes, there are many things that Amy Sequenzia wants, but pity is not one of them.

Amy knows who she is and what she is capable of. She wishes that other people did too. But usually they don't, even though they think they do, which only makes things worse. "I am a self-advocate and I can type my thoughts," she writes. "But at the moment I show up with my communication device and an aide, my credibility, in the eyes of most neurotypical people, is diminished."

It is a constant battle, both for Amy and for others in the non-speaking autistic community. "Even the ones among us who have demonstrated, many times, their capabilities, and who have succeeded despite all the hurdles a disability imposes," she complains, "these successful cases don't seem to be enough to end the myths: that a non-speaking autistic cannot self-advocate; that the so-called 'low-functioning' cannot think by themselves and cannot have ideas or opinions."

"We can, and we do," Amy asserts, adding that there "are too many neurotypical 'experts' claiming to know more about us than ourselves. They say they can make us 'better,' as if we are 'not-right' or 'wrong.' Most of them never thought about asking us what could make our lives more productive, less anxious; or trying to understand a non-speaking autistic who has not yet found a way to communicate. All the conversation has been about 'fixing' us, with the expectation that we finally look and act 'more normal.' " Such problems, she maintains, do not stem from a lack of effort. "We, autistic, have tried hard and accepted the neurotypical way of doing things to make it easier for non-autistic people to understand us, interact with us," she insists, yet there has been "very little reciprocity" from the neurotypical side, especially with respect to "the so-called 'low-functioning,' " like herself. "There is little patience in listening to us," Amy claims. "When one of us succeeds, he or she is considered an extraordinary exception."

Amy concludes with a challenge: "Look around. There are many of us trying to be heard. We did not put the 'low' in 'low-functioning' and we are speaking out. It is also up to the non-autistic to reciprocate in this communication exercise."[2]

I am inspired by Amy's words. Beyond that, I very much want to be a part of the reciprocity for which she is calling. Interviewing Amy for this book would be a great place to start, I think to myself as I ponder the next step in the project's development on a cool, breezy November afternoon in 2014. But would she consider being involved? And does she even have much of an interest in music in the first place?

I have never met Amy and I've had no direct contact with her up to this point. We do have a couple of mutual friends, though: Ibby Grace and Andrew Dell'Antonio. I contact Ibby and ask her, first, if Amy is much into music and, second, if she thinks Amy might want to take part in our book project.

On whether Amy is into music, most definitely, Ibby assures me; on whether she would want to take part, not so sure.

"Let me check with her," Ibby writes to me. She does, Amy is interested, and a few weeks later she and I meet online for our first chat session.

"So let me start by saying how much I appreciated your contribution to the *Loud Hands* volume," I begin after Amy and I have exchanged hellos. "That made a very strong impression on me, has helped shape my thinking of late, and is cited in a couple of my forthcoming publications. Thank you for writing that!"

"Thank you!" Amy replies.

"It's interesting finally getting to 'meet' you here. I know your work, of course, and I've heard about you—from Ibby, and also from Andrew. But I'd like to know a little bit more about you, your autism, your modes of functioning in the world, etc. Shall I ask specific questions or do you just want to respond in general by giving me some background on yourself?"

"Ask me [questions]," she says. "Typing can take a long time and I don't want to ramble."

"OK. First, then: How *do* you type?"

"I use facilitated communication,"[3] Amy explains. "[M]y friend supports my elbow and I type. . . ."

"So your friend is with you now?"

"Yes. We are inseparable!"

"What is her/his name?"

"Adriana," Amy informs me. ". . . [She] is my executive function."[4]

I exchange greetings with Adriana.

"So do you use all of your fingers when typing?" I ask Amy.

"No, one finger. And each letter takes the same kind of focus. That's why I don't do 'small typing.' This is my facilitated communication joke. ☺ "

"Wait. Sorry, I don't get it," I confess. "Can you explain?"

"Small talking, for speaking people. Small typing, for typists/non-speaking."

"Ah, like chit-chat!" Now I get it.

"Yes!" Amy confirms.

We move on to a new topic. "Are you able to walk?" I ask. I have heard that beyond being autistic, Amy has a number of physical disabilities. I don't know what these are or how they affect her, however.

"Yes, I'm able to walk," she answers, "but I also have cerebral palsy, so I have poor balance. I use a wheelchair sometimes. I get tired and overwhelmed; it helps."

I am also curious about Amy's use of her voice. From her *Loud Hands* piece, I know that she defines herself as "non-speaking," but I'm not sure what that means exactly.

"[So] my understanding from reading your article in *Loud Hands* is that you don't speak," I establish, "but do you use your voice for other modes of expression and communication, for example, singing?"

"No," she replies without hesitation. "I can make noises and sometimes a word comes out, like my name. But this is kind of involuntary, probably because of and related to seizure activity. I sometimes 'hum' but it is not about specific music. It is like *stimming*."

"I see. Do [you now] or did you ever try to speak, or sing? Or have you always either chosen not to, or else simply realized you could not so didn't ever try?"

"When I was little I had speech therapy and everyone wanted me to speak. I could say a few words but it was nothing like conversing. Then I learned how to type and it is so much easier [that] I don't miss not speaking, or not being able to."

"Are you able to hear, and do you understand other people's speech?" I inquire.

"I hear everything!" Amy exclaims in reply. "I only have trouble understanding when I am too overwhelmed and anxious, or after some seizures." I note that she has mentioned having seizures twice already. As I will later learn, seizures are the bane of Amy's existence: she mainly likes being autistic, but she hates having seizures—autism acceptance is a thing; seizure acceptance is not.

I shift back to the topic of Amy's typing ability. I ask her where, when, and how she first learned to type. I'm also curious to know what kind of response it generated when her parents and others first came to realize that she was communicating with them.

"I was part of a small group of children who were chosen for a facilitated communication study," Amy recounts. "I cried a lot as the facilitator tested me and then I realized that she was actually listening, or reading, my answers and that I could let her know that I was smart. My parents were there. The first thing I did was to ask them to bring me home from the luxurious institution I was living in then," she adds sarcastically. "I was eight."

"Wow, and had they taught you how to type at the institution or did you learn to do that on your own?" I ask naively, having missed the sardonic bite of Amy's last remark.

"Institutions only teach you fear and self-loathing," she asserts. "I tried to be happy with some nice people [there] but they taught me nothing. [As for] the typing, the facilitator showed me how to point, as she made my arm stable."

"The facilitator at the institution?" I ask, a bit confused.

"The facilitator came from Syracuse [University], where the facilitated communication movement in the U.S. began.[5] The study [I was in] was outside the institution [where I lived]."

I ask Amy how she learned to use a keyboard when working with the facilitator at Syracuse, and how she learned to read.

"At the time it was a letter board, not a keyboard," she replies, adding, "I learned how to read watching *Sesame Street* when I was three."

I next ask Amy a series of basic questions about her age, birthplace, where she grew up, and where she now lives.

"I am thirty-one. I was born in Miami but left when I was eleven to live in a type of group home/community in St. Louis, MO [Missouri]. It was because education in Florida for disabled kids sucked, still sucks. Then I lived in Pennsylvania and Massachusetts. I came back when I turned twenty-two because I was still considered a Florida resident and adult funding does not cross state lines. I live in Rockledge with my friend [Adriana] and her husband; we are like roommates."

"Thank you. Just two more of these 'background' questions and then we'll get into music—the fun stuff!" I promise. "First, when were you diagnosed with autism, and in what circumstances? Second, what, in your own conception, defines you as an autistic person?" I decide to tack on my obligatory "magic wand" question before posting: "Well, I lied. There's a third question as well (that I ask pretty much everyone I interview on this project): If you could wave a magic wand and make your autism 'disappear,' would you?"

Amy rattles off her answers in quick-fire succession: "Diagnosed when I was two. Usual lots of doctors stuff, first a [developmental] delay, then autism. Autism shapes my interaction with the world."

And then: "I would break the wand before anyone could wave it."

Following a brief pause, Amy continues. "The way I act, react, understand and stand in the world is because I am Autistic. Autism cannot be separated from me and is part of every aspect of my life. . . . The way I perceive people and the sound of words, it touches me internally. I feel the words and I feel people. Some people might be too intense, some might calm me down, some are like a beautiful poem. The sounds and lights affect me in a way that, if it is overwhelming, it can make me withdrawn. The fact that I don't speak makes me listen better, I guess; my body does not necessarily follow my brain commands and that causes false assumptions [about me]."

This seems the perfect moment to delve into Amy's inner musical world. I begin, outlining for her how my approach to this project "is essentially ethnomusicological and in no way 'therapeutic' or 'medical' or any such thing.

I define ethnomusicology as the study of how people make and experience music, and of why it matters to them that they do," I explain, ". . . [so I want to understand how] you make and/or experience music, and why it matters to *you* that you do (and keep in mind that you should feel free to conceptualize 'music' in the broadest and most imaginative possible terms!)."

Amy's reply comes quickly: "I think the simple answer is: I just love music. I love live music. . . . I love each instrument's voice, even though I don't know all instruments. I can see colors coming from the orchestra or choir, I can see color in movement . . . but it has to be live. I experience the words and sounds of music differently if I am listening on the radio or [to a] CD.

"I still enjoy and can see colors, but the feeling is less intense. . . . I love when someone sings to me, even someone who cannot sing well[,] because the words dance in front of me. Sometimes I can feel the music entering my blood stream and I even react in a visible way. ([Adriana] says I make some faces and my eyes change.)"

Listening to music is clearly meaningful for Amy on many levels. Moreover, she engages with it in a variety of creative ways. That is also the case for other autistic people, she insists, and for reasons having much to do with their social desires. "[M]usic is very important to many, many Autistics," she tells me, "so I believe the connection is real. We are social, we are [just] not conventional. Because our experiences with the world are so different from [those of] neurotypicals, because of sensory overload and such, we develop our own 'socialization.' Maybe music gives us the social experience because it is also so private and personal."

Amy returns to the subject of music and color. She claims, "I don't know music as a musician does. I hear some notes, I guess, and they have colors, and the colors are like waves moving above, in front and around the music makers. Sometimes it is a big rainbow dancing, sometimes one color is dominant." I ask her if she has ever heard of synesthesia.[6] She has, and it is something with which she immediately identifies.

A SYNESTHESIA INTERLUDE: AMY AND HEADSTONES

In the months to come, Amy decides to explore her self-described "synesthete" identity extensively, writing poetry and posting blog essays about her synesthesia experiences as a music listener in a range of contexts. Notably, the scope of her musical life expands during this time to include going to rock concerts, something she had previously told me would be beyond her sensory threshold.

Amy's new embrace of rock music comes via her discovery of Headstones, a Canadian, punk-influenced alternative rock band that has been together for almost thirty years. She is like a kid on a synesthesia playground when listening to Headstones recordings, an experience she first describes to me in an email of January 26, 2015, several months after the conclusion of our official dialogue sessions for this book.

"I thought you would like to know," the email begins, "I never thought I would be interested in hard rock but I was listening to some . . . and I kind of liked it. I was paying attention to the lyrics at first but then it was like seeing a ball of light, spinning, then melting into drops of light. In some loud moments I could see some notes, like, jumping behind the 'noise.' It was not live; I don't think I can handle a concert, but it was pretty. . . . [T]he band's name is Headstones. I did not listen to a lot of their music but what I experience was similar to some music from Simon and Garfunkel, some from Elvis Costello, some from Paul Simon. I know they are different styles but the notes pop up and the drops fall. The experience of the spinning ball happened with some of the music that wasn't so loud."

Three weeks later, on February 14, Amy sends me a second account of her evolving Headstones musical odyssey: "I'm listening to some more of the Headstones music and I did some research. I think they are punk rock, not hard rock, but I don't really know the difference. I realized that the [songs] I like and that I can enjoy (and that I see the notes [in]) are the ones that change[;] they have softer moments. I like the bass; I think it is the bass. The notes are more circular. And I like when instruments are introduced one by one, not all at the same time. I also listened to some of their music that is acoustic and I liked the voice of the singer. I see the movement when he changes his voice, like a high wave that then breaks. Since our interviews [last December] I am paying more attention to what happens when I listen to music, even if it is not live. And I am listening to more music too. ☺"

Amy goes public about her synesthesia a couple of months later. She writes to notify me that she has just posted a new blog entry at ollibean.com and invites me to read it. The post begins with some prefatory remarks under the heading "Synesthesia." [7]

"I am a synesthete," Amy states. "I see colors and movement to music— to all sounds actually, but music makes everything prettier. I also see words, I can feel them. My synesthetic experience has always been beautiful but I never paid extra attention to it. The colors, the movements and the feelings have always been there."

"Recently," she continues, "I have been expanding my musical experience, and I am enjoying it greatly. I am paying more attention to what I see, to what I feel.

"It is hard to explain. I wish I could paint it, but I can't. So I wrote a poem.

"The format, the capitalization, the punctuation, are an attempt to be true to my experience."

"I am writing about other songs [too]," Amy adds, "about different music styles. These were chosen first because they came to me as I began exploring my synesthesia. Each stanza references a different song."

"Music: Hugh Dillon and Canadian band Headstones," Amy specifies. A list of the songs referenced in the poem, including links to music videos that feature them, is included at the companion website (CW 10.1 ▶).

"(Warning: brief use of the f-word)," Amy's preamble concludes. The poem follows directly after that:

Music, Colors, Movement, Feelings

It starts here
Sorrytown in Durham County.
Evoking loneliness
The word feels like a gentle stroke
The melody sips in and through my body
Absorbed, it lulls me
It appeases my soul
A fading orange

The voice awakens me
Gentle, potent still
Circles—fire red
Slowly forming everywhere,
Eternity

A mighty ball of energy
Yellow, it spins
Blue
Drops
Orange
Drops
Radiating light

Van Gogh I am not
And this is my "Starry Night"

I hear circling and spinning—I see red
My stimming Autistic body squees.
The frozen motion before the bliss—Bright red
I silently scream
Fuck yeah!
Silence, no more.
It's unspoken
Yet
Liberating

Words quickly form in the air like a prism the spectrum of colors
Slowly they vanish
One by one
New words emerge
Notes... and....tunes .... glide... on... a ... rainbow
"Pinned down" to the polychromatic air

My body exhilarates
Surrounded by a cyclone of yellow and orange
I am the center
A towering cyclone of yellow and orange
Harmonious harmonica
Riveting
Ecstasy. I embrace it

I SEE a sound of sorrow
Gradually giving in to hope
I'm in a bubble
I feel empathy
In this midnight
I breathe yellow

THE LOUD NOTES come with
Previously unexpected blue
THE NOTES SOAR from behind
The cotton-like textured wall
They reveal themselves to me
Until they hide again
Allowing for words to form in the air

Music and colors and movement

In my nearly motionless body
I revel in them
I celebrate
I discover
Colors
Sounds
Feelings
Joy

CONVERSATION 2: DECEMBER 15, 2014

Back to the year 2014, Amy and I meet online for our second chat. Five days have passed since the first one.

"Last time, when we signed off," I type, "you had made the point that music is a very important part of life not just for you but for a great many autistics you know and know of. I'd like to hear more about what it is about music that makes it so significant and meaningful for you personally, and to the extent that you can surmise, to autistic people generally."

"I don't know why music is important to them; I know that many of them love music," Amy states matter-of-factly. "I know at least one who has perfect pitch, some who can understand music intuitively, one who sees music as math. There are kids who are considered 'severe' [autistics] who are music geniuses."

Amy next returns to some of the themes she raised in our first conversation. "I just feel good listening to notes, even though I don't know them [like musicians do]. It is the whole experience, the colors, the movement, the feeling. It embraces me completely. I feel the same when someone reads a poem and does it really well. The melody makes me feel things I don't always feel, like my blood running in my body."

"Last time you mentioned music entering your blood stream (I think those were your words), and just now you mentioned how musical melody can make you feel things you don't always, like your blood running in your body," I write. "This is interesting to me, in that it is a very physical, visceral response to music—which is not unusual at all—but it is physical and visceral internally. Listening to music makes me move, maybe dance, feel certain emotions, but I can't think of a time when it has brought my attention to my blood flowing through my body; if it did, I think that might be disturbing to me actually! But the way you describe that makes it sound as though it is definitely pleasurable. Is it? Can you tell me more about that feeling and how it 'connects' you to the music that brings it about?"

"I am usually not very aware of my body," Amy replies. "I don't always know when I am in pain, I can't always feel certain types of pain, I rarely know where it hurts. To simply get up from a chair is sometimes hard, as if my body forgets how to move. I don't always know that I need to go to the bathroom. So when I feel the music inside my body, when I feel my blood running with the music, it is an amazing thing. Yes, it is a good thing."

"But this experience is only strong with live music," she adds. "Recordings are not the same." I ask her why she thinks that's the case. "I never thought about that difference until this interview," she acknowledges, and then, "I have to pay attention to this."

I tell her I have some thoughts on the subject. Would she like me to share them, I ask.

"OK," she replies.

"So I have two 'theories,'" I begin. "One is that the actual physical impact of live music on your body is greater than that of recorded music—that it's a purely physical phenomenon of greater physical stimulation. The other is that there is something about the social experience/connection that actually being in a place where music is being made—seeing and in a sense 'feeling' the musicians before you, as well as the other audience members around you—that inspires a heightened emotional (maybe even spiritual?) experience of the music on your part. In this 'theory,' the elevated sense of blood flow has as much to do with the environment of the musical experience as [with] the music itself. Do either of these make sense? Or a combination of both? Or maybe these are both so wrong that it will get you thinking about what's *really* going on!"

"I think you might be right, especially about the second one," Amy responds. "Being social without the societal-imposed traditional or usual ways, being able to connect and not feeling overwhelmed by the presence of so many people, the body and mind are free from the need for regulation and the feelings are more intense. There goes, again, the theory that we are not social. And [with the music] being live, I share the experience with the musicians more intensely, even if they don't feel the same way."

CONVERSATION 3: DECEMBER 18, 2014

Amy tells me she is feeling "a little overwhelmed" when we sign on for our third and final session three days later. She explains that she has been consumed by the "Activism #FreeNeli" campaign of late, in a marathon of countless Tweets and endless blogging. The good news, she reports, is that the campaign is working, with important objectives achieved and more in the offing, but the effort has been exhausting.

I am lost. I need context. I tell Amy that I know nothing about the #FreeNeli campaign. She directs me to a report she has written on the subject, which was just recently published as a blog post at ollibean.com.[8]

I read the report. It is gut-wrenching.

Eighteen-year-old Reginald "Neli" Latson, an Autistic, intellectually disabled, African-American high school student in Virginia—a "good student . . . excelling in school"—was standing outside a library he regularly visited, waiting for it to open, when he was arrested for walking away from an approaching officer and then profiled as "a criminal, 'possibly carrying a gun.'" As Amy explains, he "did not 'comply' with the officer who approached him, already with baseless suspicion, since there was no gun. An altercation sent Neli to jail, trial and prison. He served his time, and was released." In the end, Amy suggests, "Neli served time in prison for being profiled (black young man wearing a hoodie), and for being Autistic (his reactions [in walking away from the officer] not understood)."

Things went from bad to worse for Neli following his release. Traumatized by what had happened, he ran up against the law again, violated his parole, and ended up back in jail serving hard time. There, he got into a fight with a prison guard, landing him in solitary confinement. And now, one year later according to Amy's report, Neli remains in solitary confinement, all "because he is Autistic, without supports to cope with a very stressful situation."

"Why isn't the whole country screaming against the despicable practice of putting disabled youth—mostly black—in solitary confinement?" Amy cries out. "This torturous situation will not help Neli, it will not 'teach' him or reform him. Being deprived of human contact, except for his punishers, will increase the mental stress he already experiences (Neli is also being denied radio or TV, so he does not even hear human voices)."

"Neli needs supports," Amy asserts, "which are nowhere near a solitary small room with a hole in the ground—and nothing else."

"Please, join us," she appeals.

"Follow the link and in five minutes or less you will take action to end the four years of suffering Neli has endured. Then join us on Twitter, search the hashtag #FreeNeli."

I follow the link as instructed and sign the petition, notifying Amy I have done so when I come back online with her.

"Check out Twitter," she writes proudly regarding some just-in reports. "We got him out of solitary. Now we want pardon. And thank you for your support!"

"Sure thing," I say, making a note to get onto the #FreeNeli Twitter feed once our conversation is done. "Let's pick up where we left off last time, specifically about how hearing music live is more intense for you than listening to it on a recording. Can you provide more insight on that subject?" It is an awkward shift of topic, but there is no elegant way to segue from #FreeNeli to talking about music, so I simply don't bother to try.

"I think it is because during a concert, the energy of the music comes from the stage, and initially we are just receiving," Amy speculates. "The audience starts sharing with the musicians, or choir, or singer, but it is also an individual experience. Each one of us shares with them, through music, but not with each other. To me this makes being around all the people easier. If I go to a concert of popular music, where people sing along, dance and jump, I do feel overwhelmed and cannot enjoy my music experience."

"Ah, that's a fascinating insight, Amy, and actually reminds me of another question I was meaning to ask you, specifically: What type(s) of music do you like best? My sense is that you are mainly a classical music fan? Anyhow, I do want to come back to that concert experience issue, but first, do share with me the types/genres/artists you like best, and perhaps also the kinds of music you don't really enjoy listening to/seeing."

"Classical, yes. [As for other styles,] I don't have favorite artists, but I usually enjoy James Taylor, Elvis Costello. I like musicals like *Les Miz* and *Cats*; some songs I listen to I don't even know the names. My favorite is classical music because that's when the color, [the] movement experience, is the best. When I saw *Evita*, I really liked it too. I think it also depends on who is singing. I do have fun listening to Elvis [Presley] and the Beatles, but because some [of their] lyrics are so silly."

"But you probably would *not* have enjoyed hearing Elvis or the Beatles live in concert with all those screaming girls, right?"

"No," Amy agrees, "but I would have enjoyed a private concert with them! Some [of their] songs are sweet."

"Cool. So back to the concert experience thing. As an active performer of music (and perhaps one with some 'splinter traits' of Asperger's), I can very much relate to what you're talking about from the other side. I almost always have my eyes closed when I'm playing. It's a very 'social' experience—intensely so—with the other musicians, with the audience, but I want to *hear* and *feel* the people around me, not see them. If I make eye contact while playing, I almost feel like the audience is staring at me sitting on stage naked. There is something so intimate and intense about that connection that happens through music, whether with the other musicians or the audience, which just makes it seem like too much—overload, overwhelming, excessively intense—to add in the whole visual communication thing on top of everything else." I pause, not quite sure how to wrap this thread back around. I attempt to do so, though rather feebly: "Sorry, I guess there's no question there, but do you have any response to what I just wrote? Does [it] bring to mind anything else about your own experiences with music?"

"I don't feel like I am exposed," Amy replies, "but I think I can understand. You are initially giving something and when the audience begins to share, it is a lot! To me, it is like I am immersed in colors, unless someone hits the wrong note," she writes, capping the remark with a smiley-face emoji.

"And then what happens?!" I am genuinely curious.

"I was half joking," Amy writes. "When something disrupts my experience, the colors fade, the feeling subsides. I can go back, but it is an interruption."

"So the colors, the feeling—is it like a trance experience or something like that?" I ask, reflecting as I do on powerful moments of musical transcendence I have experienced in my own life. "Do you feel you've been 'transported' to somewhere outside of everyday reality when you get, to use your word, immersed?"

"I guess it is in a way, but I am still aware of my surroundings. I can look around, see people, smile, move around. But the colors and movements make me feel things I cannot just bring up without the music."

"What about pain, or feelings of stress, sadness, worry? If you're experiencing anything like that, does being at a good concert and getting immersed in the music provide any relief from those kinds of sensations or emotions?"

"Depends on how intense they are."

"Let's say present but not super-intense. Like, say, for example, today. You've got this whole #FreeNeli thing hanging over you; you mentioned you're not doing too badly but are feeling a bit overwhelmed. If you were to go out to a concert now, and it was a really good and enjoyable one, how might that affect the way you're feeling?"

"I also have a little neck pain, so that makes me not want to go places. If no neck pain, which makes sitting quietly or in a chair that might be a little uncomfortable even more so, then I think it would help. Or having concerts where people can sit, stand or lie down. In some conferences we say that people can do whatever they need to feel not overwhelmed. We call it Autistic Safe Space."

" . . . I am getting tired," Amy posts after a brief pause in the conversation. "Need a break."

We have been going for almost ninety minutes straight by this point and Amy was already worn out when we started—and she has a sore neck.

I ought to take her cue to end the session right now, but it's all so *interesting*; I want to keep going, if only just a little bit longer.

"So I need to leave in, oh, about thirteen minutes," I tell Amy. "Do you want to take a quick breather and finish up after that for a few more minutes, or are you tired enough that we should just call it a day now?" A pushy move on my part, but Amy pushes back.

"I am really tired," she reiterates.

In other words: we are done. This time I get the message. More important, this time I honor it.

"OK, let's call it a day then," I write. "I'm going to review all of the interview material we've compiled thus far. It may be that we're all set re: what's needed for the chapter; or maybe we'll want to do at least one more session. Of course, if you do want to set up another one because you know there's more you want to share, I'm certainly happy to do that. Otherwise let me go through stuff and then let you know where I think we're at. Sound good?"

"Yes, it's good."

"Great. Have a great weekend, and good luck with the FreeNeli effort. Kudos to you for taking the lead on that. Bye for now; I'll be in touch!"

"Thank you! You have a good weekend too!"

"Thanks, and Happy Holidays!"

MEETING AMY

It's a little after 9:00 in the morning on June 12, 2015, and I am about to meet Amy Sequenzia in person for the first time. Both of us are in Atlanta for the Society for Disability Studies Conference, where we will be participating on a panel called "Autistic Musicians, Autistic Musicking" with our good friends Ibby Grace and Andrew Dell'Antonio about three hours from now. First, though, we are all going to have breakfast together.

My wife Megan and I enter the hotel restaurant, and I recognize Amy immediately. She is seated in a wheelchair next to a large nook booth, flanked on the one side by her friend Adriana and on the other by Ibby and Andrew. I walk over to Amy to introduce myself, but suddenly I have no idea what to do. Her head is cocked awkwardly to the side. Her eyes seem locked in place gazing at some invisible object, almost as though she is in a trance. I am embarrassed to admit it, but I simply cannot rectify that this Amy and the Amy I have gotten to know so well online are the same person.

"Amy is having a hard time today," Adriana informs me, apparently picking up on my disorientation. "She's had several seizures in the last few hours and she is really feeling bad. She has to conserve her energy for the panel later. She'll be fine, but she just has to keep everything low-key for now."

"Of course," I say. I tell Amy how great it is to finally meet her, how much I've enjoyed getting to know her through our chat sessions, how excited I am about the panel and the book and all the other stuff we've worked on together. There is a fleeting moment when she seems to be acknowledging me—a glance in my direction, maybe a tiny nod of the head—but it is subtle. It may have just been my imagination.

After a while, though, it all seems fine. The food is delicious and our server even orders me up a batch of fresh-baked, gluten-free biscuits—a rare and unexpected treat. There is such a warm feeling of camaraderie within our little group, and Amy is an integral part of it. Between the breakfast, the friendly banter, and some excited if slightly anxious last-minute planning for the panel, we find our communal groove. And along the way, I trade in my initial awkwardness for a new appreciation of just who Amy is, that is, precisely the same person I have known and admired all these years, just now sharing breakfast with me on a morning that has certainly brought its challenges but will hopefully get better as the day unfolds.

Just after 12:00 noon, our panel begins. Andrew presents first, then Ibby, then me, and finally Amy. She has been still and mainly inactive throughout the session, but when the time comes to speak, a sudden change comes over her. Amy leans forward in her wheelchair, her right elbow aloft and supported by Adriana, and places her index finger on the screen of a specially equipped iPad. Then she starts to type, and her voice—that is, the automated computer voice that speaks for her—comes out. The words are full of power, grace, and beauty. They wrap themselves around ideas and images that have been flowing through the air all session long, first bringing them down to earth, later floating them skyward again but with renewed poignancy and profundity.

Amy is in full stride, and watching her write, hearing her *speak*, is a thing to behold. Yes, Amy Sequenzia is in the house, and no one in her presence is ever going to forget it.

NOTES

1. "Non-Speaking, 'Low-Functioning'" (Sequenzia 2012, 159).
2. "Non-Speaking, 'Low-Functioning'" (Sequenzia 2012, 159–61).
3. A 1994 report of the American Speech-Language-Hearing Association, or ASHA (American Speech-Language-Hearing Association 1994), describes facilitated communication (FC) as "a technique in which physical, communication, and emotional support is provided by a *facilitator* to an individual with a

communication disorder *(communicator)*. With assistance, the communicator points to symbols such as letters, pictures and/or objects." In the same report, the following is stated: "Professionals, parents, and others have reported unexpected communication and literacy skills from individuals considered to have severe communication impairments. Some of these individuals had also been diagnosed as severely to profoundly intellectually disabled. Professionals and others have questioned the extent to which such outcomes reflect the actual abilities of individuals using this method (communicators) and not the unwitting contributions of individuals (facilitators) who are supporting them physically, emotionally, and communicatively during interactions." This has generated a great deal of controversy and debate across many sectors (Biklen 2005; Donvan and Zucker 2016).

    With respect to the larger debates over FC, those are beyond the scope of what I am prepared to address here. With respect to Amy's case in particular, however, I have by now established a long enough track record of communicating with her and observing her directly in the process of writing (using both FC and another platform called Rapid Prompt Method, or RPM) to confirm beyond the shadow of any doubt that the words and ideas attributed to her, in this book and in her many published writings, are unequivocally her own.

4. As defined by Blythe Corbett and colleagues in an article in the journal *Psychiatry Research*, "Executive function (EF) is an overarching term that refers to mental control processes that enable physical, cognitive, and emotional self-control . . . and are necessary to maintain effective goal-directed behavior. . . . Executive functions generally include response inhibition, working memory, cognitive flexibility (set shifting), planning and fluency. . . . Deficits in EF are frequently observed in neurodevelopmental disorders, including autism and attention deficit hyperactivity disorder (ADHD)" (Corbett et al. 2009). Happé and colleagues also provide enlightening perspectives on executive function issues in ASD and ADHD (Happé et al. 2006).

5. See the introductory chapter of Douglas Biklen's book *Autism and the Myth of the Person Alone* (Biklen 2005) for the author's own account of the facilitated communication program at Syracuse University and its history. Biklen was the founding director of that program.

6. Simon Baron-Cohen and colleagues published a 2013 article in the journal *Molecular Autism* in which it was demonstrated that the prevalence of synesthesia among subjects with autism spectrum conditions was almost three times greater than that of non-autistic subjects in control groups (Baron-Cohen et al. 2013).

7. The poem and its accompanying blog post text, reproduced here with the author's permission, may be accessed at ollibean.com (Sequenzia 2015). All of Amy's published work can be found on her personal blog, "Non-Speaking Autistic Speaking" (Sequenzia 2017).

8. "#FreeNeli" (Sequenzia 2014).

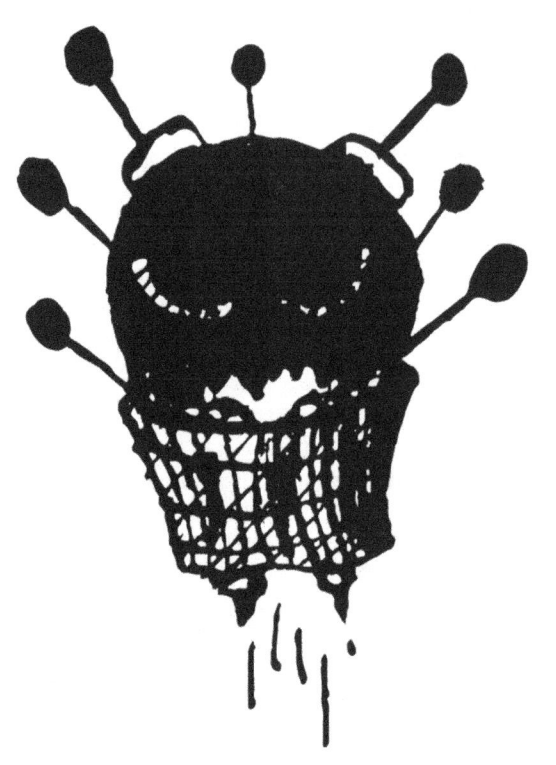

CHAPTER 11

Addison Silar

. . . when I put the music on I get a creative spark-type thing, 'cause usually it's hard for me to think, and when I get that creative spark I honestly couldn't tell you what comes through my head, but I feel I'm able to take the song and in a sense manipulate it and put it into words.

Addison Silar (2014)

I first met Addison Silar[1] on the day of his birth. He and my son Isaac were born two days apart at Tallahassee Memorial Hospital in July of 1999. My wife Megan had met Addison's mother, Tanya, in a prenatal exercise class a few months before that. The two moms-to-be became good friends. Our families grew close, and when the boys were little we would often get them together for play dates.

Addison was diagnosed with Asperger's syndrome at the age of five. Social situations had always been difficult for him but his problems escalated after he began kindergarten. Staying organized and on task in school was challenging from the start, and navigating the social intricacies of the school environment even more so. To make matters worse, Addison was the biggest kid in his class, and being a gentle and sensitive boy by nature he was a frequent target of bullying. These various difficulties prompted Tanya and her husband Matt to seek professional help for their son, which ultimately led to his Asperger's diagnosis. Eventually the Silars moved north to Chicago but Megan and Tanya stayed in touch, and on their annual winter pilgrimages south to visit relatives in Florida, Tanya, Matt, Addison, and Addison's little sister, Adriana, would always pay us a visit as well.

On one such occasion in January of 2014, Addison, Matt, and I are sitting at the dining room table after eating lunch. Addison is now fifteen and cuts an imposing figure at about 6'3". He looks like a tough offensive lineman on a high school football team, but his sweet nature and gentle expression defy that image.

Matt tells me that Addison has been working hard on his first novel and encourages his son to tell me about it. Addison is happy to comply. The book is a science fiction piece called "The Unfortunate Project," he tells me, following up with a detailed account of the plot and main characters.[2] It sounds really good; I tell him I'll be eager to read it once it's done.

But what captures my attention most of all is Addison's evocative description of his writing process. Music is a big part of it, he explains. He doesn't just listen to music while writing; nor is it enough to say just that music inspires his writing, or even that it helps to shape the content of his words and ideas. It is much more than any of that, for Addison claims that when he "writes to music," what he is doing is quite literally writing the music he hears *into* the fictional worlds he invents—textually, emotionally, and atmospherically.

I am fascinated by both the concept and Addison's explanation of it. Might it be possible to follow up with a Google Hangouts interview for a book I am writing on music and autism, I ask him, checking with Matt and Tanya as well to see what they think of the idea.

Addison is very excited, as are his parents. It will be several months before everything falls into place, but finally it does, and in mid-June Addison and I have our first chat session.

CONVERSATION 1: JUNE 12, 2014

In preparation for our dialogue, I ask Addison three days ahead to send me a playlist of the music he has been writing to in his work on "The Unfortunate Project." He's busy with other things, however, and the playlist doesn't show up in my inbox until a few minutes before we're scheduled to begin. I click on the link for the first song and start listening to it just as our chat is getting under way.

"I'm listening to Of Monsters and Men's 'Dirty Paws' now," I inform Addison. "Can you give me about ten or fifteen minutes to quickly check out the other tunes on the list, too, before we begin chatting? I think my questions for you will be better that way."

"Sure," he replies.

I move quickly through the list (which is included at the companion website: CW 11.1 ▶). I don't want to keep Addison waiting too long; closer listenings can wait until later. Beyond "Dirty Paws," there are YouTube links to six other selections and I devote a minute or two to each of them: Dot Exe's remix of the Nightcore tune "Monster"; "Welcome Home," by Coheed and Cambria; "Ain't No Rest for the Wicked" and "Tiny Little Robots," both performed by Cage the Elephant (Addison notes, "'Tiny Little Robots' was not originally done by Cage the Elephant, but I like their version of it"); and "Shatter Me" and "Radioactive," featuring the innovative violinist and performance artist Lindsey Stirling, who is joined on the first number by guest vocalist Lzzy Hale and on the second by the a cappella group Pentatonix.

"Let me say first off that I really like your taste in music!!" I type once we are back online together. "I like every one of these pieces . . . very cool stuff, and very eclectic too!"

"Thanks."

"My first question is about 'Radioactive.' So this is a cover of the original version by Imagine Dragons, correct?" I am familiar with Imagine Dragons' recording of "Radioactive," but this Stirling rendition with Pentatonix is new to me.

"Yes," Addison confirms.

"And you prefer this version, right?"

"Yeah."

"I do, too, but I'm curious about why you do. Can you explain?"

"I like that version because it is more acoustic and has a group of singers harmonizing instead of one singer who ends up being auto-tuned at least half the time," he replies, "and I guess I like the fact that everybody [performing] is getting a part that people enjoy, instead of just the singer or just the guitarist."

"Good explanation. So . . . I must confess that 'Radioactive' is the only tune on your list that I recall having heard before." It's embarrassing for me to admit to Addison how out of date I am. "So this is a great lesson in interesting new music for me. Thanks for that! How did you narrow the list down to just these seven selections? Would you say that each one of them is representative of a different style or genre that you like? I ask because each is quite different from the next."

"I narrowed them down [by] trying to pick the ones I really enjoy, but that also show how I don't usually like the trends to be set. I would rather stick with different music, all with a meaning that I can follow, if that makes sense."

"Yes, it makes sense," I assure him, "but let me ask you to clarify a couple of things. What do you mean by 'I don't usually like the trends to be set'?

Do you mean that you generally prefer music that is not in the mainstream of popular music?"

"That's it, but also, when there's a trend like 'Gangnam Style' or 'Harlem Shake'—stuff like that—I tend to stay away from it 'cause it stays for a week." Addison is exaggerating—both "Gangnam Style" and "Harlem Shake" topped the pop charts for months—but his point is well taken. "It's all people talk about and I usually don't like that kind of music, 'cause it's overplayed and too many people think that music is the best. And then the next new trend comes and everybody moves with it."

"Right, that makes sense," I concur. "So the thing that intrigues me about your relationship to music is what we talked about the last time you and your family were down here visiting Tallahassee. Most of the other people I'm collaborating with on this project either play music or write music, but you write fiction *to* music. Can you first give a brief synopsis of the novel you're writing, and then describe how music functions so integrally in your writing process?"

"Well, my book is basically a book about a kid who goes through all this trauma and unexpected behaviors, but he's able to cope with it even if he can't take any more of it. And music plays into the process: one, it helps my speed and typing; two, sometimes I incorporate the emotion of music into my book."

" . . . Can you give me a more detailed description of the book's plot, the main character, the kinds of traumas and 'unexpected behaviors' of that main character?"

"The plot is [about] a colony that has moved from earth because the sun went cold and they got marooned on a planet that killed most of the people off very quickly with poisonous gases, and the main character is a struggling scientist who has a friend who is always taking him on insane adventures. Skip a couple spoilers. We end up in a simulation of his childhood, and a couple examples of the unexpected struggles are the hallucinations he experiences through the book and the revealing of the name of his real wife in the simulation[;] and some of the [other] struggles are the mass killing of a crime syndicate which he did with his partners. I'm trying to stay away from spoilers."

"Wow. Sounds great!" I exclaim. "Was the title inspired by the 'Series of Unfortunate Events' book series [by Lemony Snicket] or is that just a coincidence?"

"No, it was coincidence."

"So now tell me about the main character (I mean, beyond what you've already explained). Name, traumas, unexpected behaviors. What's he all about? Also, how old is he?"

"His name is Alexander and his name changes throughout the book, from Alexander to Xander to Alex back to Alexander. Some other traumas are"—Addison continues in bullet list form:

- The killings that an alter ego he has encountered has done
- A government revolution
- Fighting off insanity
- And fighting off his demons

"And [as for] unexpected behaviors," he adds to wrap up, those involve "most of what the alter ego has done."

"Cool. So let's get into the music aspect now," I suggest. "How does your writing process work? Do you select particular pieces, artists, or albums that you know are 'right' for what you are planning to write, put that music on, and then let the writing flow? Or do you just put on, say, a particular radio station you like and let the music come at you randomly, inspiring you as it will to write in a particular way or take the story in a certain direction? (Note: I'm not implying that it's *either* of the above, but just putting those out there as 'examples' of what I mean by your 'writing process in relation to music.' Does that make sense?)"

Addison jumps right in with his reply, ignoring my parenthetical remarks. "I usually put on a radio station that I enjoy and it is actually more of a mix," he explains. "If I begin to not enjoy the music, I'll switch to music I already have [in my collection] and put one song on and repeat [it] until I run out of ideas, [after] which I either go back to radio or choose a different song."

"OK, so it's kind of a combination."

"Yeah."

"Can you take me through a particular episode of your writing to music [process]. For example, Lindsey Stirling's 'Shatter Me': Have you used that one in your writing of "The Unfortunate Project'?"

"Yes I have."

"OK, great. Now was that one that just came on the radio or is it one from your collection that you put on and listened to repeatedly as you were writing?"

"I found out about it from a friend and decided to get it myself after hearing a minute of it, and [then I] turned it on, repeated, and listened."

"How many times do you think you listened to it repeatedly in a single writing session?"

"Ten to twenty times."

"Was that just one writing session or did you write to that song during multiple sessions?"

"One writing session. I could say I have written one to three pages just listening to that song. I have found that I can't write a lot more than two pages in a day. Because of the strain."

"Strain on the brain, the body, the eyes?"

"Yeah."

"So all of the above then!"

"Yeah."

"Could you email me what you wrote while listening to 'Shatter Me'? Looking it over would help me ask intelligent questions about your writing to music process—that's why I ask."

"Sure, but it's very unedited and very crude."

"No worries. I just want to get the gist of it," I assure him. "If we decide to include all or part of it in [our] book, we'll make sure it's edited and refined to your satisfaction. And we'll be sure to delete any potential spoilers as well! ☺"

"Ok, thank you."

Moments later, the promised passage from "The Unfortunate Project" arrives in my inbox. I paste the text into our transcript and read: "Alexander walked out of the hospital calm, cool, and collected, but his head started to tremble, his bandages unwrapped, and he fell as he placed himself on the floor thinking he was tired, knowing he might not wake up, but he didn't care. His life has gone to shambles, his whole persona has changed, and for god's sake he just killed another man without remembering how, what, where, or who—only with the memory that he had killed somebody. He sat in this doubtlessness knowing this time, knowing his whole life has turned from solid rock to molten steel. He continued to fade away, each second turning slower and slower as he yelled as hard as he could to try and get help, but nobody came. He lied down on the concrete right down the street from the hospital. He sat there for hours, only being able to communicate through his own thoughts.

"'Hey kid, get up,' a calm woman said, with a very soothing tone.

"Alexander sat up, his body aching immediately, bumped into a clam shell full of water, and saw a young woman approximately in her twenties with a bright shining katana engraved with gold on her belt, and a claymore on her back.[3] She once again took her clam shell full of water and made him drink, then laid him back onto a surprisingly comfortable jungle bed made out of vines, cloth, and some rope. The woman sat him up about an hour later and created an incision into his right hand with her sewing needle, then grabbed her small tweezers and took out what seemed to be a sort of microchip while Alexander screamed in pain. The woman said while covering his mouth with her hand, 'Shh, they will hear you.'

"Alexander nodded in reply while watching his hand stop bleeding and heal itself. The woman spoke again, this time with a more hasteful tone. 'You will be fine, you don't have to trust me just yet, but I would like you to just follow my orders so we can fix this quick.' Alexander replied not with a nod but with words, 'I trust you,' even though he had no idea who she was or what was happening. All he knew was she saved his life, and he had practically no choice at the moment as he nodded back into unconsciousness."

"That's great stuff, Addison!" I exclaim. "I read it once on its own, then a second time with 'Shatter Me' playing in the background. Now I want to listen to 'Shatter Me' by itself. Then I'll have a few more questions for you, OK?"

"OK."

I hit the "Play" button and let the opening sounds of Stirling's recording envelop me. In the opening verse, lead vocalist Lzzy Hale sings, "I pirouette in the dark / I see the stars through me / Tired mechanical heart / Beats 'til the song disappears." The music is dark, brooding, understated. It hints at something bigger to come as Stirling's violin weaves in and out of the vocal line.

That something bigger arrives with the first chorus, which brings a dramatic surge of energy as Hale sings "Somebody shine a light / I'm frozen by the fear in me" before exploding into the song's catchy hook line: "Somebody make me feel alive, and shatter me!" A second chorus follows immediately, this one with new lyrics—"So cut me from the line / Dizzy, spinning endlessly," leading to a climactic reprise of the ". . . shatter me!" hook.

After the second chorus, the arrangement dives full speed into a searing improvised violin solo by Stirling, and from there into the second verse, which is sung over a double-time rock groove while the established harmonic motion remains stable. Later in the arrangement, the anticipation grows once more through a bridge section, which unfolds over a rising bass line with the lyrics "If I break the glass, then I'll have to fly / There's no one to catch me if I take a dive / I'm scared of change, and the days stay the same / The world is spinning but only in gray." The bridge repeats, but with richly harmonized vocals enhancing the texture the second time through. This ultimately leads to a rousing coda in which the hook is repeated multiple times while Stirling's solo violin soars above the fray with ever-growing intensity.

A number of striking connections between "Shatter Me" and "The Unfortunate Project" occur to me. I imagine what it must have felt like for Addison to write about Alexander waking up in the hospital and getting rescued by the katana-bearing, twenty-something heroine with this powerful song streaming into his consciousness and permeating the fabric of his words.

"Wow. I see lots of really interesting potential links between that song and what you wrote," I relate to Addison, "but I want you to tell me how it all came together as you yourself recall. Can you kind of replay the tape and share with me how things took shape? Did you start listening first and then start writing? Or were you writing and then suddenly realized this was the song you needed to guide you? Is it mainly the words of the song or the music itself or both (or certain aspects of one or the other) that motivated you to write? I'm fascinated and very curious. Please enlighten me on how all this worked, in as much detail as you can remember."

"It is aspects from everything," Addison types back, "but my personal explanation would be [that] when I put the music on I get a creative spark-type thing, 'cause usually it's hard for me to think, and when I get that creative spark I honestly couldn't tell you what comes through my head, but I feel I'm able to take the song and in a sense manipulate it and put it into words."

What a wonderful way of articulating how the process works, I think to myself. I highlight it for future reference.

Next, I ask Addison how his process takes shape: Is it something that unfolds more-or-less spontaneously as he listens and writes along or does it happen in a different way?

"It's not exactly spontaneous," Addison replies. "It's more of just interpretation; it's not spontaneous because it does take me some time to think."

"The seven songs that you sent me [on the playlist]—have you used all of those to aid you in your writing of the book?"

"Yes, I have."

"And have they all been ones that you used in a similar way to 'Shatter Me,' i.e., listening to them repeatedly as you write and interpreting them into the fabric of your story?"

"Yes."

I ask Addison if he can provide me with "a run-down of the kinds of things you wrote in connection with each of those songs, or at least two or three of them."

"For 'Ain't No Rest for the Wicked,' there is a part where Alexander has to take on a whole crime syndicate practically by himself," he recounts. "For 'Dirty Paws,' there is a part where Alexander gets reunited with his town. I can't really say more about that part because of spoilers. And 'Monster' inspired the setting for the very beginning of the story."

"Thanks. That's great. I want to go back to something you wrote to me earlier," I type, then copy and paste his "creative spark-type thing" remarks into a dialogue box for his reference: ". . . when I put the music on I get a creative spark-type thing, 'cause usually it's hard for me to think, and when I get that creative spark I honestly couldn't tell you what comes through my head, but I feel I'm able to take the song and in a sense manipulate it and put it into words."

"Yes, what exactly would you like to know?" Addison inquires after reading his words back to himself.

"So when the creative spark ignites," I continue, "does it make you better able to think *because* it's usually hard for you to think at other times or is it the opposite: the creative spark *makes* it hard for you to think, so that you no longer know what's going on in your head, but something comes out (in your writing) anyhow? Which one is it, or is it something else altogether?"

"It does both," Addison explains. "It makes it harder to think but easier to get a clear thought through."

"That's an interesting paradox!"

"Yeah."

"Do you also listen to music when you're doing other kinds of work, like when you're doing, say, math or science homework?"

"Yes, I listen to it with homework, reading, math, [computer] programming. A lot of stuff."

"And in those other contexts, is the process similar? Sometimes just letting what comes happen on a favorite radio station, other times selecting from your own music and listening to particular songs repeatedly?"

"Yeah, it's the same system."

"Interesting. I'm wondering, though, since the music penetrates into what you do so deeply—at least when you're writing fiction—isn't that a problem in reading? If you're reading for content to do a book report, for example, I could imagine the story you are reading blurring together with the story of the song you're listening to at the same time, so that you would end up with a 'Nightcore's "Monster" meets Huckleberry Finn' plot synopsis of the Mark Twain novel."

I wonder if that last bit will warrant a "hahaha" or an "LOL" response from Addison. It doesn't. I continue.

"Do you ever have such problems or are you able to process music differently when you're writing fiction vs. doing other kinds of work [in which] you don't have as much creative freedom?"

"There are points where I can't exactly concentrate on the book I'm reading, but I have learned if I don't know exactly what I'm reading [I can] just read it over again. And why do I do it if it is sometimes distracting?" Addison asks rhetorically. "Because it's even more distracting without."

I am intrigued by this last comment. "More distracting to read without music, you mean?" I ask.

"Yeah."

"How so?"

"Things are even more unexpected without music."

How very interesting, I say to myself. Definitely something to follow up on during our next session.

CONVERSATION 2: JUNE 19, 2014

I waste little time getting back to Addison's "Things are even more unexpected without music" comment when we meet for our second chat a week later.

"Hi, Addison. How are you?"

"Good. You?"

"Great, thanks. So last time we chatted, right near the end of the conversation, we were talking about how you listen to music while you read, and I asked you if that was challenging sometimes, since, as I wrote, 'I could imagine the story you are reading blurring together with the story of the song you're listening to at the same time.' And you replied, 'And why do I do it if it is sometimes distracting? . . . Because it's even more distracting without,' and then you added, 'Things are even more unexpected without music,' which I found really interesting. Could you expand on how and why that is the case?"

Addison is clear and to the point in responding: "With music I have just one or two things to focus on at a time and without it I'm being bombarded with a lot more than I can handle, usually noise [and] different conversations going on at the same time, and other distracting mishaps."

"So the music helps you tune out the 'noise' of life?" I ask.

"Yes."

"When was the first time you remember 'writing to music,' that is, writing while listening to music and having the music enter into the process and [into] the content of the writing itself?"

"I believe about a year or two ago."

"How did it happen that first time?"

"At first it was just to help me focus. After a while I realized I was using it as a source for my writing."

"So you were trying to write something and having a hard time concentrating, so you put on some music to shut out the other noisy distractions, and it was only after that that you became aware of the music serving this other, inspirational purpose? Am I understanding correctly?"

"Yes, it wasn't as fast [as that], but that's pretty much what happened."

"So it was a gradual thing. Didn't happen on the first occasion you experimented with using music as a focus aid. Right?"

"Yeah."

"How long in-between starting to use music to help you focus and the first time you recognized it was becoming a creative resource? Days, a week, a month?"

"Around five or six months after."

"Ah, so quite a while. And by that time, I assume that you were well convinced of its usefulness as a focus aid, yes?"

"Yes."

"Can you remember the first time it became something more—a creative inspiration? What were you listening to? What were you writing? Was the music already 'slipping in' to the writing before you were consciously aware of it, or was it more like you thought, 'Wow, I think I could use music as a creative spark for my writing,' and *then* it started happening after that? Try to recreate the first time it all 'clicked' in as much detail as you can!"

"I started writing my book and I started to notice that the moods of my music directly correlated with what I was writing down, and it was [like that] before [too] but I didn't notice. I just noticed that a lot of my papers [for school] were longer and more accurate with music rather than without."

"OK, great, so with the book, was the correlation with music something that was happening (and that you were aware of) right from the beginning of the writing process?"

"Yes."

"So right from the beginning you were 'using' music to write the book, yes?"

"Yes."

"What was the first song you used?"

"The first piece I listened to—I can tell you the band, Five Finger Death Punch[;] don't remember the song . . . but that part [of the book] is kind of dark and dreary so I would narrow it down to 'Wrong Side of Heaven.' It also fits the story, not just the mood."

"OK, so can you take me back in time to that first experience of writing [to] 'Wrong Side of Heaven'? What did it feel like? Was the inspiration more coming from the music itself, the energy of it, the words?"

"OK, to me it kind of just felt natural. I didn't really think differently."

"Yes, that's the hard part of 'explaining' art, isn't it? As a musicologist, I struggle with that every day—trying to put into words experiences that kind of defy them. Yet that analytical piece is important to help other people understand how we work and think. I know it's difficult, but if you can, try to put into words those feelings and experiences you had when you first came to the revelation that you could *be* a writer, and that [the] music could help you get there! In fact, I'm asking you to tell a story—it doesn't have to be perfectly 'accurate' actually; more important is that the story captures the essence of what it *feels* like for you to write to music."

"Well, I do know that it gave me a sense of clarity, but yet I would have racing thoughts at the same time," Addison remembers. "It felt like I knew what I was doing instead of the writer's block I would get without music. It felt natural but it created a whole new process for me, which made a sense of order." Addison's next move catches me entirely by surprise. "And [instead of] a story, I could probably do a quick poem."

"THAT PLACE YOUR HEART DESIRES"

Within seconds, a poem flashes onto my screen (a recording of Addison reciting it may be heard at the companion website: CW 11.2 ▶). The poetry is striking:

> That place your heart desires
> It is shaped to your being
> It has everything you want
> And nothing you need
> It belongs with you
> Wherever you go
> To help people that you don't know
> Whatever you do
> In your mind
> Shape your world
> Of candy and gold
> For you fall
> To wonderland
> The land of
> Imagination
> Wonder
> Responsibility
> The place you save
> The world you destroy
> Now journey to
> Wonderland
> The land of mine

"Wait. Did you just write that right now?!" I ask Addison in astonishment.

"I used an unfinished poem and thought I could do something off of that," he replies.

"But it's your poem, yes?"

"Yes it is."

"It's great! Did you write the poem to music?"

"Yes I did."

"What song?"

"Lindsey Stirling—'Shatter Me.'"

I can't help but smile. Everything is coming full circle.

"Nice! When did you write it?" I ask.

"About a month ago."

"I love it, especially that line 'It has everything you want and nothing you need.' That pretty much captures what 'art' is all about, I think. Beautiful! It brings another thought to mind as well. It seems to me that people with Asperger's and other ASCs are subjected to way too much of what other people think they need and *don't* get enough opportunities to just be the way *they* want to be, on their own terms, regardless of what they 'need.' Your poem, to me at least, speaks to that experience as well. What do you think?"

"Well, I can agree with you, but then there are also points where autism kids etc., at least for me, we don't have the structure [we need] sometimes, but we have people to watch our backs when we go too far."

"So those people, they're kind of like the music is in your writing?"

"Yeah."

"If they get the balance right, they can free you to unleash your creativity and passion, but they can also help you keep things in order when the freedom gets to be too much?"

"Yes," Addison affirms.

I take a deep breath and smile again. Of all the lessons Addison has taught me in these conversations, this is perhaps the most valuable one of all.

NOTES

1. Addison Silar is a pseudonym, as are the names used in the chapter for his parents and his sister.
2. Science fiction writing and fandom have long figured prominently in autistic culture. On this topic, see Steve Silberman's *NeuroTribes* (Silberman 2015, 223–47).
3. The katana and claymore are different types of swords. The former was traditionally associated with Japanese samurai warriors; the latter is a traditional Scottish weapon.

CHAPTER 12

Conclusion

"Living with Autism Shouldn't Be Hard"

It is not possible to separate the autism from the person—and if it were possible, the person you'd have left would not be the same person you started with.

Jim Sinclair (1993)[1]

The national conversation on autism "has increased in tone and fervor" in recent years, claims Ari Ne'eman, adding that "we who are the targets of this discussion have not been consulted. To those who believe in the motto of the disability rights movement—'Nothing About Us, Without Us!'—this situation has to change" so that "autistic people can enjoy the same rights, opportunities and quality of life as any of our neurotypical peers."[2]

So how do we get there? Certainly autistic people need jobs, education, health care, housing, transportation, safe living environments, civil rights, and legal protections in order to enjoy a good quality of life, just as other people do. Yet there is abundant evidence indicating that such needs simply are not being met for a great many individuals on the autism spectrum, and, moreover, that the most pressing challenges they face often have less to do with their autistic "symptoms" per se than with problems "built into the ways that society treats people who don't meet the standard expectations of 'normal.'"[3]

Changing the situation demands that autistic voices be heard, loud and clear and often, and perhaps even more important, that they be truly *listened* to: carefully, seriously, compassionately, and by as large and wide-ranging an audience as possible. As Joyce Davidson and Michael Orsini have written, what we "know about autism needs to be informed by a deep appreciation for what individuals living on the spectrum have to say about what it means to be autistic," and, I would add, by a deep appreciation for what they have to say about music, or about disability rights, synesthesia, or most any other subject that matters to them as well.[4]

To read about Zena Hamelson's musical stimming, Mara Chasar's spinny-chair therapy, Donald Rindale's ideas for autistic rights legislation, Ibby Grace's bawdy Irish singing, Graeme Gibson's view of world music as a spectrum of numerous genres, Maureen Pytlik's silent being and compassionate listener, Gordon Peterson's ambivalence toward his musical "superpower," Amy Sequenzia's break-the-wand autistic pride, or Addison Silar's musically infused science fiction is to be reminded, again and again, of the integral humanity we all share, be we autistic, neurodiverse, neurotypical, or neuro-anything-else.

The varied ways in which the people in this book make and experience music, as well as the different reasons it matters to them that they do, invite us to explore a range of expressions of autistic personhood and musicality that can contribute greatly to meeting the priorities of autism acceptance and neurodiversity. When Donald recalls the musical experiences of his youth being "a welcome refuge from the interpersonal engagements of the outside world," since music, unlike many people in his life, "did not laugh, or judge, or make nasty comments" at his expense, he is tapping into a special capacity of music to uplift the human spirit, even in the face of those who would defeat it. When Amy describes the words of a song dancing before her eyes as she listens to a friend singing to her, she reveals a brighter side of that human spirit, one in which compassion and joy merge in the socialness of shared musical expression. Maureen's colorful accounts of meaningful connections and moments of cathartic self-liberation achieved through West African music and dance reveal a further instance of such brightness. Music also serves as an essential bridge to social relationship for Graeme, linking him deeply to people he might otherwise have never gotten to know, from professional musicians like Randy Raine-Reusch and Rene Hugo Sanchez, to his mechanical engineer friend Daniel Ouellet, to the virtual community of world music enthusiasts who visit him at his website.

Gordon's and Zena's musical pursuits have at times moved them into an entirely different realm of social connection, not one of relationships with actual living people, but rather with the living creations of their powerful imaginations: the denizens of Gordon's "time-ribbon" world of antiquity; the members of the "Band of Brothers" who play all the different instruments in Zena's radically reconfigured Artism Ensemble. Dotan, too, revels in the rich, creative world of his imagination, though in his case the outcome can take on a more formalized character. I am thinking here in particular of a recital of his that I attended, in which he performed Mussorgsky's *Pictures at an Exhibition*. His flawless execution, dazzling technique, and evocative interpretation brought to life so vividly the pictures of the work's title—the Old Castle, the Marketplace in Limoges, the Catacombs, the Great Gate of Kiev—that I felt as though I was right there in the gallery with him, and with Mussorgsky too, taking it all in. I have heard *Pictures* performed many times, but never before has the effect been so powerful.

As for Ibby, "thinking in music" is no mere intellectual abstraction; it is the foundation of an autistic worldview and way of life, one that enables her to perceive that which others cannot, to hear the voices of those who do not speak, the songs of those who do not sing. And then there is Addison, who can channel a popular song by Lindsey Stirling into the basis of a science fiction novel or into a poem that contains an essential lesson for everyone: "That place your heart desires, it is shaped to your being. It has everything you want and nothing you need. It belongs with you wherever you go, to help people that you don't know."

Music, poetry, stories, and conversations are not substitutes for rigorous science, impactful legislation, or progressive public policy in the struggle for autistic rights, but beyond their own inherent value, they can pave the way for new research, new laws, and new policies that make a real difference. They cannot solve the world's problems in and of themselves, but they can direct our collective attention toward recognizing what those problems are, and from there toward forms of vigorous critical engagement that motivate viable solutions.

Taking part in conversations, and in the process committing ourselves to really listening to what other people have to say, puts us in position to find common ground from which to move forward in common purpose toward the common good. Along the way, perhaps we start to distance ourselves from the tragic patterns of divisiveness, prejudice, intolerance, and denial of the humanity of others that darken the record of human history at every turn. In the firm embrace of our shared humanity, we advance toward forms of empathy and understanding that benefit us all; in its absence, we can only regress.

My collaborators and I believe firmly that what we have to say through the conversations shared in this book is important for people to hear. Our greatest hope is that by sharing our stories as we have—by speaking for ourselves—we can contribute in some meaningful way to making a future world that not only accepts neurodiversity but celebrates it as a hallmark of our shared humanity.

FINAL WORDS, FROM MARA

Mara Chasar is wise beyond her years. She understands that there is so much that matters, that there are so many things that must happen to make this a good world for people like her to live in. She knows that none of it will come easily, that problems abound for people on the autism spectrum across virtually every domain of social, cultural, legal, economic, political, and professional life. For Mara, life is at times overwhelming. It is sometimes scary. With so much to attend to, so many obstacles in the way, so many prejudices to combat, it can all appear as an impossible jumble of challenges and frustrations.

But Mara has a gift for cutting through the clutter, and she knows that the creation of a better world—for her and for everyone—is not so far out of reach. She reminds us that it really is not all that complicated:

Living with Autism shouldn't be hard
And we don't want to make it hard
So even if you can't
Just try to understand
That all we need from the world is acceptance, inspiration, and love.

NOTES

1. From the reprint of "Don't Mourn for Us" published in *Loud Hands* (Sinclair 2012b).
2. Quotations are from "The Future (and the Past) of Autism Advocacy" (Ne'eman 2012, 88–90). On the twentieth-century history of the disability rights movement, see *Nothing About Us Without Us* (Charlton 1998).
3. *NeuroTribes* (Silberman 2015, 458).
4. *Worlds of Autism* (Davidson and Orsini 2013, 24).

REFERENCES CITED

"#ActuallyAutistic People React to Autism Speaks 'Change' in Mission Statement."
2016. Blog. *Boycott Autism Speaks*. October 14. https://boycottautismspeaks.
wordpress.com/2016/10/14/actuallyautistic-people-react-to-autism-speaks-
change-in-mission-statement/.

Allison, Theresa. 2010. "Transcending the Limitations of Institutionalization
through Music: Ethnomusicology in a Nursing Home." Doctoral Dissertation
(Ethnomusicology), University of Illinois, Urbana-Champaign.

American Psychiatric Association. 2000. *Diagnostic and Statistical Manual of Mental
Disorders: DSM-IV-TR*. 4th ed., text rev. Washington, DC: American Psychiatric
Association.

American Psychiatric Association. 2013. *Diagnostic and Statistical Manual of Mental
Disorders: DSM-5*. 5th ed. Washington, DC: American Psychiatric Association.

American Speech-Language-Hearing Association. 1994. "Technical Report: Facilitated
Communication." Prepared by the ASHA Subcommittee on Facilitated
Communication of the Ad Hoc Committtee on Auditory Integration Training
and Facilitated Communication. American Speech-Language-Hearing
Association. http://www.asha.org/policy/TR1994-00139.htm.

Bakan, Michael B. 2009. "Measuring Happiness in the 21st
Century: Ethnomusicology, Evidence-Based Research, and the New Science of
Autism." *Ethnomusicology* 53 (3): 510–18.

Bakan, Michael B. 2012. *World Music: Traditions and Transformations*. 2nd ed.
New York: McGraw-Hill.

Bakan, Michael B. 2014a. "Ethnomusicological Perspectives on Autism,
Neurodiversity, and Music Therapy." *Voices: A World Forum for Music Therapy* 14
(3). https://voices.no/index.php/voices/article/view/799.

Bakan, Michael B. 2014b. "Neurodiversity and the Ethnomusicology
of Autism." *College Music Symposium* 54. http://symposium.
music.org/index.php?option=com_k2&view=item&id=1067
3:neurodiversity-and-the-ethnomusicology-of-autism&Itemid=128.

Bakan, Michael B. 2014c. "The Musicality of Stimming: Promoting Neurodiversity in
the Ethnomusicology of Autism." *MUSICultures* 41 (2): 133–61.

Bakan, Michael B. 2015a. "'Don't Go Changing to Try and Please Me': Combating
Essentialism through Ethnography in the Ethnomusicology of Autism."
Ethnomusicology 59 (1): 116–44.

Bakan, Michael B. 2015b. "Being Applied in the Ethnomusicology of Autism." In *The Oxford Handbook of Applied Ethnomusicology*, edited by Svanibor Pettan and Jeff Todd Titon, 278–316. New York: Oxford University Press.

Bakan, Michael B. 2016a. "Toward an Ethnographic Model of Disability in the Ethnomusicology of Autism." In *The Oxford Handbook of Music and Disability Studies*, edited by Blake Howe, Stephanie Jensen-Moulton, Neil Lerner, and Joseph N. Straus, 15–36. New York: Oxford University Press.

Bakan, Michael B. 2016b. "Music, Autism, and Disability Aesthetics." *Journal of the American Musicological Society*, Colloquy: "On the Disability Aesthetics of Music" (Convenors: Blake Howe and Stephanie Jensen-Moulton), 69 (2): 548–53.

Bakan, Michael B., Benjamin D. Koen, Megan Bakan, Fred Kobylarz, Lindee Morgan, Rachel Goff, and Sally Kahn. 2008. "Saying Something Else: Improvisation and Facilitative Music-Play in a Medical Ethnomusicology Program for Children on the Autism Spectrum." *College Music Symposium* 48: 1–30.

Bakan, Michael B., Benjamin Koen, Fred Kobylarz, Lindee Morgan, Rachel Goff, Sally Kahn, and Megan Bakan. 2008. "Following Frank: Response-Ability and the Co-Creation of Culture in a Medical Ethnomusicology Program for Children on the Autism Spectrum." *Ethnomusicology* 52 (2): 163–202.

Baron-Cohen, Simon, Donielle Johnson, Julian Asher, Sally Wheelwright, Simon E. Fisher, Peter K. Gregersen, and Carrie Allison. 2013. "Is Synaesthesia More Common in Autism?" *Molecular Autism* 4: 40. doi:10.1186/2040-2392-4-40.

Barz, Gregory F. 2006. *Singing for Life: HIV/AIDS and Music in Uganda*. New York: Routledge.

Barz, Gregory F., and Judah M. Cohen, eds. 2011. *The Culture of AIDS in Africa: Hope and Healing in Music and the Arts*. New York: Oxford University Press.

Bascom, Julia. 2012a. "Foreword." In *Loud Hands: Autistic People, Speaking*, edited by Julia Bascom, 6–11. Washington, DC: Autistic Press/Autistic Self Advocacy Network.

Bascom, Julia, ed. 2012b. *Loud Hands: Autistic People, Speaking*. Washington, DC: Autistic Press/Autistic Self Advocacy Network.

Baum, Fran, Colin MacDougall, and Danielle Smith. 2006. "Participatory Action Research." *Journal of Epidemiology & Community Health* 60 (10): 854–57. doi:10.1136/jech.2004.028662.

Bernier, Raphael, and Jennifer Gerdts. 2010. *Autism Spectrum Disorders: A Reference Handbook*. Santa Barbara: ABC-CLIO.

Biklen, Douglas. 2005. *Autism and the Myth of the Person Alone*. New York: New York University Press.

Bohlman, Philip V., ed. 2013. *The Cambridge History of World Music*. Cambridge: Cambridge University Press.

Brown, Walter A., Karen Cammuso, Henry Sachs, Brian Winklosky, Julie Mullane, Raphael Bernier, Sarah Svenson, Deborah Arin, Beth Rosen-Sheidley, and Susan E. Folstein. 2003. "Autism-Related Language, Personality, and Cognition in People with Absolute Pitch: Results of a Preliminary Study." *Journal of Autism and Developmental Disorders* 33 (2): 163–67. doi:10.1023/A:1022987309913.

Campbell, Patricia Shehan. 2010. *Songs in Their Heads: Music and Its Meaning in Children's Lives*. 2nd ed. New York: Oxford University Press.

Campbell, Patricia Shehan, and Trevor Wiggins, eds. 2013. *The Oxford Handbook of Children's Musical Cultures*. New York: Oxford University Press.

Charlton, James I. 1998. *Nothing About Us Without Us: Disability Oppression and Empowerment*. Berkeley: University of California Press.

Corbett, Blythe A., Laura J. Constantine, Robert Hendren, David Rocke, and Sally Ozonoff. 2009. "Examining Executive Functioning in Children with Autism Spectrum Disorder, Attention Deficit Hyperactivity Disorder and Typical Development." *Psychiatry Research* 166 (2–3): 210–22.

Danielou, Alain. 1968. *The Ragas of Northern Indian Music*. London: Barrie and Rockliff.

Davidson, Joyce, and Michael Orsini, eds. 2013. *Worlds of Autism: Across the Spectrum of Neurological Difference*. Minneapolis: University of Minnesota Press.

Dell'Antonio, Andrew, and Elizabeth J. Grace. 2016. "No Musicking about Us without Us!" *Journal of the American Musicological Society*, Colloquy: "On the Disability Aesthetics of Music" (Convenors: Blake Howe and Stephanie Jensen-Moulton), 69 (2): 553–59.

Diament, Michelle. 2016. "Autism Speaks No Longer Seeking Cure." *Disability Scoop: The Premier Source for Developmental Disability News*. October 14. https://www.disabilityscoop.com/2016/10/14/autism-speaks-no-longer-cure/22884/.

Dirksen, Rebecca. 2012. "Reconsidering Theory and Practice in Ethnomusicology: Applying, Advocating, and Engaging beyond Academia." *Ethnomusicology Review* 17. http://ethnomusicologyreview.ucla.edu/journal/volume/17/piece/602.

Dohn, Anders, Eduardo A. Garza-Villarreal, Pamela Heaton, and Peter Vuust. 2012. "Do Musicians with Perfect Pitch Have More Autism Traits than Musicians without Perfect Pitch? An Empirical Study." *PLoS ONE* 7 (5): e37961.

Donvan, John, and Caren Zucker. 2016. *In a Different Key: The Story of Autism*. New York: Crown.

Edelson, Stephen M. n.d. "Self-Stimulatory Behavior." *Autism Research Institute*. https://www.autism.com/symptoms_self-stim.

Edwards, Jane, ed. 2016. *The Oxford Handbook of Music Therapy*. New York: Oxford University Press.

Edwards, Jane, Gregory F. Melchor-Barz, and Bussakorn Binson. 2015. "Collaborating Together: Finding the Emergent and Disruptive In and Between the Fields of Music Therapy and Medical Ethnomusicology." *Voices: A World Forum for Music Therapy* 15 (3). https://voices.no/index.php/voices/article/view/856.

Fein, Elizabeth. 2012. "The Machine Within: An Ethnography of Asperger's Syndrome, Biomedicine, and the Paradoxes of Identity and Technology in the Late Modern United States." Doctoral Dissertation (Anthropology/Comparative Human Development), University of Chicago.

Frisch, Michael. 2006. "Oral History and the Digital Revolution: Toward a Post-Documentary Sensibility." In *The Oral History Reader*, edited by Robert Perks and Alistair Thomson, 2nd ed., 102–14. London: Routledge.

Gibson, Deborah. 2011. "The Early Lexical Acquisition of a Child with Autism Spectrum Disorder." Doctoral Dissertation (Language and Literacy Education), University of British Columbia.

Gibson, Graeme. 2015. *Museumofworldmusic.com: The Exploration of Traditional, Ethnic, "World Music" and Experimental or Custom-Made Musical Instruments*. museumofworldmusic.com.

Gold, Christian. 2011. "Special Section: Music Therapy for People with Autistic Spectrum Disorder." *Nordic Journal of Music Therapy* 20 (2): 105–7.

Grace, Elizabeth J. 2012a. "Labels; Also, Intense Teaching Is Realer than 'Cure.'" Blog. *Tiny Grace Notes (Ask an Autistic)*. October 23. http://tinygracenotes.blogspot. com/2012/10/labels-also-intense-teaching-is-realer.html.

Grace, Elizabeth J. 2012b. "'It Hurts My Ears' Part One." Blog. *Tiny Grace Notes (Ask an Autistic)*. November 30. http://tinygracenotes.blogspot.com/search.

Grace, Elizabeth J. 2013. "Autistethnography." In *Both Sides of the Table: Autoethnographies of Educators Learning and Teaching With/In (Dis)ability*, edited by Phil Smith, 89–102. New York: Peter Lang.

Grace, Elizabeth J. 2014. "Your Mama Wears Drover Boots." In *Criptiques: Exploring the Provocative Side of Disability*, edited by Caitlin Wood, 11–23. criptiques.com.

Grace, Elizabeth J., Aiyana Bailin, Zach Richter, Allegra Stout, and Alyssa Z. 2013. "Intersectionalities in Autistic Culture(s): A Discussion Instigated by This Posse of Autistics and Friends." In *Program Abstract*, 42. Orlando, FL, Society for Disability Studies 26th Annual Conference.

Grandin, Temple. 2006. *Thinking in Pictures: My Life with Autism*. 2nd ed. New York: Vintage Books.

Grandin, Temple, and Richard Panek. 2013. *The Autistic Brain: Thinking across the Spectrum*. New York: Houghton Mifflin Harcourt.

Grandin, Temple, and Margaret M. Scariano. 1986. *Emergence: Labeled Autistic*. Novato, CA: Arena Press.

Griffin, Edward, and David Pollak. 2009. "Student Experiences of Neurodiversity in Higher Education: Insights from the BRAINHE Project." *Dyslexia* 15 (1): 23–41. doi:10.1002/dys.383.

Hacking, Ian. 2006. "Making Up People." *London Review of Books*, August 17.

Hammel, Alice M., and Ryan M. Hourigan. 2013. *Teaching Music to Students with Autism*. New York: Oxford University Press.

Happé, Francesca, Rhonda Booth, Rebecca Charlton, and Claire Hughes. 2006. "Executive Function Deficits in Autism Spectrum Disorders and Attention-Deficit/Hyperactivity Disorder: Examining Profiles across Domains and Ages." Edited by Ami Klin and Simon Baron-Cohen. *Brain and Cognition*, Special Issue: The Cognitive Neuroscience of Asperger Syndrome, 61 (1): 25–39.

Happé, Francesca, and Uta Frith, eds. 2010. *Autism and Talent*. Oxford: Oxford University Press.

Harrison, Klisala. 2012. "Epistemologies of Applied Ethnomusicology." *Ethnomusicology* 56 (3): 505–29.

Harrison, Klisala, Svanibor Pettan, and Elizabeth Mackinlay, eds. 2010. *Applied Ethnomusicology: Historical and Contemporary Approaches*. Newcastle upon Tyne, UK: Cambridge Scholars Publishing.

Headlam, Dave. 2006. "Learning to Hear Autistically." In *Sounding Off: Theorizing Disability in Music*, edited by Neil Lerner and Joseph N. Straus, 109–20. New York: Routledge.

Heidegger, Martin. 2008. *Being and Time*. Translated by John Macquarrie and Edward S. Robinson. New York: HarperPerennial/Modern Thought.

Hofstadter, Douglas R. 1979. *Gödel, Escher, Bach: An Eternal Golden Braid*. New York: Basic Books.

Howe, Blake, and Stephanie Jensen-Moulton. 2016. "Introduction." *Journal of the American Musicological Society*, Colloquy: "On the Disability Aesthetics of Music" (Convenors: Blake Howe and Stephanie Jensen-Moulton), 69 (2): 525–30.

Howe, Blake, Stephanie Jensen-Moulton, Neil Lerner, and Joseph N. Straus, eds. 2016. *The Oxford Handbook of Music and Disability Studies*. New York: Oxford University Press.

Human, Erin. 2016. "Cognitive Dissonance in a Different Key." Blog (a review of *In a Different Key: The Story of Autism* [2016], by John Donvan and Caren Zucker). *NeuroQueer: Queering Our Neurodivergence, Nerodiversifying Our Queer*. March 10. http://neuroqueer.blogspot.com/2016/03/cognitive-dissonance-in-different-key.html.

Jensen-Moulton, Stephanie. 2006. "Finding Autism in the Compositions of a 19th-Century Prodigy: Reconsidering 'Blind Tom' Wiggins." In *Sounding Off: Theorizing Disability in Music*, edited by Neil Lerner and Joseph N. Straus, 199–215. New York: Routledge.

Kanner, Leo. 1943. "Autistic Disturbances of Affective Contact." *Nervous Child* 2: 217–50.

Koen, Benjamin D., ed. 2008. *The Oxford Handbook of Medical Ethnomusicology*. New York: Oxford University Press.

Koen, Benjamin D., Michael B. Bakan, Fred Kobylarz, Lindee Morgan, Rachel Goff, Sally Kahn, and Megan Bakan. 2008. "Personhood Consciousness: A Child-Ability-Centered Approach to Socio-Musical Healing and Autism Spectrum 'Disorder.'" In *The Oxford Handbook of Medical Ethnomusicology*, edited by Benjamin D. Koen, 461–81. New York: Oxford University Press.

Locke, David. 1987. *Drum Gahu: A Systematic Method for an African Percussion Piece*. Crown Point, IN: White Cliffs Media Press.

Maloney, S. Timothy. 2006. "Glenn Gould, Autistic Savant." In *Sounding Off: Theorizing Disability in Music*, edited by Neil Lerner and Joseph N. Straus, 121–36. New York: Routledge.

Marrero, Elyse. 2012. "Performing Neurodiversity: Musical Accommodation by and for an Adolescent with Autism." Master's Thesis (Ethnomusicology), Florida State University.

"Mission." 2016. *Autism Speaks*. https://www.autismspeaks.org/about-us/mission.

Molnar-Szakacs, Istvan, and Pamela Heaton. 2012. "Music: A Unique Window into the World of Autism." *Annals of the New York Academy of Sciences* 1252 (1): 318–24. doi:10.1111/j.1749-6632.2012.06465.x.

Mottron, Laurent, Isabelle Peretz, Sylvie Belleville, and N. Rouleau. 1999. "Absolute Pitch in Autism: A Case Study." *Neurocase* 5 (6): 485–501.

Ne'eman, Ari. 2012. "The Future (and the Past) of Autism Advocacy, or Why the ASA's Magazine, *The Advocate*, Wouldn't Publish This Piece." In *Loud Hands: Autistic People, Speaking*, edited by Julia Bascom, 88–97. Washington, DC: Autistic Press/Autistic Self Advocacy Network.

Nietzsche, Friedrich Wilhelm, and Walter Arnold Kaufmann. 1974. *The Gay Science; with a Prelude in Rhymes and an Appendix of Songs*. Translated by Walter Arnold Kaufmann, with commentary. New York: Random House.

Nitzberg, Dotan. 2012. "How to Teach Piano to People with Asperger." Unpublished Lecture Script, Novi Sad, Serbia. https://www.youtube.com/watch?v=g7LTFboZAqk.

Perks, Robert, and Alistair Thomson, eds. 2006. *The Oral History Reader*. 2nd ed. London: Routledge.

Pettan, Svanibor, and Jeff Todd Titon, eds. 2015. *The Oxford Handbook of Applied Ethnomusicology*. New York: Oxford University Press.

Reschke-Hernández, Alaine E. 2011. "History of Music Therapy Treatment Interventions for Children with Autism." *Journal of Music Therapy* 48 (2): 169–207.

Ritchie, Donald A. 2015. *Doing Oral History*. 3rd ed. New York: Oxford University Press.

Sacks, Oliver. 1995. *An Anthropologist on Mars: Seven Paradoxical Tales*. New York: Alfred A. Knopf.

Sequenzia, Amy. 2012. "Non-Speaking, 'Low-Functioning.'" In *Loud Hands: Autistic People, Speaking*, edited by Julia Bascom, 159–61. Washington, DC: Autistic Press/Autistic Self Advocacy Network.

Sequenzia, Amy. 2014. "#FreeNeli." Blog. *Ollibean*. December 17. https://ollibean.com/freeneli/.

Sequenzia, Amy. 2015. "Synesthesia: 'Music, Colors, Movement, Feelings.'" Blog. *Ollibean*. April 22. https://ollibean.com/synesthesia/.

Sequenzia, Amy. 2017. Blog. *Non-Speaking Autistic Speaking*. http://nonspeakingautisticspeaking.blogspot.com/.

Sequenzia, Amy, and Elizabeth J. Grace, eds. 2015. *Typed Words, Loud Voices*. Fort Worth, TX: Autonomous Press.

Sibley, Kassiane A. 2013. "Kassiane A. Sibley's Open Letter to Identity Police (Part 1)." Blog. *NeuroQueer: Queering Our Neurodivergence, Neurodiversifying Our Queer*. September 13. http://neuroqueer.blogspot.com/2013/09/kassiane-sibleys-open-letter-to.html.

Silberman, Steve. 2015. *NeuroTribes: The Legacy of Autism and the Future of Neurodiversity*. New York: Avery.

Simpson, Kate, and Deb Keen. 2011. "Music Interventions for Children with Autism." *Journal of Autism and Developmental Disorders* 41: 1507–14.

Sinclair, Jim. 2012a. "Why I Dislike 'Person First' Language." In *Loud Hands: Autistic People, Speaking*, edited by Julia Bascom, 223–24. Washington, DC: Autistic Press/Autistic Self Advocacy Network.

Sinclair, Jim. 2012b. "Don't Mourn for Us." In *Loud Hands: Autistic People, Speaking*, edited by Julia Bascom, 15–21. Washington, DC: Autistic Press/Autistic Self Advocacy Network.

Singer, Judy. 1999. "'Why Can't You Be Normal for Once in Your Life?' From a 'Problem with No Name' to the Emergence of a New Category of Difference." In *Disability Discourse*, edited by Marian Corker and Sally French, 59–67. Buckingham, UK: Open University Press.

Small, Christopher. 1998. *Musicking: The Meanings of Performing and Listening*. Middletown, CT: Wesleyan University Press.

Smith, Phil, ed. 2013. *Both Sides of the Table: Autoethnographies of Educators Learning and Teaching With/In (Dis)ability*. New York: Peter Lang.

Straus, Joseph N. 2011. *Extraordinary Measures: Disability in Music*. New York: Oxford University Press.

Straus, Joseph N. 2013. "Autism as Culture." In *The Disability Studies Reader*, edited by Lennard J. Davis, 4th ed., 460–84. New York: Routledge.

Straus, Joseph N. 2014. "Idiots Savants, Retarded Savants, Talented Aments, Mono-Savants, Autistic Savants, Just Plain Savants, People with Savant Syndrome, and Autistic People Who Are Good at Things: A View from Disability Studies." *Disability Studies Quarterly* 34 (3). http://dsq-sds.org/article/view/3407.

Titon, Jeff Todd. 1992. "Music, the Public Interest, and the Practice of Ethnomusicology." *Ethnomusicology* 36 (3): 315–22.

Titon, Jeff Todd. 2011. "The Curry Lecture: Applied Ethnomusicology." Research Blog. *Sustainable Music: A Research Blog on the Subject of Sustainability, Sound and Music*. April 24. https://sustainablemusic.blogspot.com/2011/04/curry-lecture-applied-ethnomusicology.html.

Van Buren, Kathleen J. 2010. "Applied Ethnomusicology and HIV and AIDS: Responsibility, Ability, and Action." *Ethnomusicology* 54 (2): 202–23.

Walker, Nick. 2012. "Throw Away the Master's Tools: Liberating Ourselves from the Pathology Paradigm." In *Loud Hands: Autistic People, Speaking*, 225–37. Washington, DC: Autistic Press/Autistic Self Advocacy Network.

Walker, Nick. 2014. "What Is Autism?" Blog. *Neurocosmopolitanism: Nick Walker's Notes on Neurodiversity, Autism, and Cognitive Liberty*. March 1. http://neurocosmopolitanism.com/what-is-autism/.

"Wrong Planet." 2017. *Wrong Planet*. wrongplanet.net.

ADDITIONAL READING

Aigen, Kenneth S. 2002. *Playin' in the Band: A Qualitative Study of Popular Music Styles as Clinical Improvisation*. New York: Nordoff-Robbins Center for Music Therapy, Steinhardt School of Education, New York University.

Aigen, Kenneth S. 2012. "Community Music Therapy." In *The Oxford Handbook of Music Education*, edited by Gary E. McPherson and Graham F. Welch, 2: 138–54. New York: Oxford University Press.

American Music Therapy Association. 2012. "Music Therapy as a Treatment Modality for Autism Spectrum Disorders." American Music Therapy Association. http://www.musictherapy.org/assets/1/7/MT_Autism_2012.pdf.

Ariel, Cindy N., and Robert A. Naseef, eds. 2006. *Voices from the Spectrum: Parents, Grandparents, Siblings, People with Autism, and Professionals Share Their Wisdom*. London: Jessica Kingsley.

Bagatell, Nancy. 2010. "From Cure to Community: Transforming Notions of Autism." *Ethos* 38 (1): 33–55.

Bakan, Michael B. 1999. *Music of Death and New Creation: Experiences in the World of Balinese Gamelan Beleganjur*. Chicago: University of Chicago Press.

Barron, Judy, and Sean Barron. 2002. *There's a Boy in Here: Emerging from the Bonds of Autism*. Arlington, TX: Future Horizons.

Barz, Gregory F., and Timothy J. Cooley, eds. 2008. *Shadows in the Field: New Perspectives for Fieldwork in Ethnomusicology*. 2nd ed. New York: Oxford University Press.

Becker, Judith. 2004. *Deep Listeners: Music, Emotion, and Trancing*. Bloomington: Indiana University Press.

Bergmann, Thomas. 2016. "Music Therapy for People with Autism Spectrum Disorder." In *The Oxford Handbook of Music Therapy*, edited by Jane Edwards, 186–209. New York: Oxford University Press.

Brezis, Rachel. 2012. "Autism as a Case for Neuroanthropology: Delineating the Role of Theory of Mind in Religious Experience." In *The Encultured Brain: An Introduction to Neuroanthropology*, edited by Daniel H. Lende and Greg Downey, 291–314. Boston: MIT Press.

Bruscia, Kenneth E. 1987. *Improvisational Models of Music Therapy*. Springfield, IL: Charles C. Thomas.

Carlson, Licia. 2009. *The Faces of Intellectual Disability: Philosophical Reflections*. Bloomington: Indiana University Press.

Carrico, Alexandria Heaton. 2015. "Constructing a Two-Way Street: An Argument for Interdisciplinary Collaboration through an Ethnomusicological Examination of

Music Therapy, Medical Ethnomusicology, and Williams Syndrome." *Voices: A World Forum for Music Therapy* 15 (3). https://voices.no/index.php/voices/article/view/825.

Cascio, M. Ariel. 2012. "Neurodiversity: Autism Pride among Mothers of Children with Autism Spectrum Disorders." *Intellectual and Developmental Disabilities* 50 (3): 273–83. doi:10.1352/1934-9556-50.3.273.

Cascio, M. Ariel. 2014. "New Directions in the Social Study of the Autism Spectrum: A Review Essay." *Culture, Medicine, and Psychiatry* 38 (2): 306–11.

Chernoff, John Miller. 1993. *Hustling Is Not Stealing: Stories of an African Bar Girl.* Chicago: University of Chicago Press.

Clarkson, Ginger. 1994. "Creative Music Therapy and Facilitated Communication: New Ways of Reaching Students with Autism." *Preventing School Failure* 38 (2): 31.

Crafts, Susan D., Daniel Cavicchi, and Charles Keil. 1993. *My Music: Explorations of Music in Daily Life.* Middletown, CT: Wesleyan University Press.

Crapanzano, Vincent. 1980. *Tuhami, Portrait of a Moroccan.* Chicago: University of Chicago Press.

Davis, Lennard J., ed. 2013. *The Disability Studies Reader.* 4th ed. New York: Routledge.

Edgerton, Cindy Lu. 1994. "The Effect of Improvisational Music Therapy on Communicative Behaviors of Autistic Children." *Journal of Music Therapy* 31 (1): 31–62.

Edwards, Jane, and Susan Hadley. 2007. "Expanding Music Therapy Practice: Incorporating the Feminist Frame." *Arts in Psychotherapy* 34 (3): 199–207.

Eyal, Gil, Brendan Hart, Emin Onculer, Neta Oren, and Natasha Rossi. 2010. *The Autism Matrix.* Cambridge, UK: Polity Press.

Feld, Steven. 1987. "Dialogic Editing: Interpreting How Kaluli Read Sound and Sentiment." *Cultural Anthropology* 2 (2): 190–210.

Feld, Steven. 2012. *Sound and Sentiment: Birds, Weeping, Poetics, and Song in Kaluli Expression.* 3rd ed. Durham, NC: Duke University Press.

Fenn, John, ed. 2003. *Folklore Forum*, Special Issue: *Applied Ethnomusicology*, 34 (1–2): 119–31.

Garland-Thomson, Rosemarie. 1997. *Extraordinary Bodies: Figuring Physical Disability in American Culture and Literature.* New York: Columbia University Press.

Garland-Thomson, Rosemarie. 2013. "Integrating Disability, Transforming Feminist Theory." In *The Disability Studies Reader*, edited by Lennard J. Davis, 4th ed., 333–53. New York: Routledge.

Grinker, Roy Richard. 2007. *Unstrange Minds: Remapping the World of Autism.* New York: Basic Books.

Grinker, Roy Richard. 2010. "Commentary: On Being Autistic, and Social." *Ethos* 38 (1): 172–78.

Gunderson, Frank. 2010. *Sukuma Labor Songs from Western Tanzania: "We Never Sleep, We Dream of Farming."* Leiden: Brill.

Hadley, Susan, ed. 2006. *Feminist Perspectives in Music Therapy.* Gilsum, NH: Barcelona.

Hadley, Susan. 2014. "Shifting Frames: Are We Really Embracing Human Diversities?" *Voices: A World Forum for Music Therapy* 14 (3). https://voices.no/index.php/voices/article/view/801/666.

Harvey, Trevor. 2009. "Virtual Garage Bands: Collaborative Cybercommunities of Internet Musicians." Doctoral Dissertation (Ethnomusicology), Florida State University.

Hayes, Tommy. 2016. "Music Therapy in Special Education." In *The Oxford Handbook of Music Therapy*, edited by Jane Edwards, 176–85. New York: Oxford University Press.

Hendriks, Rudd. 2012. *Autistic Company*. Translated by Lynne Richards. Amsterdam: Rodopi.

Jaarsma, Pier, and Stellan Welin. 2012. "Autism as a Natural Human Variation: Reflections on the Claims of the Neurodiversity Movement." *Health Care Analysis* 20 (1): 20–30. doi:10.1007/s10728-011-0169-9.

Jellison, Judith A., and Patricia J. Flowers. 1991. "Talking about Music: Interviews with Disabled and Nondisabled Children." *Journal of Research in Music Education* 39 (4): 322–33.

Kapp, Steven K., Kristen Gillespie-Lynch, Lauren E. Sherman, and Ted Hutman. 2012. "Deficit, Difference, or Both? Autism and Neurodiversity." *Developmental Psychology* 49 (1): 59–71. doi:10.1037/a0028353.

Keil, Charles, and Steven Feld. 1994. *Music Grooves*. Chicago: University of Chicago Press.

Kern, Petra. 2004. "Making Friends in Music: Including Children with Autism in an Interactive Play Setting." *Music Therapy Today* 5 (4): 1–43.

Kingsbury, Henry. 1988. *Music, Talent, and Performance: A Conservatory Cultural System*. Philadelphia: Temple University Press.

Koen, Benjamin D. 2009. *Beyond the Roof of the World: Music, Prayer, and Healing in the Pamir Mountains*. New York: Oxford University Press.

Lawson, Wendy. 2000. *Life behind Glass: A Personal Account of Autism Spectrum Disorder*. London: Jessica Kingsley.

Lerner, Neil, and Joseph N. Straus, eds. 2006. *Sounding Off: Theorizing Disability in Music*. New York: Routledge.

Lubet, Alex. 2011. *Music, Disability, and Society*. Philadelphia: Temple University Press.

Miller, Jean Kerns. 2003. *Women from Another Planet? Our Lives in the Universe of Autism*. Bloomington: First Books.

Miller, Kiri. 2012. *Playing Along: Digital Games, YouTube, and Virtual Performance*. New York: Oxford University Press.

Mitchell, Frank, Charlotte J. Frisbie, and David P. McAllester. 1978. *Navajo Blessingway Singer: The Autobiography of Frank Mitchell, 1881–1967*. Albuquerque: University of New Mexico Press.

Monje, Michael Scott Jr. 2015. *Defiant*. Fort Worth, TX: Autonomous Press.

Mukhopadhyay, Tito Rajarshi. 2011. *How Can I Talk If My Lips Don't Move? Inside My Autistic Mind*. New York: Arcade.

Murray, Stuart. 2008. *Representing Autism: Culture, Narrative, Fascination*. Liverpool: Liverpool University Press.

Nadesan, Majia Holmer. 2005. *Constructing Autism: Unraveling the "Truth" and Understanding the Social*. New York: Routledge.

National Disability Rights Network. 2009. "School Is Not Supposed to Hurt: Investigative Report on Abusive Restraint and Seclusion in Schools." Washington, DC: National Disability Rights Network. http://www.ndrn.org/images/Documents/Resources/Publications/Reports/SR-Report2009.pdf.

Nettl, Bruno. 1995. *Heartland Excursions: Ethnomusicological Reflections on Schools of Music*. Urbana: University of Illinois Press.

Nettl, Bruno. 2015. *The Study of Ethnomusicology: Thirty-Three Discussions*. 3rd ed. Urbana: University of Illinois Press.

Neumeier, Shain. 2012. "Inhumane beyond All Reason: The Torture of Autistics and Other People with Disabilities at the Judge Rotenberg Center." In *Loud Hands: Autistic People, Speaking*, edited by Julia Bascom, 204–19. Washington, DC: Autistic Press/Autistic Self Advocacy Network.

Nordoff, Paul, and Clive Robbins. 1977. *Creative Music Therapy: Individualized Treatment for the Handicapped Child*. New York: John Day.

Ochs, Elinor, Tamar Kremer-Sadlik, Karen Gainer Sirota, and Olga Solomon. 2004. "Autism and the Social World: An Anthropological Perspective." *Discourse Studies* 6 (2): 147–83.

Ochs, Elinor, Tamar Kremer-Sadlik, Olga Solomon, and Karen Gainer Sirota. 2001. "Inclusion as Social Practice: Views of Children with Autism." *Social Development* 10 (3): 399–419.

Ochs, Elinor, Olga Solomon, and Laura Sterponi. 2005. "Limitations and Transformations of Habitus in Child-Directed Communication." *Discourse Studies* 7 (4–5): 547–83.

Osteen, Mark. 2008. *Autism and Representation*. New York: Routledge.

Pavlicevic, Mercédès, and Gary Ansdell, eds. 2004. *Community Music Therapy*. London: Jessica Kingsley.

Porcello, Thomas. 1996. "Sonic Artistry: Music, Discourse, and Technology in the Sound Recording Studio." Doctoral Dissertation (Anthropology), University of Texas at Austin.

Prince, Dawn Eddings. 2010. "An Exceptional Path: An Ethnographic Narrative Reflecting on Autistic Parenthood from Evolutionary, Cultural, and Spiritual Perspectives." *Ethos* 38 (1): 56–68.

Prince-Hughes, Dawn. 2002. *Aquamarine Blue 5: Personal Stories of College Students with Autism*. Athens, OH: Swallow/Ohio University Press.

Prince-Hughes, Dawn. 2004. *Songs of the Gorilla Nation: My Journey through Autism*. New York: Harmony.

Prizant, Barry M., Amy M. Wetherby, Emily Rubin, Amy C. Laurent, and Patrick Rydell. 2006. *The SCERTS Model: A Comprehensive Educational Approach for Children with Autism Spectrum Disorders*. Baltimore, MD: Paul H. Brookes.

Ralston, D. Christopher, and Justin Ho. 2010. "Introduction." In *Philosophical Reflections on Disability*, edited by D. Christopher Ralston and Justin Ho, 1–18. Dordrecht: Springer.

Rice, Timothy. 1994. *May It Fill Your Soul: Experiencing Bulgarian Music*. Chicago: University of Chicago Press.

Robison, John Elder. 2007. *Look Me in the Eye: My Life with Asperger's*. New York: Crown.

Rolvsjord, Randi. 2004. "Therapy as Empowerment: Clinical and Political Implications of Empowerment Philosophy in Mental Health Practices." *Nordic Journal of Music Therapy* 13 (2): 99–111.

Rutter, Michael. 2013. "Changing Concepts and Findings on Autism." *Journal of Autism and Developmental Disorders* 43: 1749–57.

Ruud, Even. 1998. *Music Therapy: Improvisation, Communication, and Culture*. Gilsum, NH: Barcelona.

Sacks, Oliver. 2008. *Musicophilia: Tales of Music and the Brain*. 2nd ed. New York: Random House.

Shakespeare, Tom. 2013. "The Social Model of Disability." In *The Disability Studies Reader*, edited by Lennard J. Davis, 4th ed., 214–21. New York: Routledge.

Shore, Stephen. 2003. *Beyond the Wall: Personal Experiences with Autism and Asperger Syndrome*. 2nd ed. Shawnee Mission, KS: Autism Asperger Publishing.

Siebers, Tobin. 2008. *Disability Theory*. Ann Arbor: University of Michigan Press.

Silverman, Chloe. 2012. *Understanding Autism: Parents, Doctors, and the History of a Disorder*. Princeton: Princeton University Press.

Silvers, Anita. 2010. "An Essay on Modeling: The Social Model of Disability." In *Philosophical Reflections on Disability*, edited by D. Christopher Ralston and Justin Ho, 19–36. Dordrecht: Springer.

Sirota, Karen Gainer. 2010. "Narratives of Distinction: Personal Life Narrative as a Technology of the Self in the Everyday Lives and Relational Worlds of Children with Autism." *Ethos* 38 (1): 93–115.

Solomon, Olga. 2010. "Sense and the Senses: Anthropology and the Study of Autism." *Annual Review of Anthropology* 39: 241–59.

Solomon, Olga. 2010. "What a Dog Can Do: Children with Autism and Therapy Dogs in Social Interaction." *Ethos* 38 (1): 143–66.

Solomon, Olga, and Nancy Bagatell. 2010. "Introduction—Autism: Rethinking the Possibilities." *Ethos* 38 (1): 1–7.

Sordyl, Samantha. 2005. "Creating an Asperger's Community." *Washington Post*, December 20. http://www.washingtonpost.com/wp-dyn/content/article/2005/12/17/AR2005121700899.html.

Sterponi, Laura. 2004. "Construction of Rules, Accountability and Moral Identity by High-Functioning Children with Autism." *Discourse Studies* 6 (2): 207–28.

Sterponi, Laura, and Allesandra Fasulo. 2010. "'How to Go On': Intersubjectivity and Progressivity in the Communication of a Child with Autism." *Ethos* 38 (1): 116–42.

Stige, Brynjulf. 2002. *Culture-Centered Music Therapy*. Gilsum, NH: Barcelona.

Stige, Brynjulf, Gary Ansdell, Cochavit Elefant, and Mercédès Pavlicevic. 2010. *Community Music Therapy in Action and Reflection*. Surrey, UK: Ashgate.

Straus, Joseph N. 2014. "Music Therapy and Autism: A View from Disability Studies." *Voices: A World Forum for Music Therapy* 14 (3). https://voices.no/index.php/voices/article/view/785.

Straus, Joseph N. 2016. "Modernist Music and the Representation of Disability." *Journal of the American Musicological Society*, Colloquy: "On the Disability Aesthetics of Music" (Convenors: Blake Howe and Stephanie Jensen-Moulton), 69 (2): 530–36.

Tammet, Daniel. 2007. *Born on a Blue Day: A Memoir (Inside the Extraordinary Mind of an Autistic Savant)*. New York: Free Press.

Tenzer, Michael. 2000. *Gamelan Gong Kebyar: The Art of Twentieth-Century Balinese Music*. Chicago: University of Chicago Press.

Titchkosky, Tanya. 2007. *Reading and Writing Disability Differently: The Textured Life of Embodiment*. Toronto: University of Toronto Press.

Treloyn, Sally. 2016. "Music in Culture, Music as Culture, Music Interculturally: Reflections on the Development and Challenges of Ethnomusicological Research in Australia." *Voices: A World Forum for Music Therapy* 16 (2). https://voices.no/index.php/voices/article/view/877.

Vander, Judith. 1996. *Songprints: The Musical Experience of Five Shoshone Women*. Urbana: University of Illinois Press.

Walworth, Darcy DeLoach. 2007. "The Use of Music Therapy within the SCERTS Model for Children with Autism Spectrum Disorder." *Journal of Music Therapy* 44 (1): 2–22.

Whipple, Jennifer. 2004. "Music in Intervention for Children and Adolescents with Autism: A Meta-Analysis." *Journal of Music Therapy* 41 (2): 90–106.

Wikan, Unni. 1990. *Managing Turbulent Hearts: A Balinese Formula for Living.* Chicago: University of Chicago Press.

Williams, Donna. 1992. *Nobody, Nowhere: The Extraordinary Autobiography of an Autistic.* New York: Harper Collins.

Wood, Caitlin, ed. 2014. *Criptiques: Exploring the Provocative Side of Disability.* Criptiques.com.

INDEX

Bascom, Julia, 6, 51. *See also Loud*
Hands: Autistic People, Speaking
Bell, Liz, 7–10
curing autism, debate over, 8–9
Bernstein, Leonard, 163. *See also* Pytlik,
Maureen
Sonata for Clarinet and Piano, 163
Biklen, Douglas, 6, 17n15, 217n5
Black, Rebecca, 61, 63
Bleuler, Eugen, 16n2
Buddhism, 182–183
Brahms, Johannes, 99. *See also*
Nitzberg, Dotan
Paganini Variations, Vol. II, 99
Brown, Lydia, 19n37

Cage the Elephant (band), 221. *See also*
Silar, Addison
"Ain't No Rest for the Wicked" (song),
221, 226
"Tiny Little Robots" (song), 221
Campbell, Patricia Shehan, 16n8
Carleton University, 5, 139, 166
West African Rhythm Ensemble
(WARE), 156
Chasar, Lia, 31, 32–33
Chasar, Mara, 2–3, 22, 23, 30–38,
234, 236
Artism Ensemble, 31–32, 36–37
Asperger's diagnosis, 31
autism acceptance, opinions on,
34, 236
autism awareness, opinions on, 34
Autism Speaks, opinions on, 34–35
biography of, 31–32
curing autism, opinions
on, 34–35, 37
emotions, opinions on, 37
Exploratory World Music Playground
(E-WoMP), 31
Music-Play Project, 31
music composition, 36
normalcy, opinions on, 31, 36
parents of, 31, 32–33
"Purple Eggs and Ham" (composition),
32. *See also* Dr. Seuss, *Green Eggs
and Ham*
social interaction, 37
Society for Disability Studies
Conference, 32

spinny chairs, 33, 34–36
stimming, opinions on, 35–36
cognitive flexibility, 151
Coffeebot, 22, 36. *See also* Artism
Ensemble
Coheed and Cambria (band), 221
"Welcome Home" (song), 221
conversation
challenges of, 163
foundation of book, as, 3
mutually transformative duet, as, 7
value in social activism, 235–236
Corbett, Blythe, 217n4
Corzine, Jon, 7. *See also* Bell, Liz
Criptiques, 74–75

Danielou, Alain, 130
*The Ragas of Northern Indian
Music*, 130
Davidson, Joyce, 234
Debussy, Claude, 100. *See also*
Nitzberg, Dotan
Prelude no. 12, Vol.1: Minstrels, 100
Dell'Antonio, Andrew, 16n6, 74, 202,
215, 216
Deng, Haiqiong, 24, 27–28. *See also*
Artism Ensemble; zheng
dance
music and, 80
West African, experience of, 147, 148,
149, 154, 160, 161. *See also* Pytlik,
Maureen
*Diagnostic and Statistical Manual of
Mental Disorders*, 5th edition,
(*DSM-5*), xxin2
dialogue
issues of power in, 144
re-presented vs. represented, 2
disability law, 44
disability rights movement, 233, 236n2.
See also Ne'eman, Ari
disability studies, xxin2
Donvan, John, xxin2, 8, 18n25
Dot Exe (band), 221. *See also*
Nightcore (band)
"Monster" (song), 221
Dr. Seuss, 32
Green Eggs and Ham, 32. *See also*
Chasar, Mara, "Purple Eggs and
Ham" (composition)

E. S., 22, 23, 36. *See also* Artism
    Ensemble
Edelson, Stephen, 21. *See also* autism,
    stimming
ethnomusicology, xix, 1–2, 3, 80
    applied, xxiin 5, 7, 17n16, 46
      publications on, xxin5
    autism, of, 1–2, 45, 58–59
    children, of, 16n8. *See also* Campbell,
      Patricia Shehan
    definition, 58, 175, 206
    medical, publications on, xxiin4
executive function, 203, 217n4
Exploratory World Music Playground
    (E-WoMP), 22–25, 31

facilitated communication, 203,
    204–205, 216n3, 217n5
    Syracuse University, and, 205, 217n5
Fein, Elizabeth, 15n1, 17n11. *See also*
    autism, labeling
Florida State University, xix, 4, 16n7, 41,
    95, 170
    gamelan of, 111–112, 170
Frith, Uta, 13–14, 18n32

Gibson, Deborah, 4, 17n2, 122–124, 135
Gibson, Graeme, 4–5, 120–137, 234
    African guitar music, on, 133
    aphasia, 125
    biography of, 125–126
    bouzouki, on, 127, 136
    classic autism diagnosis, 4, 122, 125
    classical music (Western), opinions on,
      124, 133
    Greek music, on, 127, 129
    Indian classical music, on, 126–127,
      130, 133
      raga (raaga), on, 126, 127, 130, 133
    instrument building, 129
      Ouellet, Daniel, 131, 234
    instrument collection, 125–126
    living with autism, perspectives on,
      134, 135
    modes (in different music traditions),
      opinions on, 126–127
    museumofworldmusic.com
      (website), 4
    musical ability, 125, 134
    musical performance, 124, 129

    musical preferences, 124, 133
    music and emotion, experience of,
      132–133
    music composition, 130
    music theory, on, 128, 130
    Myanmar, music of, 127
    perfect pitch, 125
    parents of, 122
    Peruvian music, on, 131
    questions list for, 123
    red-winged blackbird, photograph
      of, 136
    social relationships, 131, 234
    wildlife photography, on, 122, 129,
      135, 136
    world music, perspectives on, 4,
      126–127, 128–129, 133–134
Gold, Alison, 61
Google Hangouts (online chat platform),
    43, 48, 127, 128, 170, 220
Gould, Glenn, 1, 118n5
    S. Timothy Maloney, on, 16n4
Grace, Elizabeth J. (Ibby), 3, 15, 16n6,
    18–19n37, 68–92, 147, 202, 215,
    216, 234, 235
    alexithymia, 74–75, 83
    Artism Ensemble, 69, 71
    autism acceptance, 72
    autistic musical phenomenology, 74
    autistic self-advocacy, 15
    Celtic music, performance of, 77–78
    children of, 86–87
    "codependence song"
      (composition), 76
    Criptiques, 74, 86
    compositional process, 75–76
    family of, 77, 84–87, 89
    "Fool's Sonnet" (poem), 90–91
    hearing people as music, on, 81–82,
      83–84, 147
    Hob Nob (band), experiences as
      member of, 77–78
    "Intersectionalities in Autistic
      Culture(s): A Discussion
      Instigated by This Posse of
      Autistics and Friends", 69
      panelists, 70
      Richter, Zach, 71–72
        autism awareness vs. autism
        acceptance, 72

CPSIA information can be obtained
at www.ICGtesting.com
Printed in the USA
BVHW072358040122
624993BV00003B/13